T0074703

Advanced Digital Imaging Laboratory Using MATLAB®

IOP Series in Imaging Engineering

Series Editor

Leonid P Yaroslavsky
School of Electrical Engineering, Tel Aviv University, Tel Aviv, Israel

Images are the main source of information for humans, and the development of imaging methods and devices has always been at the forefront of technological progress. By the beginning of the 21st century a new branch of modern technology had formed: imaging engineering. The goal of the *IOP Series in Imaging Engineering* is to supply students and practitioners in academia and the imaging industry with the most up-to-date texts and reference books in the field. Encompassing imaging devices and systems, image acquisition, reconstruction and processing and the diverse applications of modern imaging systems, the series consists of compact textbooks and reference books written at a level accessible to graduate students. Authors are encouraged to take advantage of the features made possible by electronic publication to enhance the reader experience through the use of colour, animations, video and incorporating supplementary files in their work.

Advanced Digital Imaging Laboratory Using MATLAB®

Second edition

Leonid P Yaroslavsky
Professor Emeritus, School of Electrical Engineering, Tel Aviv University, Tel Aviv, Israel

IOP Publishing, Bristol, UK

Online supplementary data files are available at http://ej.iop.org/images/books/978-0-7503-1233-2/live/bk978-0-7503-1233-2suppdata.zip.

ISBN 978-0-7503-1233-2 (ebook)
ISBN 978-0-7503-1234-9 (print)
ISBN 978-0-7503-1235-6 (mobi)

DOI 10.1088/978-0-7503-1233-2

Version: 20160901

IOP Expanding Physics
ISSN 2053-2563 (online)
ISSN 2054-7315 (print)

British Library Cataloguing-in-Publication Data: A catalogue record for this book is available from the British Library.

Published by IOP Publishing, wholly owned by The Institute of Physics, London

IOP Publishing, Temple Circus, Temple Way, Bristol, BS1 6HG, UK

US Office: IOP Publishing, Inc., 190 North Independence Mall West, Suite 601, Philadelphia, PA 19106, USA

Contents

Preface to the second edition

The present book is a second and substantially extended edition of the book published under the same name in 2014. The major extensions include the following:

- Chapters 'Image digitization' and 'Digital computational imaging' are supplemented with new exercises that illustrate image general irregular and sparse sampling and modern ideas of image sparse approximation, as well as new exercises that demonstrate aliasing artifacts in 2D and 3D (spatial/temporal) sampling.
- Chapters 'Image digitization', 'Methods of image perfecting' and 'Methods of image enhancement' are extended to color and stereo images and are supplemented with corresponding new exercises.
- Chapter 'Image resampling and building continuous image models' is supplemented with new exercises that illustrate perfect image re-scaling with arbitrary scale factors.
- Questions for self-testing are correspondingly updated and extended.
- The narrative part of the book is substantially extended and complemented by verbal formulations and intuitive explanations of major theoretical results that underlie the exercises, which makes the book more self-containing.
- The total number of exercises is increased from 87 to 105.
- All exercises are re-edited and re-checked.
- The bank of test images is very substantially extended to include, in particular, color and stereoscopic images.

Preface

This book is a textbook of MATLAB® based exercises in all major topics of digital imaging: image digitization, digital image formation and computational imaging, image resampling and building continuous image models, image statistical characterization and noise diagnostics, statistical image models and pattern formation, image correlators for detecting and localization of objects, image restoration and perfecting, image enhancement. The book is addressed to students, researchers and practitioners in imaging engineering and applications. Its goal is to help readers to master digital imaging on both fundamental theoretical and practical levels. It is based on courses that have been tauught by the author in Tel Aviv University and at a number of other Universities in Europe and Japan during last 15 years.

Author biography

Leonid P Yaroslavsky

Leonid P Yaroslavsky, MS (summa cum laude, 1961), PhD (1968), Dr Sc. Habilitatus in Physics and Math (1982), OSA Fellow. From 1965 till 1983, the head of the Digital Image Processing and Digital Holography Group at the Institute for Information Transmission Problems (IITP), Russian Academy of Sciences. From 1983 till 1995, the founder and head of the Laboratory of Digital Optics at the IITP. From 1995 till 2008, a full professor at the Faculty of Engineering, Tel Aviv University. Currently a professor emeritus. A visiting professor at the University of Erlangen, Germany; National Institute of Health, Bethesda, MD, USA; Institute of Optics, Orsay, France; Institute Henri Poincaré, Paris, France; International Centre for Signal Processing, Tampere University of Technology, Finland; Agilent Laboratories, Palo Alto, CA, USA; Gunma University, Kiryu, Japan; Autonomous University of Barcelona, Spain. Supervised 20 PhD candidates. An author and editor of more than 20 books and numerous peer-reviewed publications on digital image processing and digital holography.

IOP Publishing

Leonid P Yaroslavsky

Chapter 1

Introduction

1.1 General remarks about the book

This is an unusual book. It is a book of exercises, exercises in digital imaging, the technology and engineering of creation of images by means of digital processing of sensor data retrieved in a digital form, one of the most important and rapidly developing branches of modern information technology. Studying digital imaging engineering, mastering this profession and working in the area is not possible without obtaining practical skills based on fundamental knowledge in the subject. The present book is aimed at providing a technical support for this. It contains exercises on all major topics of digital imaging for students, researchers in experimental sciences and, generally, for all practitioners in imaging engineering. It is based on courses that have been taught by the author at Tel Aviv University and at a number of other universities of Europe and Japan during last 15 years.

The key features of the book are the following.

1. The book supports studying and mastering of all fundamental aspects of digital imaging from image digitization to image resampling, recovery, parameter estimation, restoration and enhancement.
2. Exercises are designed and implemented in MATLAB®, which is commonly used in electrical engineering community.
3. MATLAB® source codes for exercises are provided (available at http://ej.iop.org/images/books/978-0-7503-1233-2/live/bk978-0-7503-1233-2suppdata.zip), which enables readers to modify them, if necessary, for particular needs, to design new exercises and, in addition, to use them for solving particular image processing tasks.
4. Exercises are supported by clear and intuitive explanations of the relevant theory.
5. Test signals and images provided in the book as well as the methodology of the experiments will be useful for readers in their further studies and practical work.

Altogether the book contains 105 exercises that are grouped in eight chapters according to their subjects. They are listed in table 1.1

Table 1.1.

Chapter 2 Image digitization

Discretization

1 Energy compaction capability of transforms
2 Image band limitation
3 Estimating image effective bandwidth
  Sampling artifacts: 1D
    4 Strobe-effect
    5 Moiré and Strobe-effect
  Sampling artifacts: 2D
    6 No anti-aliasing pre-filtering
    7 Anti-aliasing pre-filtering
8 Sampling artifacts: 3D
9 Ideal versus non-ideal sampling
  Irregular and random sampling
    10 Spectra of irregularly sampled images
    11 Reconstruction of sparsely sampled images by means of interpolation of nearest neighbors
12 Discretization of stereoscopic images
13 Discretization of color images

Quantization

  Quantization of achromatic images
    14 Image 'scalar' quantization and false contours
    15 Vision sensitivity threshold
    16 Quantization in the dynamic range
    17 Uniform versus Lloyd-Max quantization
    18 Image 'scalar' quantization with noise
    19 Quantization of image spectra

  Quantization of color images
    20 Quantization of RGB components
    21 Quantization of YUV components

  Quantization of stereoscopic images
    22 Quantization of depth map
    23 Quantization of UV components

Image data compression

  Predictive coding
    24 Prediction errors: 1D and 2D prediction
    25 DCPM coding: 1D versus 2D prediction
26 Transform coding

Chapter 3 Digital image formation and computational imaging

27 Image recovery from sparse samples
28 Recovery of images with occlusions

Table 1.1. (*Continued.*)

Numerical reconstruction of holograms		
	29	Reconstruction of a simulated Fresnel hologram
	30	Reconstruction of a real off-axis hologram
	31	Comparison of Fourier and Convolutional reconstruction algorithms
32	Image reconstruction from projections	
Chapter 4 Image resampling and building continuous image models		
Signal/image subsampling through fractional shifts		
33	1D signal	
34	2D signal	
Image resampling using 'continuous' image model		
	35	Extracting image arbitrary profiles
	36	Image local zoom
	37	Image resampling according to pixel *X*/*Y* displacement maps
	38	Cartesian-to-polar coordinate transformation
39	Three step image rotation algorithm	
Comparison of image resampling methods		
40	Point spread functions and frequency responses of numerical interpolators	
41	Multiple rotations	
42	Image multiple zoom-in/zoom-out	
Comparison of numerical differentiation and integration methods		
43	Discrete frequency responses of numerical differentiators and integrators	
44	Comparison of numerical differentiation methods	
45	Iterative differentiation/integration	
Chapter 5 Image and noise statistical characterization and diagnostics		
46	Image histograms: Histograms of achromatic images	
47	Image histograms: Histograms of color images	
48	Image local moments and order statistics	
Pixel attributes and neighborhoods		
49	Pixel statistical attributes	
50	Pixel neighborhoods	
Image autocorrelation functions and spectra		
51	Image autocorrelation function	
52	Image power spectra	
Image noise		
	Additive noise	
	53	Additive wide-band noise
	54	Additive narrow-band noise: Banding noise
	55	Additive narrow-band noise: Moiré noise

(*Continues*)

Table 1.1. (*Continued.*)

56	Impulsive noise
57	Speckle noise
Empirical diagnostics of image noise	
58	Wide-band noise
59	Moiré noise
60	Banding noise
Chapter 6 Statistical image models and pattern formation	
PWN-model	
61	Binary spatially inhomogeneous texture with controlled local probabilities of 'ones'
62	Spatially inhomogeneous texture with controlled variances ('multiplicative noise')
63	Spatially inhomogeneous texture with controlled local histograms
LF-model	
	64 'Ring of stars', circular and ring-shaped spectra
	65 'Fractal' textures with 1/f type of spectrum
	66 Imitation of natural textures
	67 Spatially inhomogeneous textures with controlled local spectra
68	PWN&LF-model
69	LF&PWN-model
Evolutionary models	
70	Generating patchy patterns
71	Generating maze-like patterns
Chapter 7 Image correlators for detection and localization of objects	
Localization of a target on empty background	
	72 Localization of a target on uniform background
	73 Localization of a character in text
	74 Threshold effect in the probability of anomalous localization errors
75	Normal and anomalous localization errors
76	'Matched filter' correlator versus signal-to-clutter ratio optimal correlator
77	Local versus global signal-to-clutter ratio optimal correlators
Object localization and image edges	
78	Image 'whitening'
79	Exchange of amplitude spectra of two images
Chapter 8 Methods of image perfecting	
Correcting imaging system transfer functions	
80	Correction of imaging system amplitude transfer function
81	Correction of imaging system frequency transfer function

Table 1.1. *(Continued.)*

Filtering periodical interferences

82 Filtering in DFT domain

83 Filtering in DCT domain

84 Filtering 'banding' noise

'Ideal' and Empirical Wiener filtering for image denoising and deblurring

85 Comparison of image deblurring/denoising capabilities of the ideal and empirical Wiener filters

86 Inspection of potentials of image restoration capabilities of the ideal and empirical Wiener filters

Local adaptive filtering for image denoising: achromatic images

87 1D denoising filtering

88 2D denoising filtering: principle

89 2D denoising filtering: global versus local

90 Local adaptive filtering for image denoising: color images

91 Filtering impulsive noise using linear filters

Image denoising using nonlinear (rank) filters

92 Filtering additive noise

93 Filtering impulsive noise

Chapter 9 Methods of image enhancement

Enhancement of achromatic images

94 Contrast enhancement: unsharp masking using local means and medians

Contrast enhancement: P-th law spectra enhancement

95 Global spectrum enhancement

96 Local spectra enhancement

Contrast enhancement: P-histogram equalization

97 Global P-histogram equalization

98 Local P-histogram equalization

99 Contrast enhancement: pixel cardinalities

100 Edge extraction: Max–Min

101 Edge extraction: Size-EV

Enhancement of color images

102 Color image unsharp masking

Color histogram modification

103 RGB P-histogram equalization

104 YUV P-histogram equalization

105 Modification of color saturation and rotation of color histogram

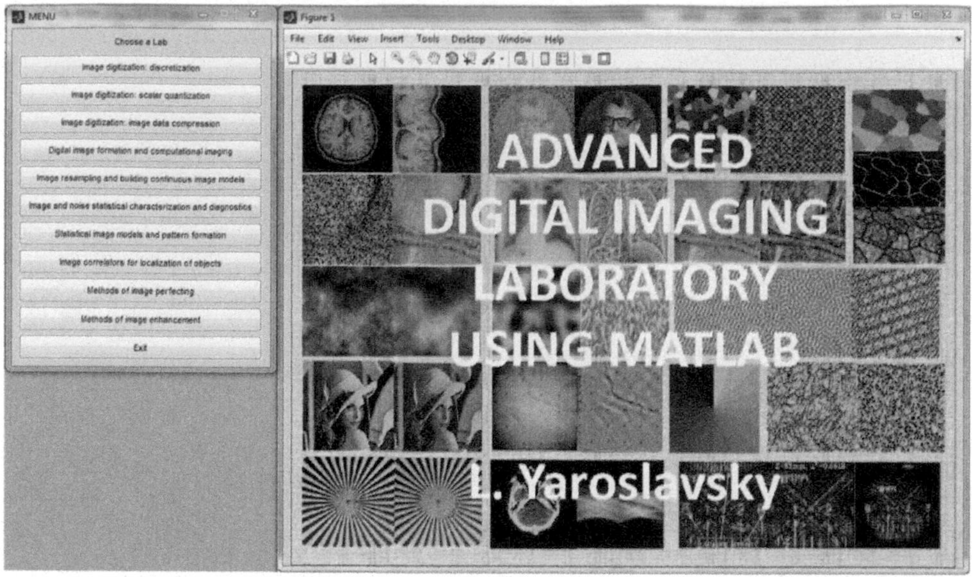

Figure 1.1. The general entrance menu.

The theoretical foundations and detailed explanations of all methods represented by exercises in this book can be found in either of the following two books:

1. Yaroslavsky L 2012 *Theoretical Foundations of Digital Imaging Using MATLAB®* (Boca Raton, FL: CRC Press)
2. Yaroslavsky 2004 *Digital holography and Digital Image Processing* (New York: Kluwer)

1.2 Instructions for readers

To use the book and conduct exercises on a reader's computer, MATLAB® should be installed on the computer, Advanced Digital Imaging Lab package that supplements the book should be copied into the computer and the MATLAB® path should be set to enable access to it from the MATLAB® command window. For some exercises, the availability of MATLAB® Signal Processing and Image Processing toolboxes is required. The package contains, in addition to program files, a set of test images in 'mat', 'tif' and 'jpg' formats. The usage for experimentation of images from users' imagedata bases is also possible. The package was tested on MATLAB® R2010b version 7.11.0.584, but earlier versions can also be used.

The start program of the package is ***Run_Labs_IOP***. The program opens the general entrance menu with a list of exercises shown in figure 1.1.

Items in this list unify sets of exercises on solving specific image processing tasks considered in the corresponding book chapter (see table 1.1). A particular set of exercises can be started by pressing the corresponding button in this menu.

Chapters 2 to 9 provide guidance for the exercises. The chapters explain the specific image processing task for which exercises of the particular chapter are designed, review basic principles underlying the corresponding methods, and give instruction for setting relevant parameters and running the exercises. It is recommended to read, before starting any particular set of exercises, the corresponding chapter.

It is also highly recommended to conduct the exercises with many different test images and with varieties of parameters of the algorithms in order to gain deeper insight into peculiarities of the algorithms and methods and their potentials and limitations, as well as how to properly set their user defined working parameters.

At the end of each chapter, questions for self-testing are offered. They are intended to induce the reader to think over the results of the exercises and formulate for him/herself what has been learned.

The author wishes the readers a fascinating journey over the land of digital imaging and will appreciate any remarks, comments and program improvements.

IOP Publishing

Leonid P Yaroslavsky

Chapter 2

Image digitization

2.1 Introduction

Exercises in this chapter address the very first problem of digital imaging, the problem of conversion of sensor signals that carry information on natural objects into digital signals that can be put in computers, stored in digital storage, transmitted through digital communication channels and eventually used for creating sufficiently perfect images. This conversion is called 'image digitization'.

Generally, image digitization can be treated as determination, for each particular image, of which image in an indexed set of all possible images that the user can distinguish one from another can be identified with that particular image. The index of this 'representative' image in the set is taken as the image digital representation. Image reconstruction from its digital representation then generates the representative image with this index. This is similar, for instance, to what we do when we describe everything in our life with words in speaking or writing.

However, in the case of images, this general procedure is, as a rule, not feasible in reality. While volume of our vocabulary is about 10^5–10^6 words, the variety of images we have to deal with in imaging is immeasurably larger. One can see that from this simple example: the number of digital images of, for instance, standard (not high definition) TV quality (500 × 500 pixels with 256 gray levels in each of three RGB channels) is $256^{3\times500\times500}$. Obviously, no technical device is capable of implementing such a huge look-up table as this number overwhelmingly exceeds the number of elementary particles in the Universe.

A solution of this problem of the image digitization complexity is found in a three-stage digitization procedure. At the first stage, called *image discretization*, continuous sensor signals are converted into a finite set of real numbers that form the *image discrete representation.*

In the second stage, called *scalar* (*element wise*) *quantization*, this set of real numbers is, number by number, converted into a set of quantized numbers, which finally results in a digital signal that can be used for reconstruction, with a certain admissible accuracy, of the initial continuous signal. In the same way as written speech is a sequence of letters selected from an alphabet, digital representation of images is a sequence of numbers that can take one of a finite set of quantized values.

In the third stage, called *image compression*, digital signals obtained after discretization and scalar quantization are subjected to 'compression' aimed at minimization of the number of binary digits (bits) sufficient to represent them and, hence, at minimization of the size of the memory required for storing images in digital storage or of the capacity of digital communication channels used for image transmission.

To study these issues, the following three corresponding sets of laboratory exercises are offered.

- Image digitization: discretization.
- Image digitization: quantization.
- Image digitization: image data compression.

2.2 Image discretization

Upon pressing the button 'Image digitization: discretization' in the main menu of exercises, the panel shown in figure 2.1 appears, which offers two groups of exercises.

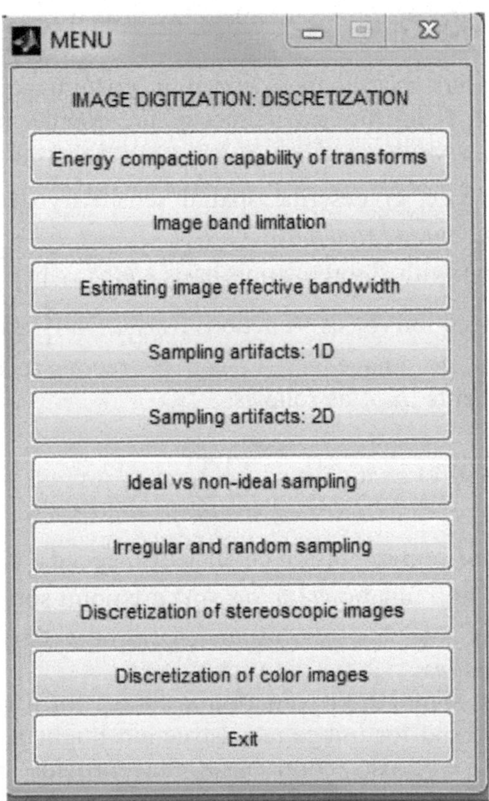

Figure 2.1. Image digitization: discretization.

The first two sets of exercises, 'Energy compaction capability of transforms' and 'Image band-limitation', illustrate the basic principle of discretization as image expansion over a set of transform basis functions. Exercises 'Estimating image effective bandwidth', 'Sampling artifacts', and 'Ideal versus non-ideal sampling' are intended for studying the most commonly used image discretization method, that of image sampling. The exercises 'Irregular and random sampling' address phenomena associated with irregular sampling grids. The last two exercises are devoted to peculiarities of discretization of color and stereoscopic images.

2.2.1 Signal discretization as its expansion over a set of basis functions

In principle, there might be many different ways of converting continuous image sensor signals into discrete ones represented by sets of real numbers. However, the technological tradition is such that technical devices used currently for such a conversion implement a method that can mathematically be modeled as computing coefficients of image signal expansion (decomposition) over a set of basis functions of a certain transform, i.e. over a set of transform template images.

The coefficients $\{\alpha_{k,l}\}$ of discrete representations of signal $a(x, y)$ are computed in image discretization devices as

$$\alpha_{k,l} = \int_X \int_Y a(x, y)\phi_{k,l}^{(\mathrm{d})}(x, y)\,\mathrm{d}x\,\mathrm{d}y \tag{2.1}$$

where (x, y) are spatial coordinates defined in the image discretization device coordinate system, $\{k, l\}$ are integer indices of the coefficients $(k, l = 1, 2, 3, \ldots.)$ and $\phi_{k,l}^{(\mathrm{d})}(x, y)$ are *discretization basis functions* defined in the same coordinate system. Functions $\phi_{k,l}^{(\mathrm{d})}(x, y)$ describe spatial sensitivity of image discretization devices, i.e. their *point spread functions*.

Image discretization with discretization basis $\left\{\phi_{k,l}^{(d)}(x, y)\right\}$ assumes that a reciprocal set of reconstruction basis functions $\left\{\phi_{k,l}^{(r)}(x, y)\right\}$ exists, with which an approximation $\hat{a}(x, y)$ to image $a(x, y)$ can be reconstructed from its discrete representation coefficients $\{\alpha_{k,l}\}$ as follows:

$$a(x, y) \approx \hat{a}(x, y) = \sum_{k=0}^{K-1}\sum_{l=0}^{L-1}\alpha_{k,l}\phi_{k,l}^{(r)}(x, y), \tag{2.2}$$

$K \times L$ is the number of representation coefficients needed for image reconstruction with a given accuracy and functions $\left\{\phi_{k,l}^{(r)}(x, y)\right\}$ are point spread functions of signal reconstruction devices (such as, for instance, computer displays), or their *reconstruction aperture functions*.

For different bases, signal approximation accuracy for a given number of basis functions $N = K \times L$ used for image reconstruction might be different. Naturally, the discretization and reconstruction bases that provide better approximation accuracy for a given N are preferable. It is customary to evaluate signal approximation accuracy in terms of preservation of *signal energy*, i.e. of integral of squared signal over its definition area. Some transforms are capable of concentrating most of the signal energy in few signal decomposition coefficients. This capability of transforms is called their *energy compaction capability*.

Theoretically, Karhunen–Loève transform and related Hotelling and singular value decomposition (SVD) transforms have the best energy compaction capability among discretization transforms. However, in practice in image processing they remain, because of implementation problems, to serve only as theoretical benchmarks, and other transforms that have fast computational algorithms, such as discrete Fourier (DCT), discrete cosine (DCT, discrete Walsh and discrete wavelet transforms, are used as discretization and, correspondingly, reconstruction transforms.

The exercise 'Energy compaction capability of transforms' provides an opportunity to compare energy compaction capability of discrete Fourier, discrete dosine, discrete Walsh and discrete wavelet transforms in application to different test images. In this exercise, spectra of images in different transforms are computed and spectral coefficients are sorted according to their magnitude. Then a certain percentage of the coefficients with the least magnitudes chosen by the user is zeroed, after which such images 'band-limited' in this way are reconstructed and displayed along with their 'band-limited' spectra to enable their visual comparison. In addition, fractions of image energy contained in the retained coefficients are computed and plotted as functions of the percentage of retained transform coefficients. The latter is a numerical measure of the transform energy compaction capability.

For experiments, several test images are prepared and an option of using other images from image data set is offered as well. The exercise can be conducted either with image frames of 256 × 256 pixels or with interactively selected image fragments of different sizes listed in the menu shown in figure 2.2.

Upon setting fragment size, the user is prompted to indicate on the chosen test image, using the cursor, the center of the fragment, after which the chosen fragment and its DFT, DCT, Walsh and Haar spectra are displayed and the user is requested to set the energy percentage threshold for retaining the largest spectral coefficients that contain this percentage of total image energy and zeroing the rest of the coefficients (figure 2.3). Finally, spectra of the fragments are supplemented by plots

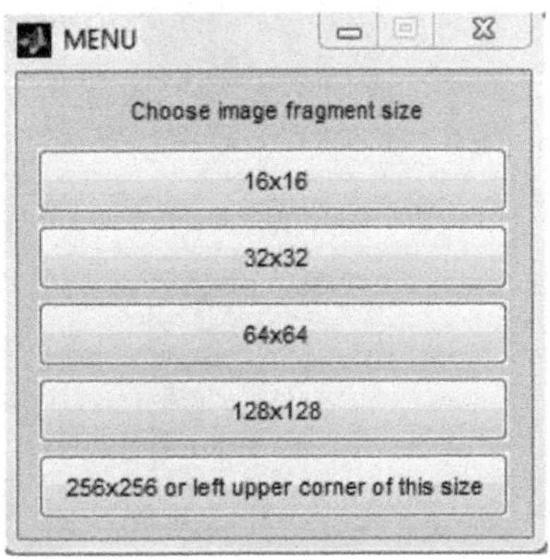

Figure 2.2. Energy compaction capability of transforms: choosing test image fragment.

of fractions of spectra energy versus fraction of their corresponding spectral coefficients and an option of displaying the above threshold spectra is offered (figures 2.4 and 2.5). The plots of fractions of spectra energy versus fraction of their corresponding spectral coefficients are numerical measures of the energy compaction capabilities of the transforms.

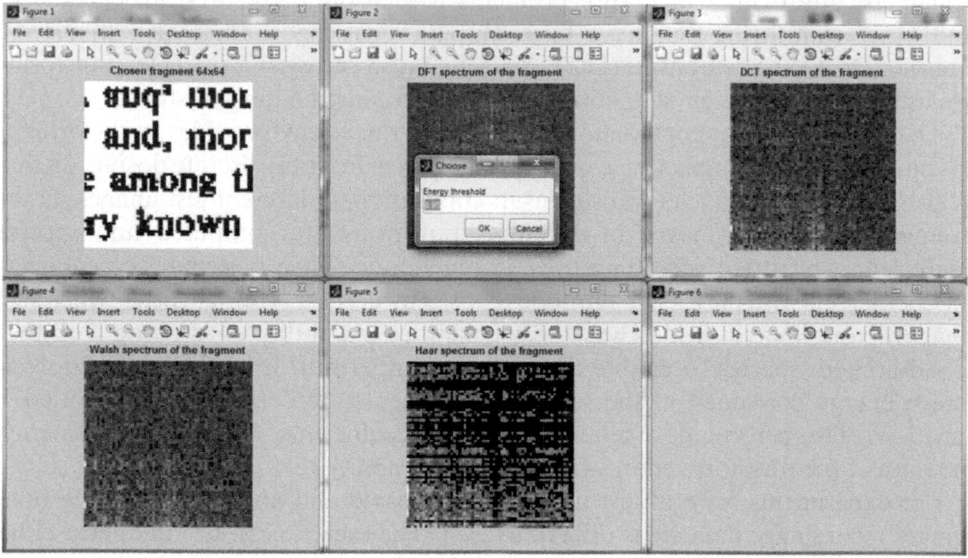

Figure 2.3. Energy compaction capability of transforms: setting energy threshold.

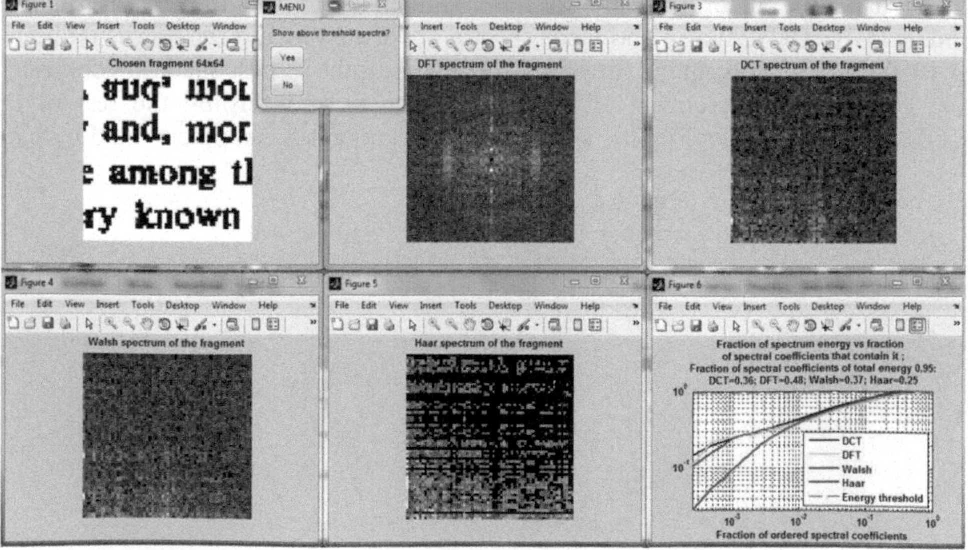

Figure 2.4. Energy compaction capability of transforms: test fragment spectra and fractions of spectra energy versus fraction of their corresponding spectral coefficients.

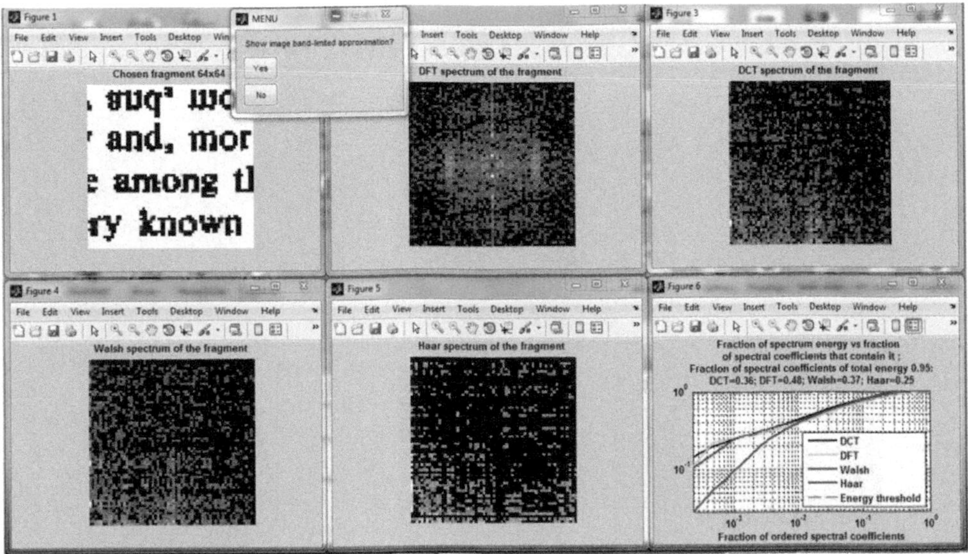

Figure 2.5. Energy compaction capability of transforms: above threshold test fragment spectra and fractions of spectra energy versus fraction of their corresponding spectral coefficients.

Image band-limitation

In the previous experiment, energy compaction capability of transforms was studied by means of zeroing a certain percentage of the image spectra smallest coefficients. This exercise provides an alternative insight into the energy compaction capability of transforms. The exercise allows us: (i) to examine how the energy of spectral coefficients depends on the degree of spectrum 'low-pass' band-limitation by a square or a pie sector, and (ii) to visually evaluate results of image band-limitation for different transforms and compare standard deviations of reconstruction errors due to spectrum band limitation by means of 'low pass' filtering. At the program start, the user is prompted to choose a test image from a list of prepared test images or from the image database. Then DFT, DCT, Walsh and Haar spectra are displayed along with plots of plots of energy of band limited image (in fraction of image total energy) versus area of a square (in fraction of image base band), which limits image bandwidth, and the user is prompted to choose displaying band limitation effects and, for this, to set fraction of base band for band limitation and band limitation shape, square or pie sector (figure 2.6).

Finally, results of the chosen band limitation in the domain of DCT, Walsh and Haar transforms are displayed for visual evaluation and comparison of standard deviations of band limitation errors (figure 2.7).

2.2.2 Image sampling

Among image discretization methods, image sampling, i.e. representation of images in the form of 2D arrays of samples taken in nodes of a uniform square sampling

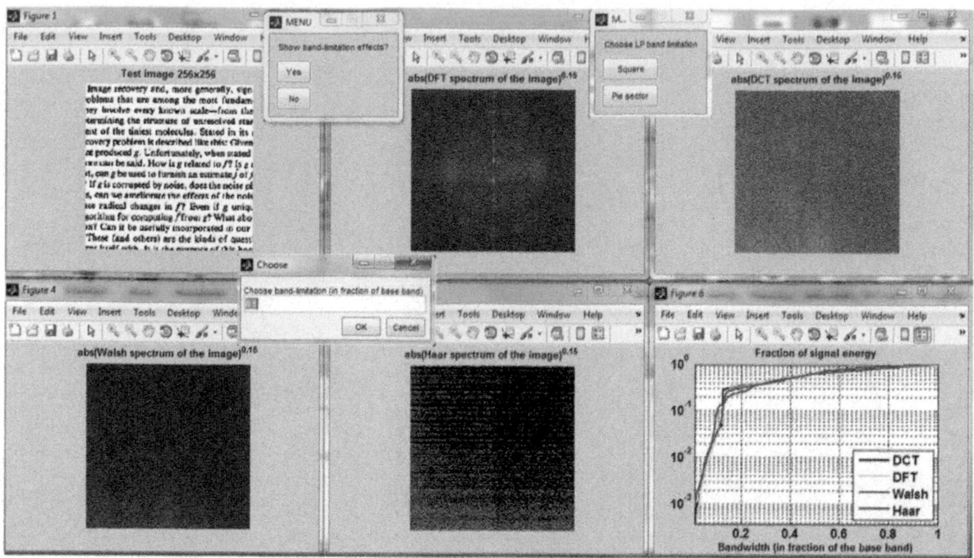

Figure 2.6. Image band-limitation: spectra of test image and plots of energy of band limited image (in fraction of image total energy) versus area of a square (in fraction of image base band), which limits image bandwidth.

Figure 2.7. Image band-limitation: test image, results of its band-limitation and band limitation errors for the case of pie sector as the band limitation shape (shown in upper left corners of error images).

lattice, is the most commonly used one. For image displays as well as for image processing software such representation is the standard.

In denotations of equation (2.1), samples of image signal $a(x, y)$ are measured using 'shift', or sampling basis functions as,

$$a_{k,l} = \int_X \int_Y a(x, y)\phi^{(s)}\left(x - k\Delta^{(s)}x, y - l\Delta^{(s)}y\right)\mathrm{d}x\,\mathrm{d}y, \tag{2.3}$$

where $(\Delta^{(s)}x, \Delta^{(s)}y)$ are sampling intervals in coordinates (x, y) and $\phi^{(s)}(x, y)$ is point spread function (*sampling aperture*) of the sampling device, such as image scanner or digital camera. Note that signal samples $\{a_{k,l}\}$ are not samples (point values) of the image $a(x, y)$ but rather point values of its copy $\tilde{a}(x, y)$

$$\tilde{a}(x, y) = \int_X \int_Y a(\xi, \eta)\phi^{(s)}(x - \xi, y - \eta)\,\mathrm{d}\xi\,\mathrm{d}\eta \tag{2.4}$$

filtered by sampling aperture $\phi^{(s)}(x, y)$ of the sampling device.

Signal reconstruction devices, such as display devices, reconstruct the image from its samples by means of summation of reconstruction shift basis functions weighted by image samples:

$$\hat{a}(x, y) = \sum_{k=0}^{K-1}\sum_{l=0}^{L-1} a_{k,l}\phi^{(r)}\left(x - k\Delta^{(r)}x, y - l\Delta^{(r)}y\right), \tag{2.5}$$

where $\Delta^{(r)}x$ and $\Delta^{(r)}y$ are corresponding sampling intervals of the image reconstruction device defined in its coordinates (x, y), and $\phi^{(r)}(x, y)$ is the reconstruction device point spread function (*reconstruction aperture*).

The reconstruction process can also be considered as filtering of a virtual signal $\tilde{\tilde{a}}(x, y) = \sum_{k=0}^{K-1}\sum_{l=0}^{L-1} a_{k,l}\delta(x - k\Delta^{(r)}x, y - l\Delta^{(r)}y)$ by reconstruction aperture of the reconstruction device:

$$\hat{a}(x, y) = \int_{-\infty}^{\infty}\int_{-\infty}^{-\infty} \sum_{k=0}^{K-1}\sum_{l=0}^{L-1} a_{k,l}\delta\left(x - k\Delta^{(r)}x, y - l\Delta^{(r)}y\right)\phi^{(r)} \times(x - \xi, y - \eta)\,\mathrm{d}\xi\,\mathrm{d}\eta, \tag{2.6}$$

where $\delta(x, y)$ is the Dirac delta function, an infinitely high and infinitely narrow impulse. A remarkable feature of the virtual signal $\tilde{\tilde{a}}(x, y)$ is that its Fourier spectrum is a periodical replication of the spectrum of the image $a(x, y)$ with periods $1/\Delta^{(s)}x$ and $1/\Delta^{(s)}y$ in the corresponding frequency coordinates.

The result of reconstruction $\hat{a}(x, y)$ is not an exact copy of the initial sampled image $a(x, y)$ unless the image is band-limited, i.e. its Fourier spectrum is zero outside the rectangle with sides $(1/\Delta^{(s)}x, 1/\Delta^{(s)}y)$ and the reconstruction device aperture performs the ideal low-pass filtering, i.e. does not pass through spectral components outside the same rectangle with sides $(1/\Delta^{(s)}x, 1/\Delta^{(s)}y)$ and, therefore, suppresses all replicas of spectrum of the virtual but one within the rectangle $(-1/2\Delta^{(s)}x \div 1/2\Delta^{(s)}x, \ -1/2\Delta^{(s)}y \div 1/2\Delta^{(s)}y)$.

Real images are not band limited. For them, minimal mean squared reconstruction error is achieved if the sampling device performs the ideal low-pass filtering as well, i.e. if it suppresses all image spectral components outside the rectangle $(-1/2\Delta^{(s)}x \div 1/2\Delta^{(s)}x, \ -1/2\Delta^{(s)}y \div 1/2\Delta^{(s)}y)$.

The rectangle $(-1/2\Delta^{(s)}x \div 1/2\Delta^{(s)}x, \quad -1/2\Delta^{(s)}y \div 1/2\Delta^{(s)}y)$ is called image *baseband*. All spectral components of the image outside the baseband will be either lost or will, due to imperfections of sampling and reconstruction devices, produce image distortions called *aliasing errors*.

In order to reduce computer memory required for storage of digitized images and image processing, time image sampling intervals should be selected to be as large as possible but not larger than is allowed by the requirements of image reconstruction accuracy. Therefore, image sampling requires evaluation of image effective bandwidth.

Estimating image effective bandwidth

Exercises in estimating image effective bandwidth are listed in the start menu (figure 2.8)

Visual readability based evaluation of effective bandwidth of image DCT spectra

This exercise provides an opportunity to visually evaluate how choosing image basebands and, correspondingly, of image sampling intervals affects the 'readability' of different images. At the start, the user is prompted to choose a test image from a list of prepared test images of any other image from the image data base. Test images in this experiment are considered as oversampled and are subjected to band-limitation in order to find out how much one can down-sample them without losses of their readability. The band limitation is implemented in the DCT domain in eight steps, from 7/8 × 7/8 to 1/8 × 1/8 of the base band. Upon choosing a test image the program displays copies of the test image one by one bandlimited in the above steps and, at the end, a test image of all its band-limited copies side by side to enable visual evaluation of an admissible degree of image band-limitation and, correspondingly, down-sampling (figure 2.9).

JPG image quality based evaluation of effective bandwidth of image DCT spectra

This exercise provides an opportunity to inspect image spectral sparsity for the same level of image approximation mean square error (RMS) as that for standard JPEG image lossy compression in MATLAB® implementation, to estimate shapes and dimensions of image DCT spectra that secure image band-limited restoration with the same or close mean square error.

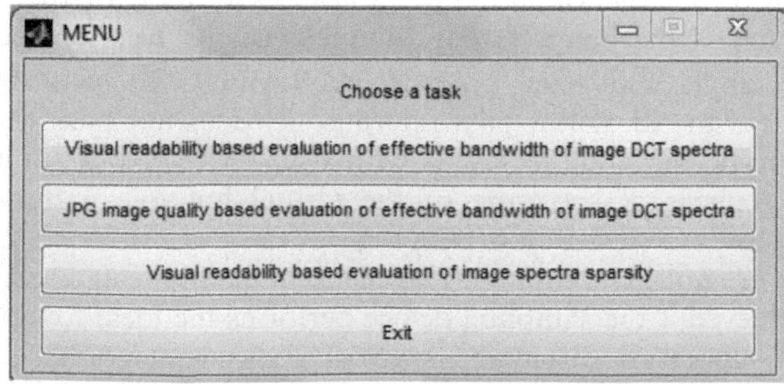

Figure 2.8. Estimating image effective bandwidth: start menu.

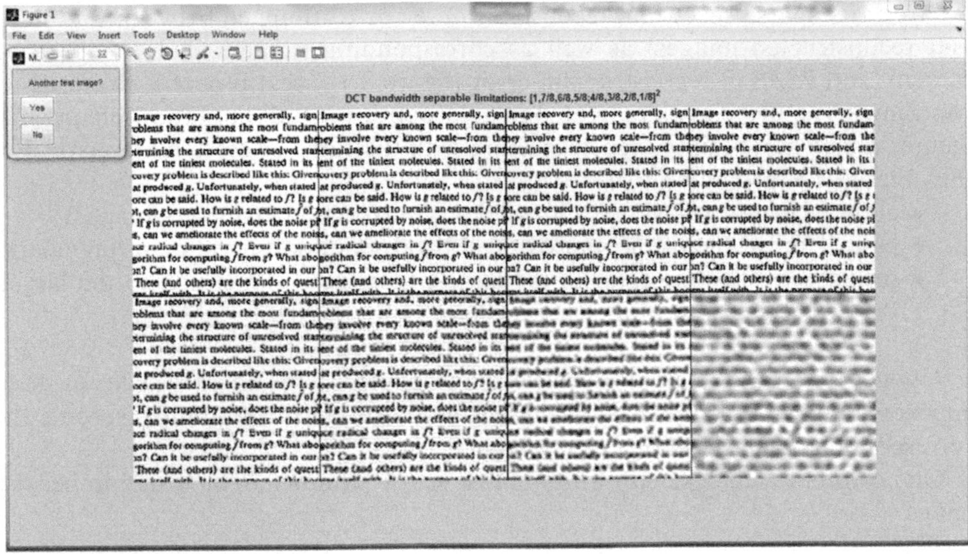

Figure 2.9. Estimating image effective bandwidth: test image and its band limited down-sampled copies with different band limitation.

Image *spectrum sparsity* is a notion defined for sampled images. As has been mentioned, digital display devices and image processing software assume by default that sampling over regular square sampling grids is used for discrete representation of images. Such sampling is as a rule far from being optimal and digital images acquired in this way are, as a rule, highly compressible. Image spectrum sparsity is a measure of image potential compressibility in terms of the sufficient number of samples.

The *discrete sampling theorem,* which assumes sampled images, states that given K samples of an image of N samples, one can approximate this image by an image with K non-zero spectral coefficients in a domain of a certain transform with mean square approximation error (MSE) equal to the energy of the rest $N - K$ transform coefficients. The approximation error is minimal if the selected K are the most intensive transform coefficients. In the case of discrete Fourier and cosine transforms, K image samples can be taken in arbitrary positions.

The relative number K/N of image spectral coefficients sufficient for image reconstruction with a given MSE is called image spectrum sparsity for this MSE. It defines potential image band limitation, which preserves the admissible accuracy of image reconstruction from its samples.

One can use in the exercise either one of several pre-prepared test images or another arbitrary image from the image database or arbitrary square image fragment. In the latter case, the chosen image is displayed and the user is prompted to choose the fragment size and, using a cursor, the fragment center. Then the program demonstrates the chosen image or its chosen fragment, its sparse spectrum for the same RMS reconstruction error as that of image JPG compression, image reconstructed from the found non-zero spectral coefficients, i.e. from its sparse spectrum, reconstruction error (difference between the initial and reconstructed images) as well as corresponding numerical data: spectrum sparsity and RMS of reconstruction error (figure 2.10) and proceeds to step 2, to choosing a regular, oval or rectangular spectrum band limitation shape that secures image band-limited reconstruction with the same or close RMS error. For this, the user is prompted to:

- either accept the RMS of admissible reconstruction error or change it
- choose the shape of the approximate band limitation (oval or rectangular)
- set aspect ratio (the ratio of the largest horizontal dimension to the largest vertical dimension) of the chosen shape.

Upon setting the requested parameters, a display with the chosen spectrum shape appears along with reconstructed images from sparse and band-limited spectra and corresponding reconstruction errors (figure 2.11).

One can repeat the exercise with another set of parameters or with another test image.

Visual readability based evaluation of image spectra sparsity

This exercise is similar to the previous one and complements it. The exercise enables analyzing spectra sparsity and approximation of image sparse spectra by standard rectangular or oval shapes more deeply. At the first display (figure 2.12) the program shows the test image chosen by the user and prompts to either accept the value of sparsity at the level of JPEG image reconstruction quality automatically found or set another value. Then the program displays the original test image

Figure 2.10. Evaluation of image bandwidth shape though spectrum sparsity (step 1). Non-zero image sparse spectrum coefficients are shown in white in the image spectrum (upper right panel).

Figure 2.11. Evaluation of image bandwidth shape though spectrum sparsity (step 2).

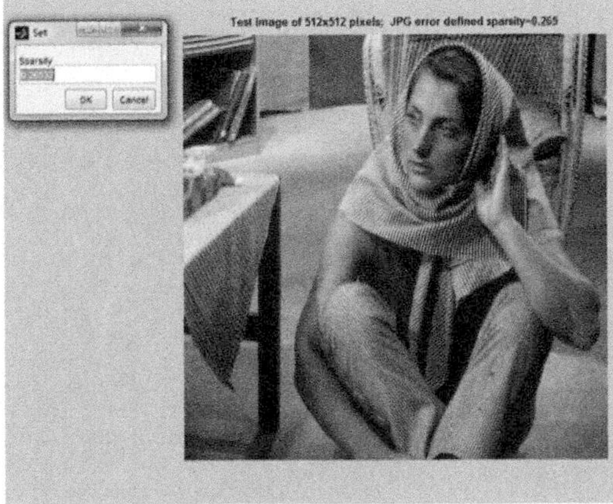

Figure 2.12. Exercise 'Visual readability based evaluation of image spectra sparsity' (step 1).

and he image reconstructed from a set of DCT spectral coefficients for the chosen spectrum sparsity and offers an option to show DCT spectra of these images (figure 2.13).

In the subsequent two steps the spectra of the images are displayed (figure 2.14), and, upon choosing the option 'Approximate sparse spectrum shape' and setting requested parameters (figure 2.15), the process and the result of the approximation (figure 2.16). Spectrum shape approximation is done by gradual enlargement of the selected shape until the error of image band limitation by the chosen shape becomes lower than the sparse approximation reconstruction error for the chosen sparsity. The final display shown in figure 2.16 contains, along with other relevant numerical

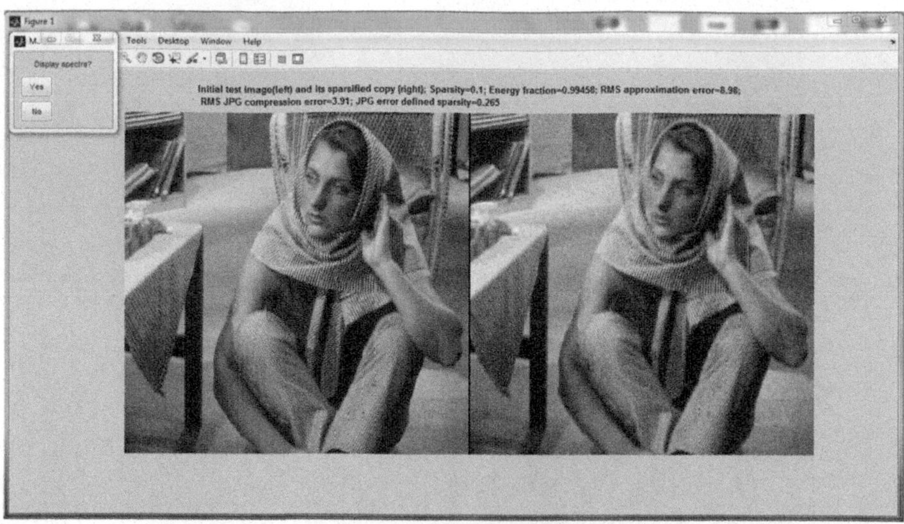

Figure 2.13. Exercise 'Visual readability based evaluation of image spectra sparsity' (step 2).

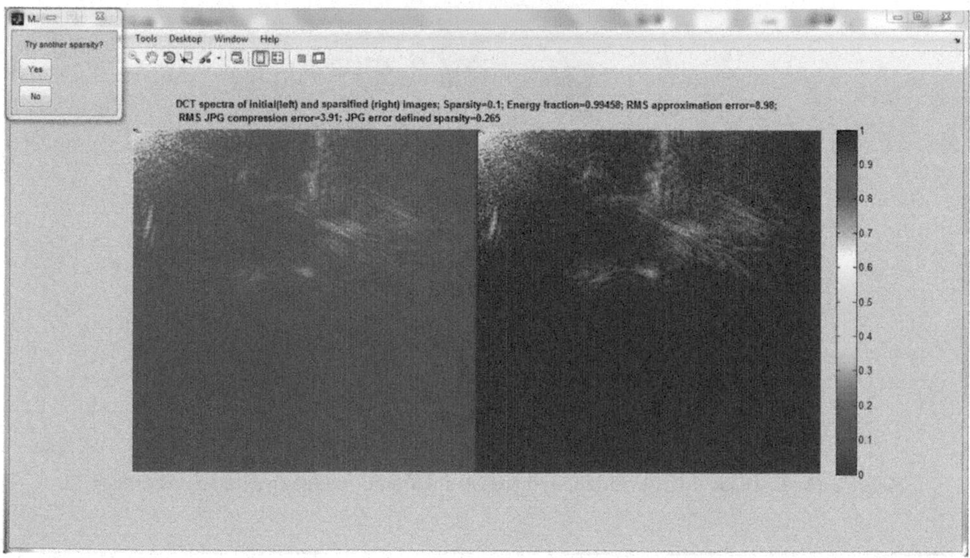

Figure 2.14. Visual readability based evaluation of image spectra sparsity: DCT spectra of test and of its sparsified copy.

parameters, an additional parameter 'Redundancy', which is the ratio of the area of the chosen shape to the number of coefficients of the sparse spectrum. According to the discrete sampling theorem, this ratio shows how much the number of samples required for reconstruction of the image band limited with the chosen shape exceeds the minimal number of samples defined by the image spectrum sparsity for the same accuracy of image reconstruction.

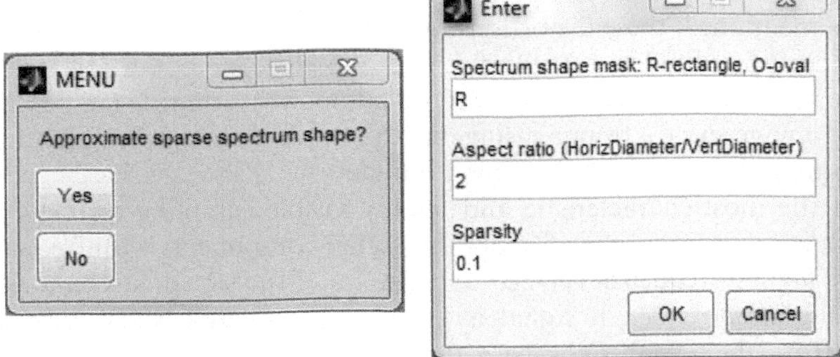

Figure 2.15. Visual readability based evaluation of image spectra sparsity: menu of parameters.

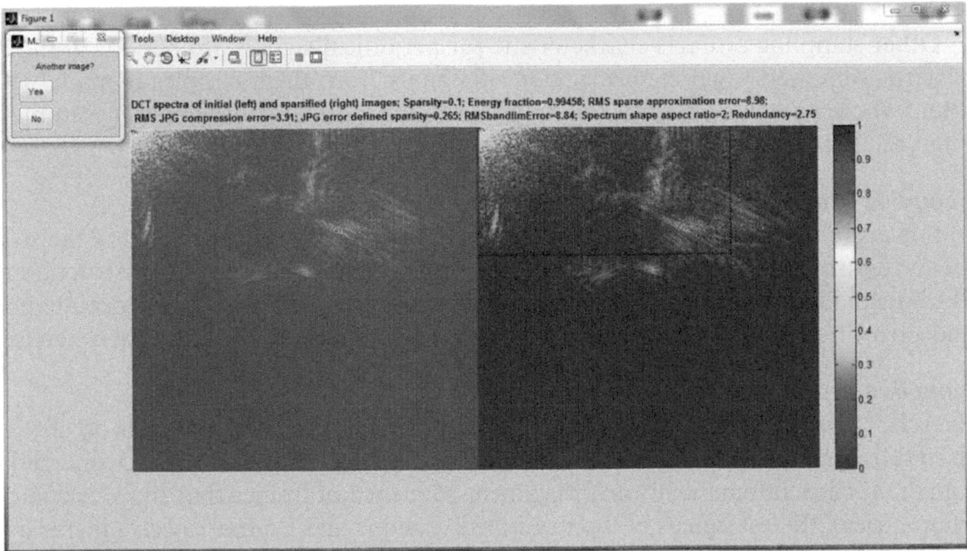

Figure 2.16. Visual readability based evaluation of image spectra sparsity (step 4): DCT spectra of test and sparsified images and chosen approximative shape of band limitation.

Sampling artifacts

Image sampling inevitably causes certain image distortions. According to the sampling theory, these distortions in the reconstructed images are due to the following reasons:

- Modifications of the image Fourier spectra due to image pre-filtering in sampling devices
- Penetration of tails of the pre-filtered image spectra periodical (with periods $(1/\Delta^{(s)}x,\ 1/\Delta^{(s)}y)$) replicas inside the image sampling baseband $(-1/2\Delta^{(s)}x \div 1/2\Delta^{(s)}x,\ \ -1/2\Delta^{(s)}y \div 1/2\Delta^{(s)}y)$; this causes spectra *aliasing*
- Penetration into spectra of reconstructed images of the image spectra periodical replicas outside the signal baseband, which are not perfectly filtered out by the 'post-filtering' in the image reconstruction device.

As was mentioned, these distortions are minimal if sampling and reconstruction apertures perform ideal low pass filtering and, therefore, do not distort image spectra within the baseband and remove all spectral components outside the baseband, thus preventing image spectra from aliasing due to sampling. Image pre-filtering with the ideal low-pass filter makes images band limited.

One of the most characteristic and readily visible sampling artifacts is stroboscopic reduction of frequency of periodical signal components with frequencies that exceed the highest frequencies $(1/2\Delta^{(s)}x,\ 1/2\Delta^{(s)}y)$ of the signal baseband. This effect is called the *strobe-effect*. If signal is properly pre-filtered, such components are removed from the signal. Otherwise their replicated copies will penetrate inside the baseband and appear with reduced frequencies. Specifically, a component with frequency $f_x > 1/2\Delta^{(s)}x$ appears in the reconstructed signal with frequency $\left(1/\Delta^{(s)}x - f_x\right)$.

Other sampling artifacts characteristic for periodical signals are periodical moiré patterns observed when reconstruction of signals from their samples is made with filters whose pass band exceeds the signal sampling baseband as defined by sampling interval. This phenomenon is called the *moiré-effect*.

Sampling artifacts 1D .
In this exercise sampling artifacts 'strobe-effect' and 'moiré effects' listed in the start menu (figure 2.17) are demonstrated on examples of sampling and reconstruction of 1D sinusoidal test signals of different frequencies with and without appropriate pre- and post-filtering. Figures 2.18 and 2.19 show examples generated in this exercise.

Sampling artifacts, 2D
Exercise 'Sampling artifacts: 2D' uses as test signals 2D sinusoidal signals of varying spatial frequencies and demonstrates sampling and reconstruction of 2D sinusoidal signals. It runs automatically and displays a sequence of frames that show circularly symmetrical 2D test signals of their sampled versions and Fourier spectra increasing in time frequencies. Two options for running the exercise are offered (figure 2.20):

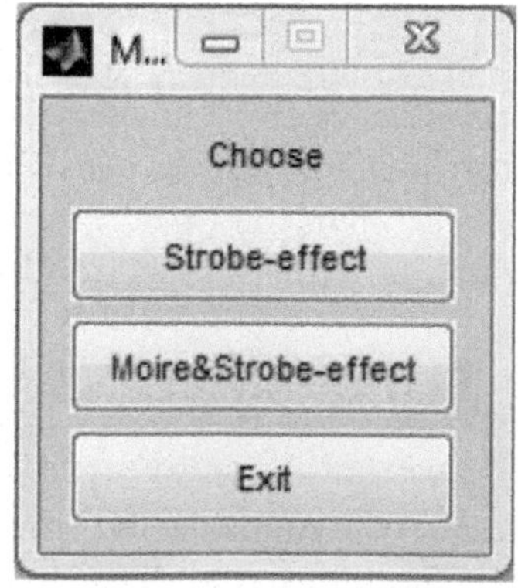

Figure 2.17. Sampling artifacts, 1D: start menu.

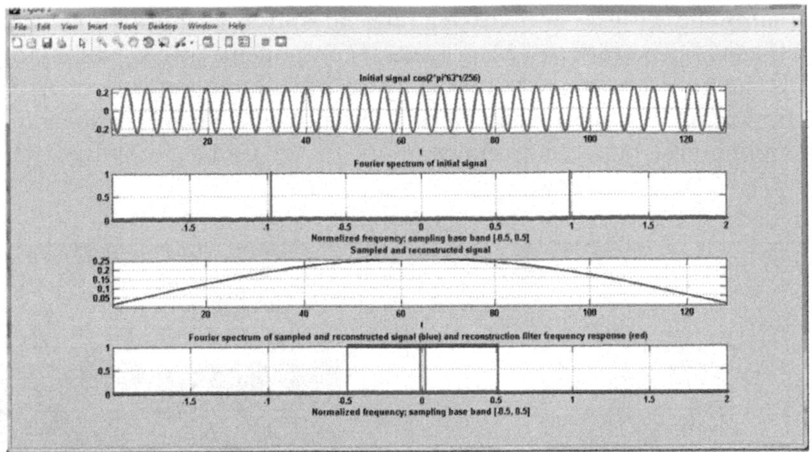

Figure 2.18. Sampling artifacts 1D: 'strobe' effect in sampling and reconstruction of an inappropriately pre-filtered sinusoidal signal, whose frequency exceeds the highest frequency of the signal baseband.

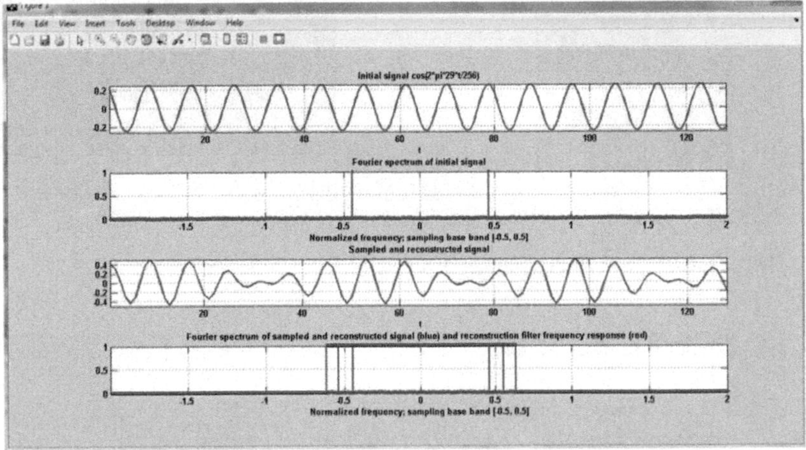

Figure 2.19. Sampling artifacts, 1D: 'moiré effect' in sampling and reconstruction of sinusoidal signals in the case of inappropriate 'post-filtering'.

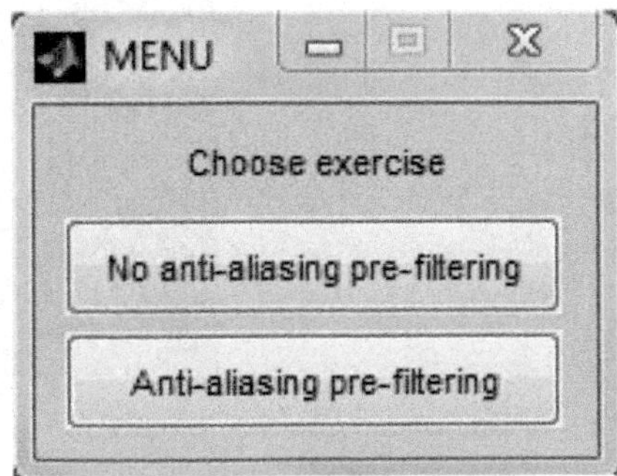

Figure 2.20. Aliasing 2D: start menu.

When sampling with no anti-aliasing filtering option is chosen, one can observe aliasing effects of penetrating aliasing spectral components into signal sampling base band, as is shown in one of the frames in figure 2.21. Sampling with no anti-aliasing filtering option allows one to observe the absence of aliasing artifacts within the signal sampling base band, as is shown in one of the frames in figure 2.22.

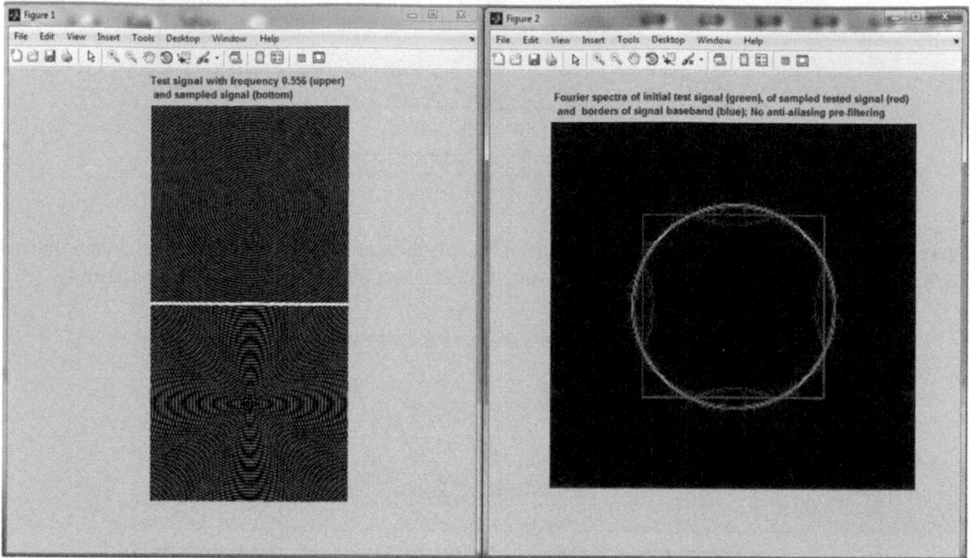

Figure 2.21. Aliasing in 2D signals: sampling with no anti-aliasing signal pre-filtering.

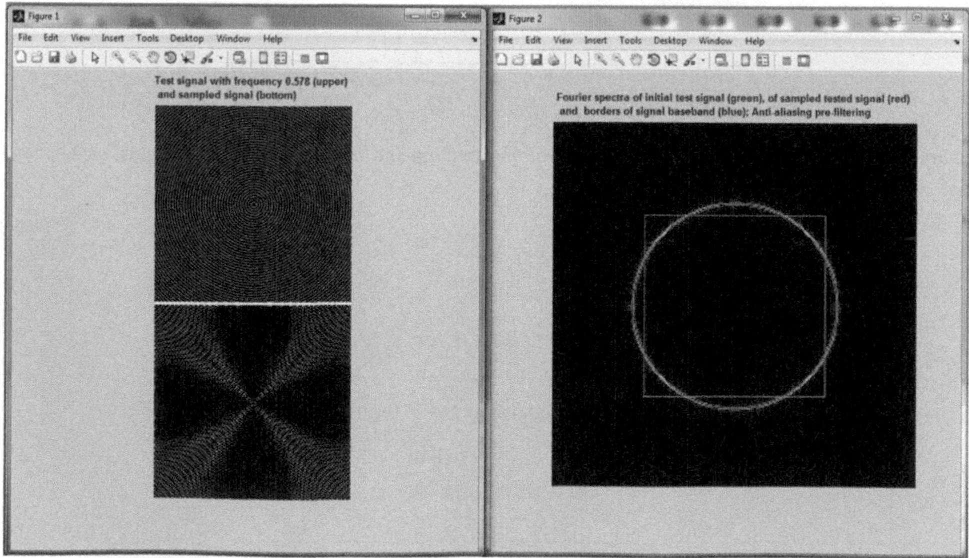

Figure 2.22. Aliasing in 2D signals: sampling with anti-aliasing signal pre-filtering.

Sampling artifacts: 3D

This exercise demonstrates aliasing strobe effects that can emerge in sampling moving objects. The program imitates sampling of rotating images by a sensor, in which the image is accessed row-wise, as takes place, for instance, in CMOS cameras. As a test image, either a pre-prepared test image of a radial resolution chart or any other image from the image database can be used. Figure 2.23 shows one of the intermediate frames of frame sequence of rotated image and its sampled copy.

Ideal versus non-ideal sampling

Appropriate pre- and post-filtering for image sampling may have a profound positive effect on performing image analysis tasks. Exercise 'Ideal versus non-ideal sampling' is intended for comparison of 'ideal' and 'non-ideal' samplings of different test images. Ideal sampling assumes image antialiasing using ideal low-pass filters for both pre-filtering before sampling and for image reconstruction from its samples. For regular image sampling over square sampling grid, frequency response of the ideal low-pass filter is equal to one within a square that encompasses image sampling base band and is zero outside this area. The same should be the frequency response of the image reconstruction interpolation filter. The ideal image sampling and reconstruction prevents aliasing errors and guarantees minimal mean square image reconstruction error. In the experiment, the user chooses a test image from a set of prepared images or for the image data base, after which the chosen test image is displayed and a menu panel for choosing image down-sampling rate in fraction of sampling rate of the test image (upper left panels in figure 2.24). Then the program displays results of down-sampling the chosen test image without and with ideal pre- and post-filtering (figure 2.24).

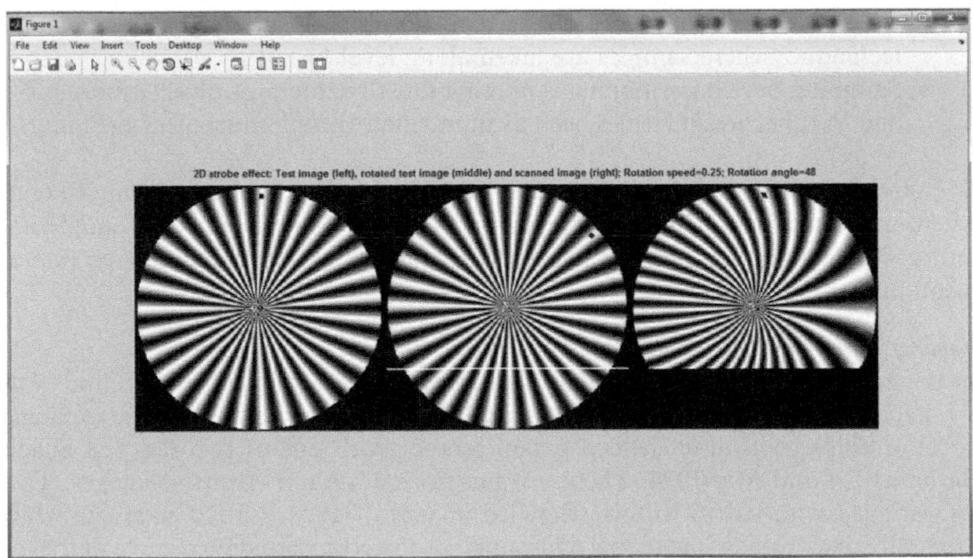

Figure 2.23. Aliasing in 3D: row-wise image acquisition.

Figure 2.24. Image sampling with ideal versus non-ideal pre- and post-filtering.

Image irregular and random sampling

There are many applications, where, contrary to the common practice of using uniform square sampling, sampled data are collected in irregular fashion. Here are some typical instances:

- Samples are taken not where the regular sampling grid dictates to take them but where it is feasible because of technical or other limitations; sometimes sample positioning might be completely irregular
- The pattern of sample disposition is dictated by physical principles of the work of the measuring device (as, for example, in interferometry or moiré-technique, where samples are taken along level lines)
- Sampling device positioning is jittering due to camera or object vibrations or due to other irregularities such as in imaging through turbulent medium.

Exercises in this group are intended to demonstrate how spectra aliasing emerges when images are sampled in an irregular way and to experiment on a simple and intuitive algorithm for reconstruction of irregularly sampled images (see pop-up menu in figure 2.25).

Spectra of irregularly sampled images

In the exercise 'Spectra of irregularly sampled images', one can work either with synthetic texture test images of 1024 × 1024 with spectra bounded by a rectangle, circle or ellipse with user defined parameters, or with one of two real test images Barbara1024 and Man1024. These test images imitate non-sampled images. They are sampled with step 8 to form sampled images of 1024 × 1024 pixels, in which every 8th pixel in each image row and column is the corresponding sample of the test image and the rest of the samples are zeros. According to the sampling theory,

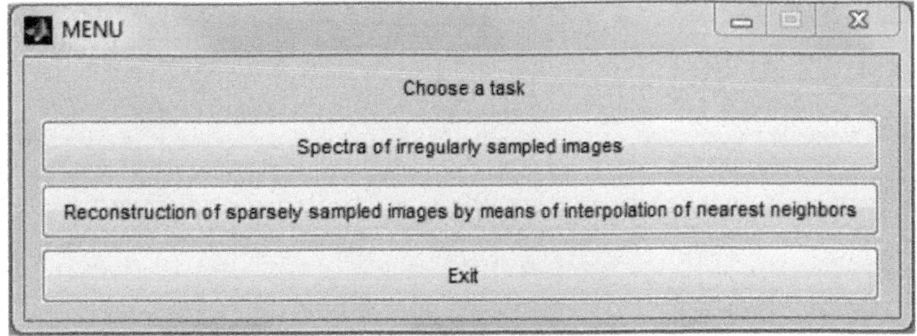

Figure 2.25. Pop-up menu of the exercise 'Image irregular and random sampling'.

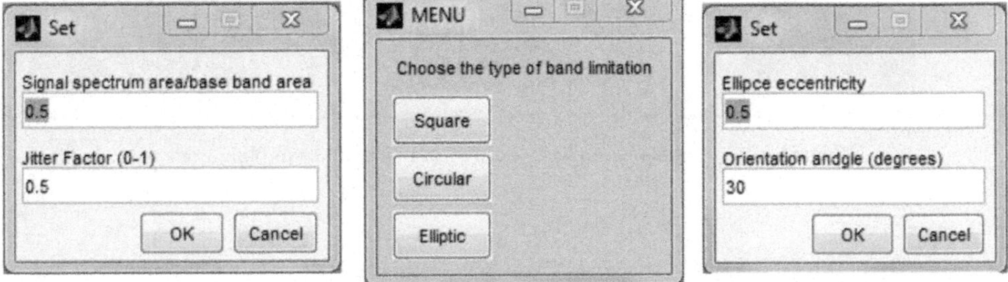

Figure 2.26. Spectra of irregularly sampled images: menus of spectrum and sampling parameters.

spectra of the sampled images are periodical replications of spectra of non-sampled images. Reconstruction of sampled images is performed by filtering out all of its spectra replicas except the central one, using the ideal low-pass filter with frequency response equal to one within the sampling base band and zero outside the base band.

When the option of a pseudo-random test image is chosen, the user is prompted to choose signal spectrum and sampling parameters (figure 2.26): the ratio of its area to the base band area, jitter factor (fraction of sampling interval, within which jitter will take place), type of the image spectrum (rectangle, circle or ellipse) and its shape parameters (aspect ratio for rectangular shape and ellipse eccentricity and orientation angle for elliptic shape).

Once setting of the parameters is completed, the program displays the chosen test image and images reconstructed by means of the ideal low pass filtering from the test images sampled uniformly, with jitter and randomly, as well as sampling grids used (figure 2.27).

After that, the options of displaying reconstruction errors (differences between initial test image and reconstructed ones, figure 2.28) and of displaying spectra of sampled images (figure 2.29) are offered.

In the spectra of sampled images one can observe the emergence of spectra aliasing, when test image spectrum bandwidth exceeds the base band as well as aliasing in spectra of images sampled with jitters or randomly.

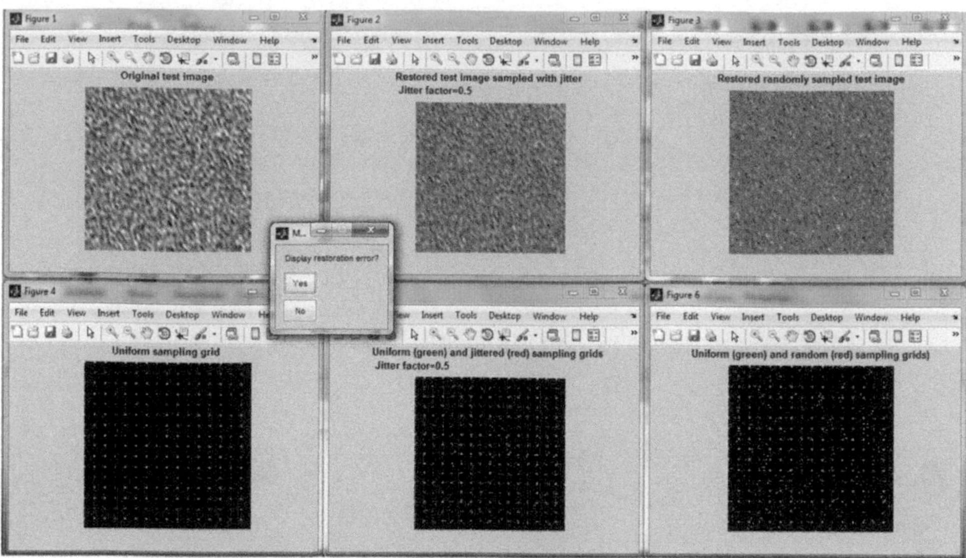

Figure 2.27. Irregular sampling: texture test image and sampling grids.

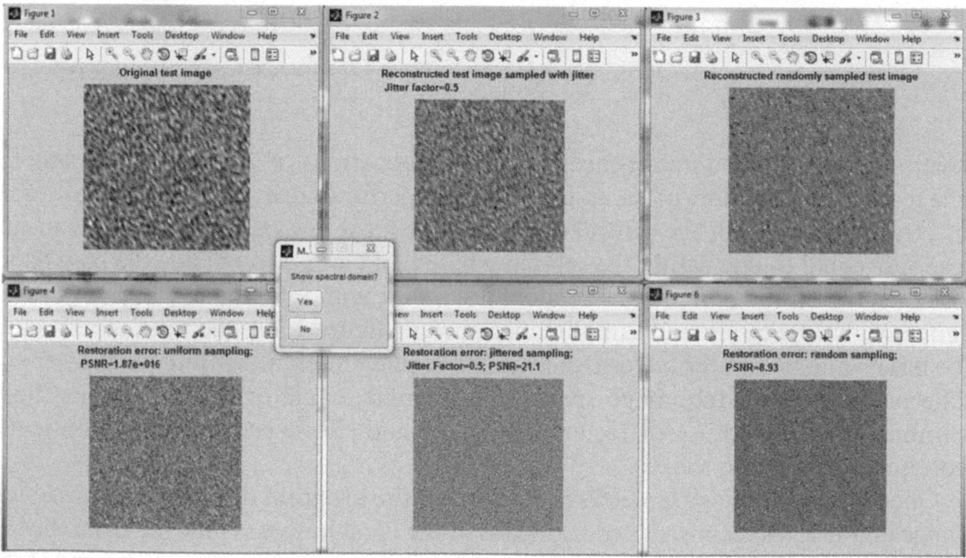

Figure 2.28. Irregular sampling: reconstruction errors.

When a real image is chosen as a test image, only setting of the jitter factor is required, and the program display, as in the previous case, the chosen test image, images reconstructed by means of ideal low pass filtering in the base band of the test images sampled with jitter and randomly, sampling grids used (figure 2.30), sampling errors (figure 2.31) and spectra of sampled images (see figure 2.32).

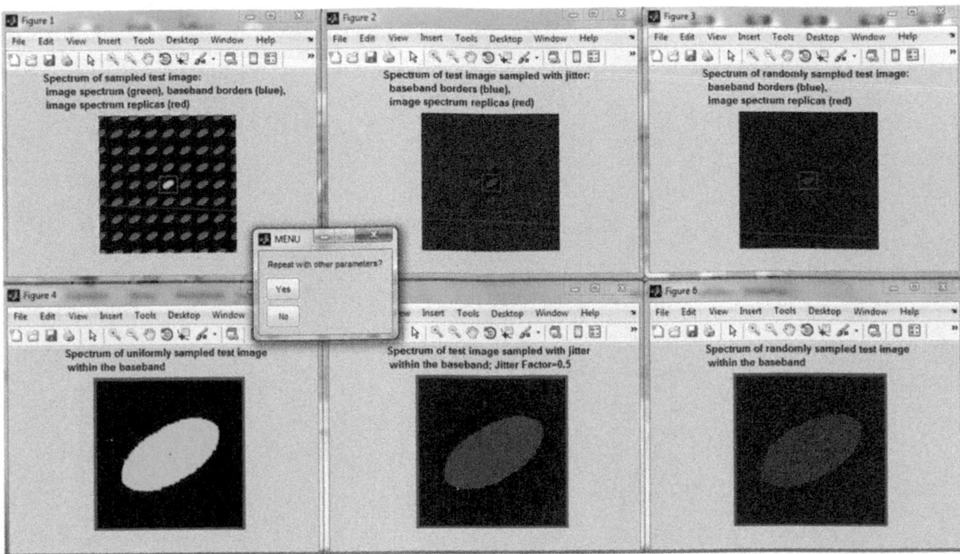

Figure 2.29. Irregular sampling: spectra of sampled texture test images.

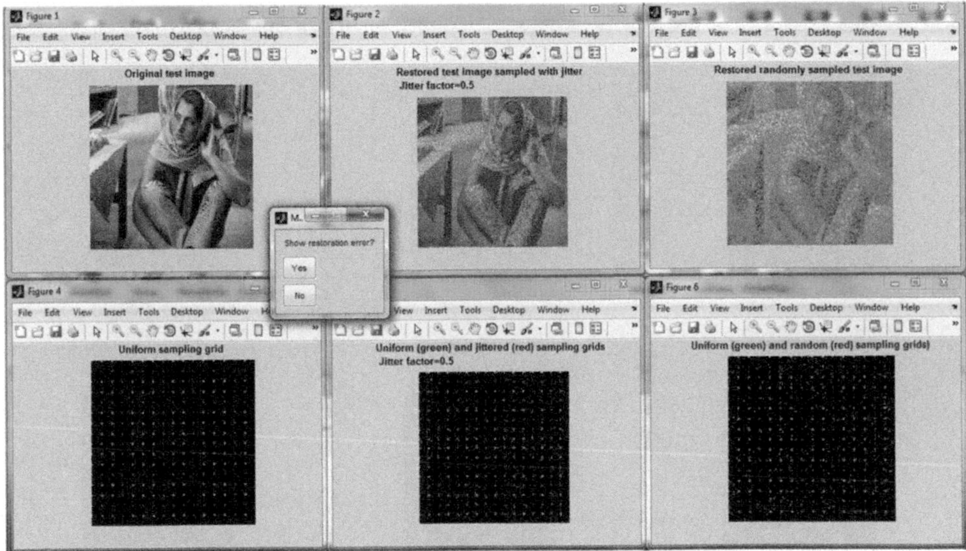

Figure 2.30. Irregular sampling: test image 'Barbara' and sampling grids.

Reconstruction of sparsely sampled images by means of interpolation of nearest neighbors

This exercise demonstrates a simple and intuitive method of reconstruction of sparsely sampled images by means of interpolation of missing samples through weighted summation of values of a certain number of available samples nearest to the interpolated one with weights inversely proportional to the distance between

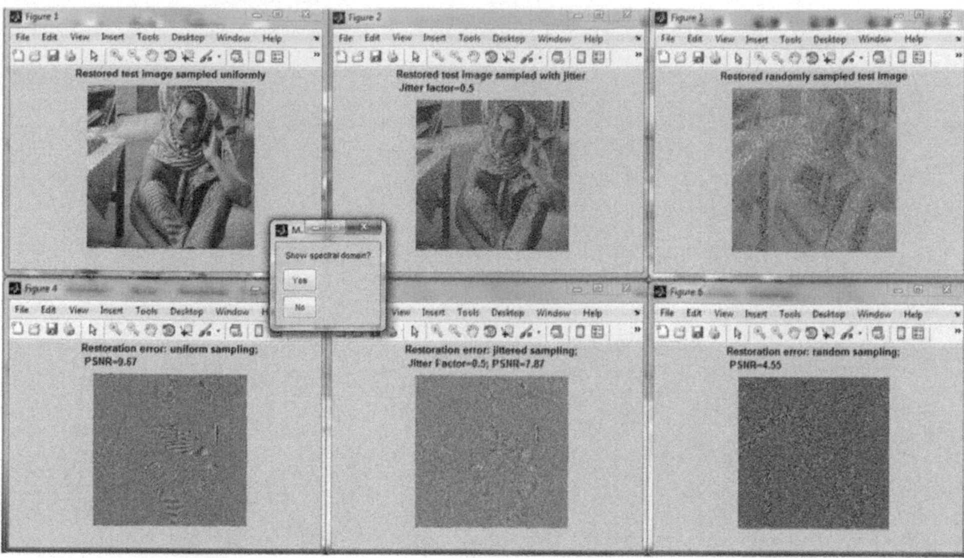

Figure 2.31. Irregular sampling: test image 'Barbara', restored images and restoration errors.

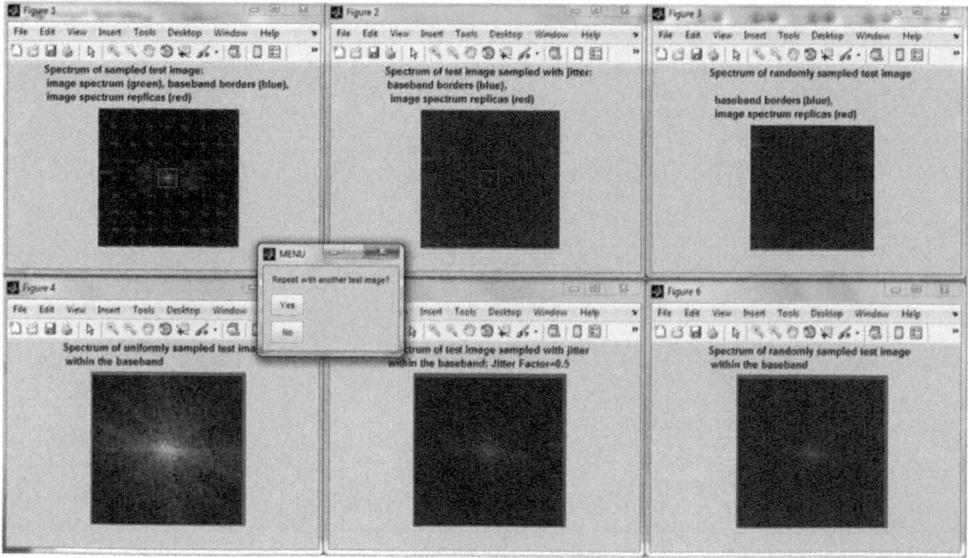

Figure 2.32. Irregular sampling: spectra of sampled test image 'Barbara'.

them. Note that this setting of weights corresponds to the envelope of the sinc-function, the point spread function (impulse response) of the ideal low pass filter, which, according to the sampling theory, is the best reconstruction filter. An exercise with a sampling theory based method of perfect image reconstruction is provided in chapter 3.

At the program start, the user is requested to set sparse sampling rate (the ratio of the number of samples taken to the total number of test image samples), the dimension of the window, from which nearest neighbors of the window central pixels will be taken for interpolation, and relative numbers of those samples (figure 2.33).

Interpolation for image reconstruction is carried out iteratively until all gaps in the sampling grid will be filled and is displayed in real time. An example of the display generated in this exercise is presented in figure 2.34.

Discretization of stereoscopic images

As is well known, to see 3D scenes one needs two images, one for the left eye and another for the right eye, taken with a parallax, i.e. from two positions slightly shifted in the horizontal direction. This, however, does not necessarily mean that both images should have the same resolving power sufficient for recognizing objects in the scene. In fact, it is sufficient if only one of two images has the required resolving power, and the second image can be very substantially blurred,

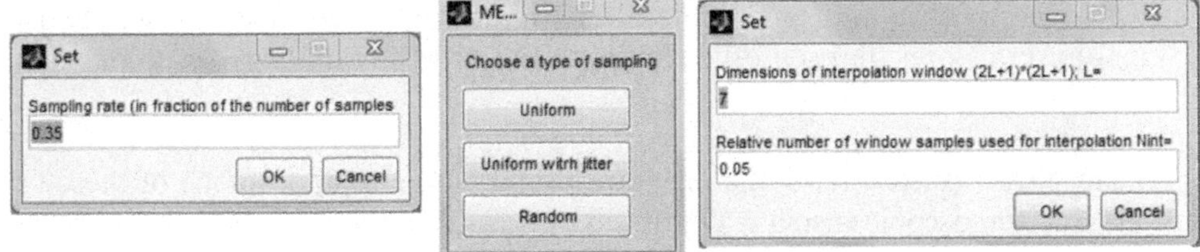

Figure 2.33. Reconstruction of sparsely sampled images by means of interpolation of nearest neighbors: parameter menu.

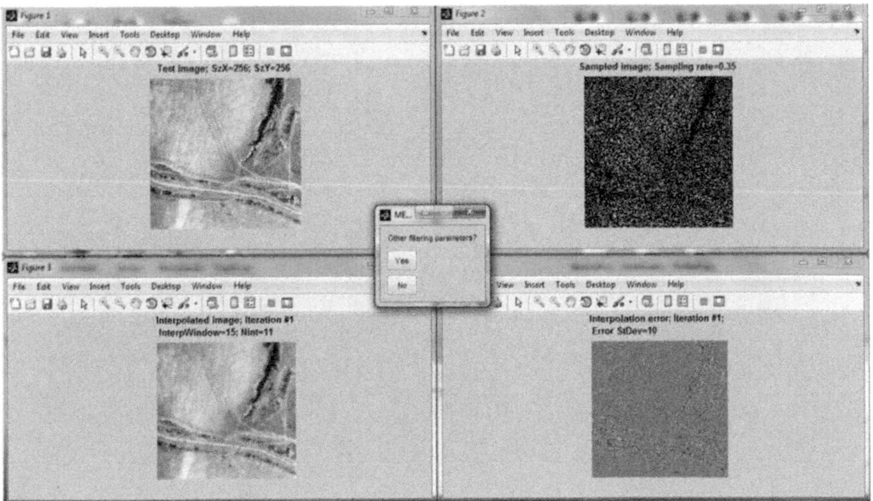

Figure 2.34. Reconstruction of sparsely sampled image by means of interpolation of nearest neighbors: final display.

which means that it can be sampled with much lower sampling rate than the first one.

Exercise 'Discretization of stereoscopic images' is intended to enable experimental evaluation of this redundancy of stereoscopic images and of a possible saving in the number of samples required for stereoscopic images.

In principle, for seeing stereoscopic images in 3D, a stereoscopic display is required. This exercise does not assume using stereoscopic displays. Instead, two options for viewing stereoscopic images for conducting the exercise are offered:

- directly viewing two stereoscopic images displayed side by side. In this case, in order to see a 3D image, one should slightly squint the eyes in such a way as to make the left eye see the right image and the right eye see the left image. This may require certain training.
- displaying stereoscopic images as color *anaglyph*, in which the red component reproduces the left image of two of them or the red component of the color left image and green and blue components reproduce the right image or the corresponding green and blue components of the right image. For viewing anaglyph, one needs color separated glasses with a red color filter for the left eye and green/blue filter for the right eye. Such glasses can be found in stores that sell office items or can be easily made from color plastic films.

At the start of the exercise, the program prompts one to choose one of these two options for stereoscopic display. When the option of side-by-side display is chosen, the user is requested to set bandwidth limitation, in fraction of the image sampling base band, for the image intended for the left eye and displays stereo images side by side for visual evaluation (figure 2.35).

Figure 2.35. Sampling stereoscopic images with substantial down-sampling of one of the images. Stereo images are displayed side by side. In order to see the scene in 3D, one should slightly squint eyes to make the left eye see the right image and the right eye see the left one.

The recommended value 0.01 corresponds to 10 fold down-sampling in each direction, i.e. 100 times fewer image samples. One can test different levels of R-component band limitation and evaluate how the band limitation affects 3D perception.

In the case of anaglyph display, an option of working with the entire image or with a 256 × 256 pixel fragment of the image is offered. In the first case, setting of bandwidth limitation for the image intended for the left eye is requested and corresponding anaglyph displayed (figure 2.36) and then the band limited component is displayed if requested (figure 2.37).

When the option of working with a 256 × 256 fragment is chosen, the user is prompted to indicate on the chosen test image, using the cursor, the center of the fragment and a set of five different values of the band-limitation factor for the best image, after which six anaglyphs are displayed side by side with obtained corresponding different band limitation factors (figure 2.38).

Figure 2.36. Sampling stereoscopic images with down-sampling of one of the images (R-component): anaglyph view. Courtesy of NASA.

Figure 2.37. Blurred R-component of anaglyph in figure 2.36. Courtesy of NASA.

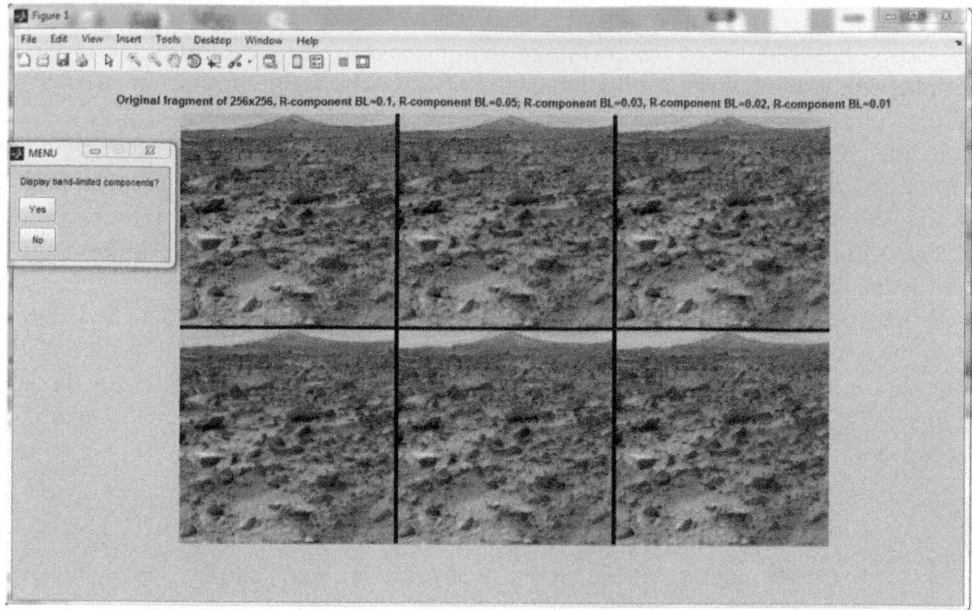

Figure 2.38. Sampling stereoscopic images with down-sampling R-component: 5 different levels of band limitation, anaglyph view. Courtesy of NASA.

Discretization of color images

Human color vision is trichromatic: the eye retina contains three types of light sensitive cells called cones that are sensitive to red, green and blue sub-bands of visible light. This why color images have three components: red (R), green (G) and blue (B) ones. The eye retina contains also achromatic light sensitive cells called rods. Rods measure light intensity over the scene image projected by eye optics on the retina. They define resolving power of vision and, therefore, they are much more densely populated in the retina, while cones provide visual cortex information on local colors of the scene. Because triplets of cones exist at one rod, sampling interval for each cone (distance between cones associated with one rode) is at least twice in each direction that of rods. In fact, the density of cones in the retina is even less than a quarter of a rod's density. This implies that resolving power of vision with respect to color is, by necessity, substantially lower than that with respect to the general light intensity.

In representation of color images by their R, G and B components, the sampling redundancy in color is hidden. For unveiling this redundancy, representation of images in a certain way transforming components is used similarly to spatially transform representation of gray scale images. One such representation is the so-called YUV-representation, in which component transformation is defined as:

$$Y = r_Y R + g_y G + b_y B;$$

$$U = Y - B = r_Y R + g_y G - \left(1 - b_y\right) B;$$

$$V = Y - R = -(1 - r_Y) R + g_y G + b_y B.$$

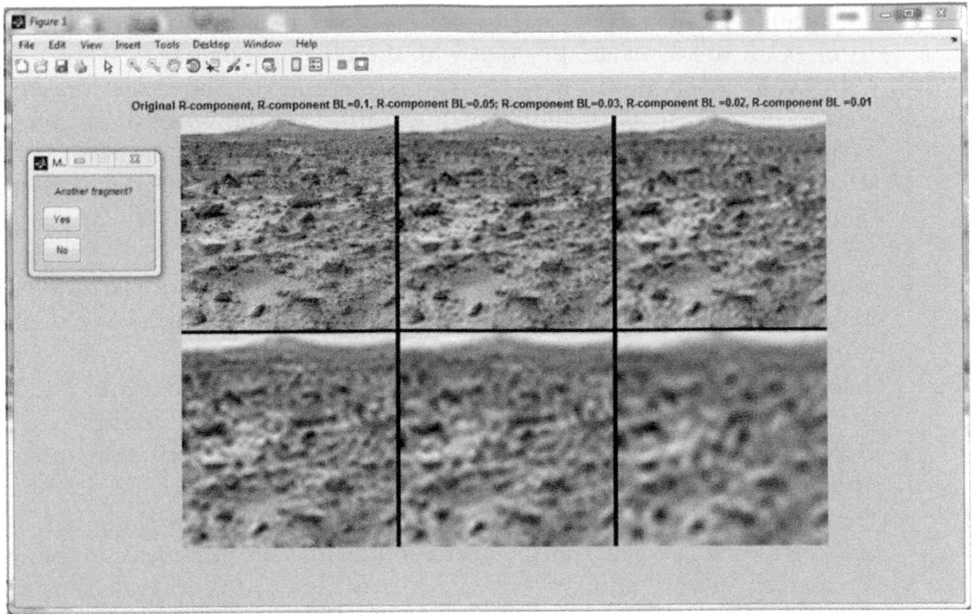

Figure 2.39. Sampling stereoscopic images with down-sampling R-component: non-blurred blurred red components. Courtesy of NASA.

There is no unified standard for values of coefficients $\left\{r_Y, g_y, b_y\right\}$, although their variations are not substantial. In the exercises, the following definition is used:

$$
\begin{aligned}
Y &= 0.3R + 0.6G + 0.1B; \\
U &= Y - B = 0.3R + 0.6G - 0.9B; \\
V &= Y - R = -0.7R + 0.6G + 0.1B;
\end{aligned}
$$

The aforementioned reduced resolving power with respect to color of images allows one to substantially down-sample U and V components. The exercise enables studying this phenomenon.

At the program start, choosing a test image for the image data set is requested, upon which the program prompts setting a down-sampling factor, fraction of image sampling base band, for U and V components, applies corresponding low-pass filters to image U- and V- components and displays the obtained image for visual evaluation. An example of the display is presented in figure 2.39.

Questions for self-testing

1. From your experiments, how would you rate, on average, DFT, DCT, Walsh and Haar Transform in terms of their energy compaction capability?
2. When is the energy compaction capability of a transform more pronounced, for image frames or for image fragments?
3. As a rule, Haar Transform has lower energy compaction capability than DCT, DFT and Walsh transforms. However, for some images and image

fragments it exhibits better energy compaction capability than other transforms. Can you associate this fact with the type of the image?
4. From your observations, how compact are groups of above the threshold transform coefficients for different transforms and how well they can be bounded by simple geometrical shapes such as rectangle or oval?
5. Were your estimations of admissive image band limitations in the exercise 'Estimating image effective bandwidth' uniform over all the sets of images you tested?
6. Suppose you have an image to scan or a scene to be photographed and you have an image scanner with a certain resolution (dots per inch) or a digital camera with a certain number of pixels per frame. How would you determine whether these devices are sufficient for doing the job? Would you need to measure image spectra to be able to make the decision?
7. Describe as many sampling artifacts you observed in the exercise 'Sampling artifacts' as you can.
8. Describe and explain distortions in images due to under-sampling that you observed while carrying out the exercise 'Ideal versus non-ideal sampling'.
9. How much, in your opinion, can one of two stereoscopic images be down-sampled without sacrificing visual 3D perception of the scenes?
10. How much, in your opinion, can one of the U and V components of color images be down-sampled without sacrificing visual perception of the scenes?

2.3 Signal scalar quantization

2.3.1 Introduction

Scalar (element-wise) quantization is the second stage of image digitization. It is applied to image discrete representation coefficients obtained as a result of image discretization. Scalar quantization implies that a finite interval has first to be specified in the entire range of magnitude of the image representation coefficients values $\{\alpha\}$ by defining their minimum $\alpha_{\min}$ and maximum $\alpha_{\max}$, and then the interval $[\alpha_{\min}, \alpha_{\max}]$ is split into a certain number Q of *quantization intervals* by defining their border values $\{\alpha^{(q)}\}, q = 0, 1, ..., Q - 1$. Quantization intervals are indexed by an integer index and, for each particular qth interval, its representative value, or *quantization level* $\aleph^{(q)}$, is chosen. For image reconstruction, all values within a particular quantization interval are replaced with its representative quantization level.

The difference $\varepsilon^{(q)} = \alpha - \aleph^{(q)}$ between true value α and its corresponding quantization level $\aleph^{(q)}$ is called *quantization error*. Quantization errors within the dynamic range are limited in the range by the size of the quantization intervals, whereas dynamic range limitation errors $\varepsilon^{(0)} = \alpha - \aleph^{(0)}$ and $\varepsilon^{(Q-1)} = \alpha - \aleph^{(Q-1)}$ may, in principle, be unlimited in value.

The arrangement of quantization intervals and assigning quantization levels is governed by requirements to the accuracy of image quantized representation, which are generally formulated in terms of certain constraints imposed on quantization errors. In the most common approach to formulating the constraints, losses due to quantization errors are evaluated on average over all possible coefficient values.

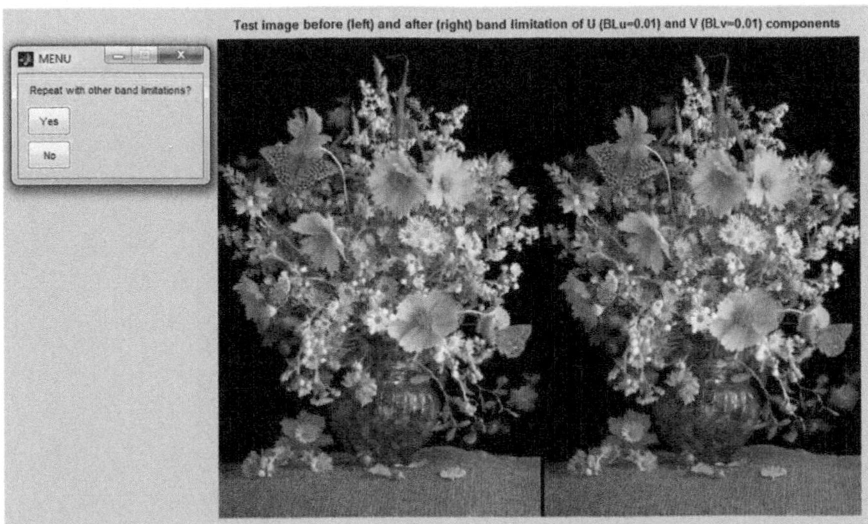

Figure 2.40. Sampling color images: low pass filtering image U- and V-components. Stereo images are displayed side by side. In order to see the scene in 3D, one should slightly squint the eyes to make the left eye see the right image and right eye see the left one.

There are two approaches to the design of optimal quantizers, which minimize losses in image representation quality due to quantization of its gray levels: a direct optimization approach and a *compressor–expander (compander)* one. The direct optimization approach assumes numerical optimization of quantization interval borders and representative quantization levels for an image data base, for a certain statistical model of image representation coefficients or for particular image frames.

Compressor–expander quantization is a simplified method of optimal non-uniform quantization, which is suited for the design of analog-to-digital convertors. With this method, the signal is subjected to a certain nonlinear pointwise transformation and after that the transformed signal values are uniformly quantized. Correspondingly, at the reconstruction stage, uniformly quantized values are subjected to a nonlinear transformation inverse to the one used for quantization.

Usually, the required non-linear pre-quantization transformation compresses the signal dynamic range, hence the name 'compressor-expander quantization'. Optimization of the compressor–expander quantization is achieved by an appropriate adjustment of the compressive nonlinear pointwise transformation.

Three groups of exercises aimed at studying scalar quantization of image gray levels, listed in the menu shown in figure 2.41, are offered.

2.3.2 Quantization of achromatic images

This group of exercises contains six exercises listed in the menu shown in figure 2.42.

Image 'scalar' quantization and 'false' contours

In quantization of image gray levels, artifacts of quantization exhibit themselves most frequently in the appearance of visible false boundaries between image patches

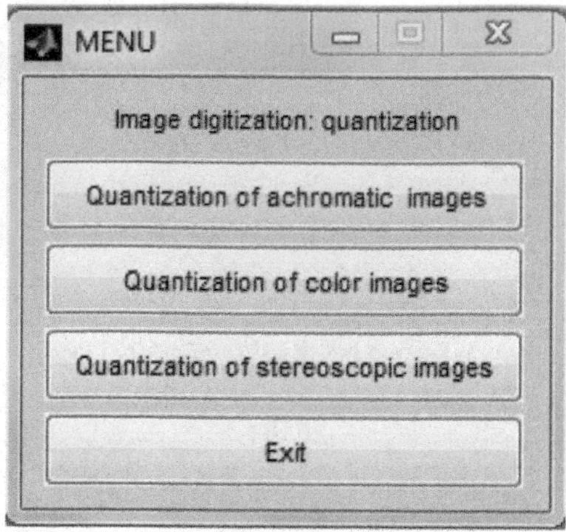

Figure 2.41. Image scalar quantization: start menu.

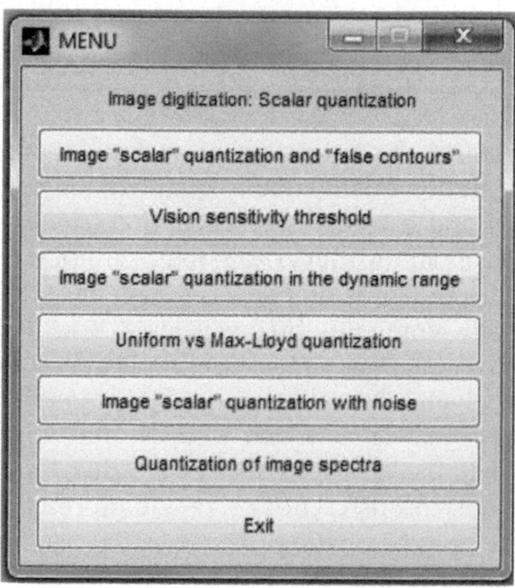

Figure 2.42. Quantization of achromatic images: start menu.

quantized to different quantization levels. They are called *false contours*. Exercise 'Image scalar quantization and "false contours"' is designed for studying this phenomenon for different test images and different numbers of quantization levels and, in particular, for evaluating how many quantization levels is sufficient for different images for their display without visible false contour. The program requests one to choose a test image from a list of prepared images or from the image database and to choose the number of quantization levels, and then it displays the chosen test image quantized to 255 gray levels, which is standard for digital images, quantized to fewer gray levels chosen by the user, histograms of both these images, and quantization error, i.e. a difference between initial and coarsely quantized images (figure 2.43).

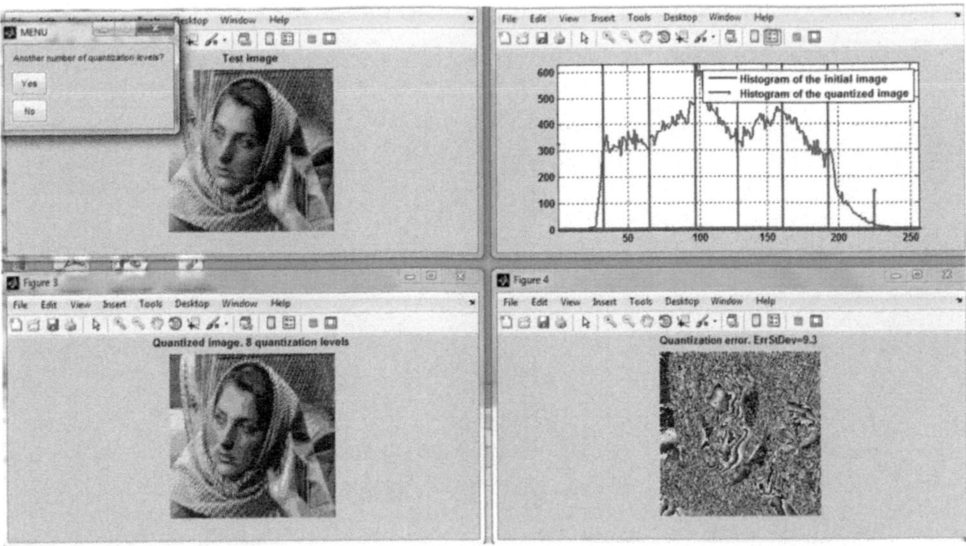

Figure 2.43. Image 'scalar' quantization and 'false' contours: final display.

Vision sensitivity threshold

A natural primary requirement for quantization of quality of images is to secure the invisibility of false contours in displayed digital images. The perceptibility of borders of constant gray level patches depends on their contrast with respect to their background and on the size of the patches. Using the exercise 'Vision sensitivity threshold' one can determine one's own visual sensitivity threshold. In the exercise, a square stimulus of a certain contrast with respect to the background is displayed in a random position within the field of view on an empty background and the viewer is prompted to confirm whether he/she has detected the stimulus.

The experiment begins with a stimulus of the smallest size of one pixel and of the lower contrast of one gray level assuming a total of 255 gray levels of image dynamic range. If the stimulus is not detected, its contrast is raised by one quantization level and the experiment is repeated until the stimulus is detected. The attained contrast is saved as the threshold visibility contrast for this stimulus size, and then a new series of tests begins with stimuli of larger sizes (3×3, 5×5, 7×7 and 11×11 pixels). After testing the stimulus of the largest size, the same is repeated for another gray level of the background. A total of three background gray levels are tested: one in the middle of the image dynamic range (gray level 128) and two in the lower half (gray level 32) and in the upper half (gray level 224) of the displayed image dynamic range 0–255. figure 2.44 is an example of visualizing the results of this exercise.

Quantization in a given range

This exercise is intended for training in image scalar quantization and specifically for experimentation in selecting limits of the image dynamic range and of the number of quantization levels. The quantization range of images is specified in terms of its ratio to the image standard deviation, and it is kept symmetrical with respect to the image

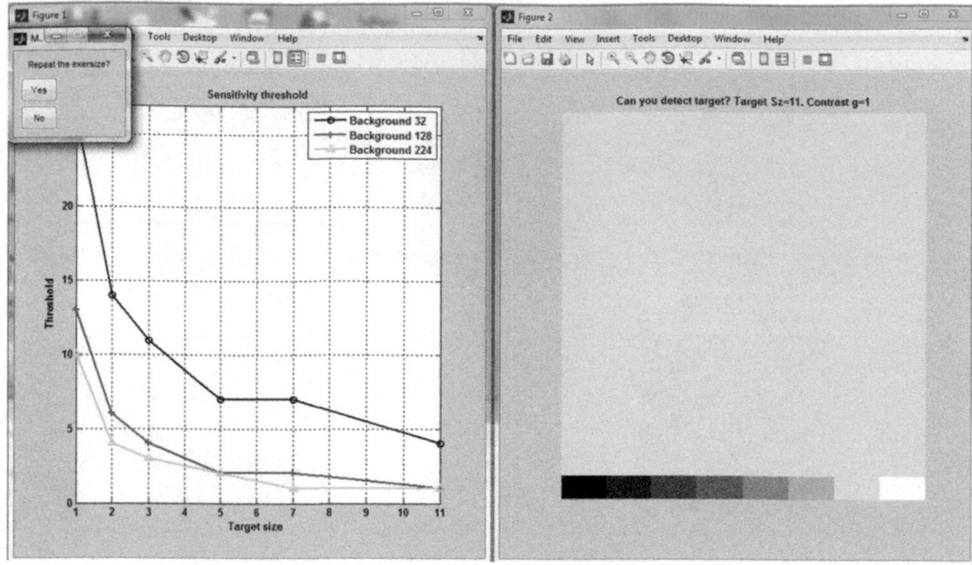

Figure 2.44. Visual sensitivity threshold: an example of the result.

mean value. The user is prompted to choose this ratio for the chosen test image and to specify the number of quantization levels within the selected dynamic range, after which the quantized test image is displayed for visual evaluation of its quality. An example of outcomes of this exercise is presented in figure 2.45.

Uniform versus Max–Lloyd quantization

The uniform arrangement of quantization levels is the simplest quantization method. It is usually implemented in analog-to-digital convertors of digital imaging devices. However, as already mentioned, uniform quantization is, in general, not optimal, and quantization errors might be, for a given number of quantization levels, reduced using appropriately adjusted non-uniform arrangement of quantization levels in the quantization range.

A quantization optimization method that minimizes, by means of non-uniform arrangement of quantization levels, the standard deviation of quantization errors is called *Max–Lloyd quantization*. The exercise 'Uniform versus Max–Lloyd quantization' enables experimental comparison of uniform and Max–Lloyd quantizations in terms of the quantization error standard deviation for a given (by the user) number of image quantization levels and for different test images, both pre-prepared and chosen by the user from the image database. Upon setting the parameters, the program displays the chosen test image, its copies quantized uniformly and using Max–Lloyd quantization and histograms of gray levels of the three images (figure 2.46).

Quantization with noise

The perceptibility of false contours in quantized images is dependent on level of noise, which is always present in image signals generated by image sensors. Noise randomizes false contours and makes them less perceptible. The exercise

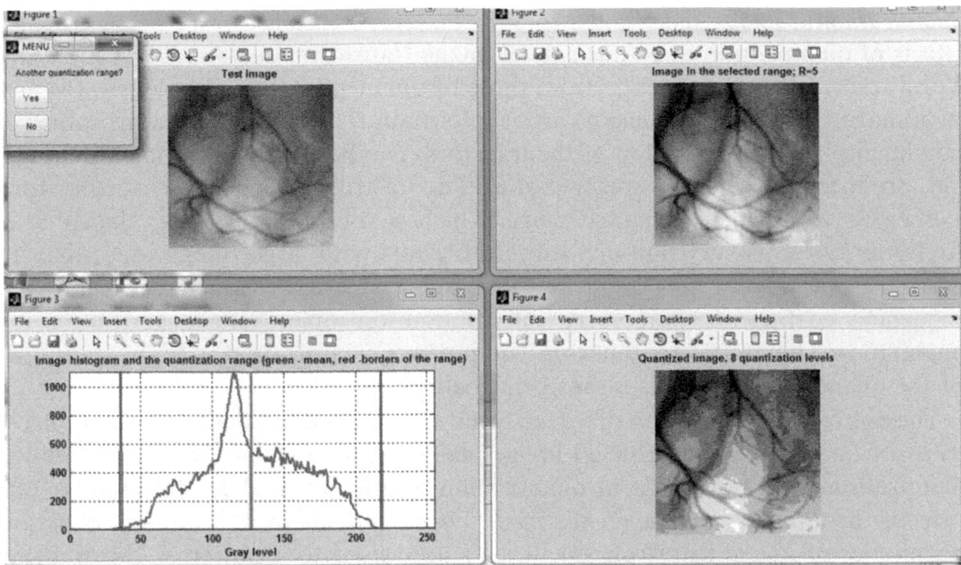

Figure 2.45. Quantization in a given range: an example of the result.

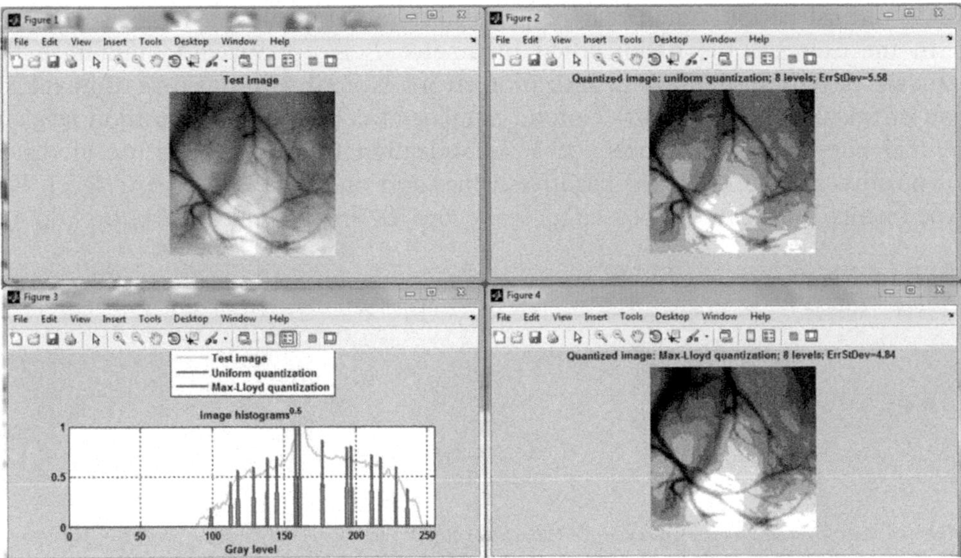

Figure 2.46. Uniform versus Max–Lloyd quantization: an example of the result.

'Quantization with noise' is intended to study this phenomenon and to determine what minimal noise level is sufficient to make false contours invisible on the chosen test image for a chosen number of quantization levels. In this experiment, a realization of random numbers with uniform distribution in the user- specified range is added to the image signal before its quantization, and the same realization is then subtracted from the quantized signal for the image display. Displayed are the chosen test image, its quantized copy and histograms of the images (figure 2.47).

Quantization of image spectra

Effects of quantization of coefficients of image transforms such as DFT, DCT and Walsh transforms differ greatly from those of quantizing pixel gray levels. Because each image transform coefficient carries information on the entire image rather on individual pixels, quantization of the transform coefficients affects the entire image and produces a kind of spotty noise. The distribution density of transform coefficients within their dynamic range, which is substantially larger than that of pixel gray levels, is very non-uniform: coefficients with larger magnitudes that are usually responsible for 'low frequency' image components are much rarer than 'high frequency' coefficients that carry information on object edges and have low magnitudes. Therefore, non-uniform compressive quantization is highly advisable for the quantization of image transform coefficients.

The exercise 'Quantization of image spectra' is intended to demonstrate improvements of quality of reconstructed images achieved with the use of a non-uniform quantization. The non-uniform quantization is implemented in the exercise in a form of the *Pth law 'compander/expander' quantization.* In *P*th law quantization, magnitudes of image transform coefficients are raised to a power $P < 1$ and then uniformly quantized to a specified (by the user) number of quantization levels within the range between zero and the maximal value of the modified coefficients. For image reconstruction, quantized coefficients are raised to the inverse power $1/P$.

In the exercise, the quantization parameter P is optimized to minimize the standard deviation of image quantization errors. Note that in this case of quantization of transform coefficients the total number of coefficient quantization levels is an odd number; for instance, for 33 quantization levels 16 levels are allocated for positive and 16 levels for negative values and one level is the 'zero' level. For experiments, one can choose either pre-prepared images or an arbitrary image

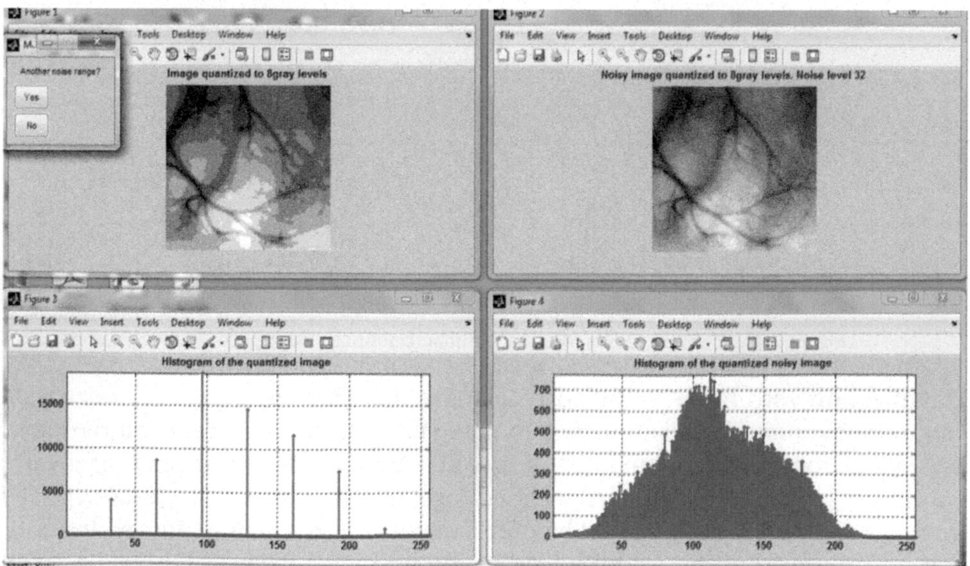

Figure 2.47. Quantization with noise: an example of the result.

from the image database. The program displays the chosen test image, the image reconstructed from uniformly quantized coefficients and the image reconstructed from quantized by *P*th low quantization with optimal value of the parameter *P* and a bar diagram of standard deviations of quantization errors versus parameter *P* of *P*th low quantization (figure 2.48).

2.3.3 Quantization of color images

Two options are offered for experimentation with quantization of color images: component-wise quantization of image RGB components or component-wise quantization of image transformed YUV- components (figure 2.49).

Quantization of RGB components, quantization of YUV components

In these exercises one can work both with pre-prepared images and images from the image data set. The program 'Quantization of RGB components' prompts one to choose a test image and to set the number of uniform quantizations individually for R, G and B image components and then displays side by side the chosen initial test image with 256 quantization levels and its quantized copy, as illustrated in figure 2.50.

As mentioned in the section 'Discretization of color images', color image representation by transformed YUV-components is more economical in terms of image discretization by sampling. The exercise 'Quantization of YUV components' enables evaluation of whether quantization of YUV-components is more economical than quantization of RGB-components. The program works and displays results similarly to the previous one (figure 2.51).

Figure 2.48. Quantization of image spectra. Results of optimization of parameter *P* of *P*th law quantization are displayed along with images reconstructed for the optimal *P* and for uniform quantization ($P = 1$).

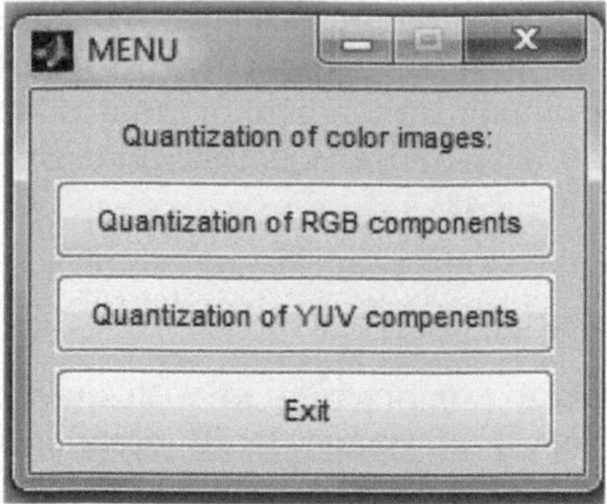

Figure 2.49. Quantization of color images: start menu.

Figure 2.50. Quantization of color image RGB components.

2.3.4 Quantization of stereoscopic images

As mentioned in the section 'Discretization of stereoscopic images', stereoscopic images are very redundant: one of two stereoscopic images can be very substantially blurred and, therefore, down-sampled without sacrificing depth perception. This redundancy is explained by the redundancy of depth maps that correspond to stereoscopic images. It turns out that depth maps not only have substantially fewer samples than is required for keeping visual sharpness of the scene observed using stereoscopic images, they can be quantized much more coarsely than their corresponding images, because depth resolving power of human stereoscopic vision is quite poor. In addition, stereo color perception of a 3D scene is governed by only one of the eyes, the one which sees a better image. The exercises 'Quantization of stereoscopic images' are intended for experimental verification of these phenomena. The corresponding two options offered for experiments in quantization of stereoscopic images are listed in the start menu shown in figure 2.52.

Figure 2.51. Quantization of color image YUV components.

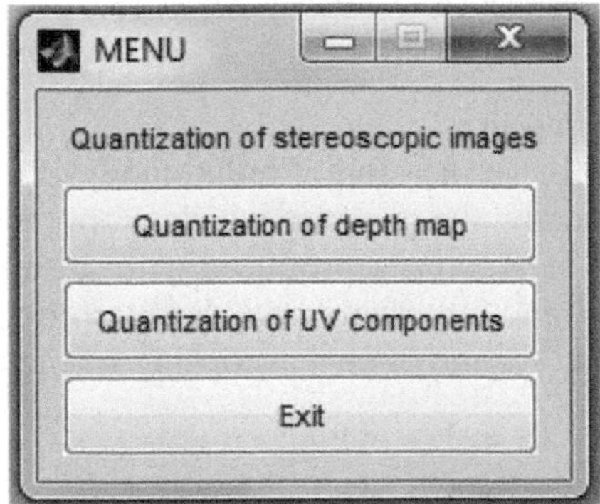

Figure 2.52. Quantization of stereoscopic image: start menu.

Quantization of depth map

For experiments in quantization of depth map, artificial stereo images are generated for a test image chosen by the user using one of two computer generated depth maps with 2D profiles, of cone and of hemisphere. Two stereoscopic images are generated: one using a non-quantized depth map, and another using a depth map, uniformly quantized to the number of quantization levels set by the user. These two images are displayed side by side as anaglyphs for viewing and visual comparison. One can change the number of depth map quantization levels and determine, by means of comparison of 3D shapes seen on the left and right images, the minimal number for which quantization effects (steps in depth of the 3D shape) become noticeable. As test images, one can use either a computer generated pseudo-random pattern, or a texture image or any other image of 256 × 256 pixels from the image database. Figure 2.53 represents an example of a generated display. Note that viewing anaglyphs using red–blue glasses may require several seconds of accommodation.

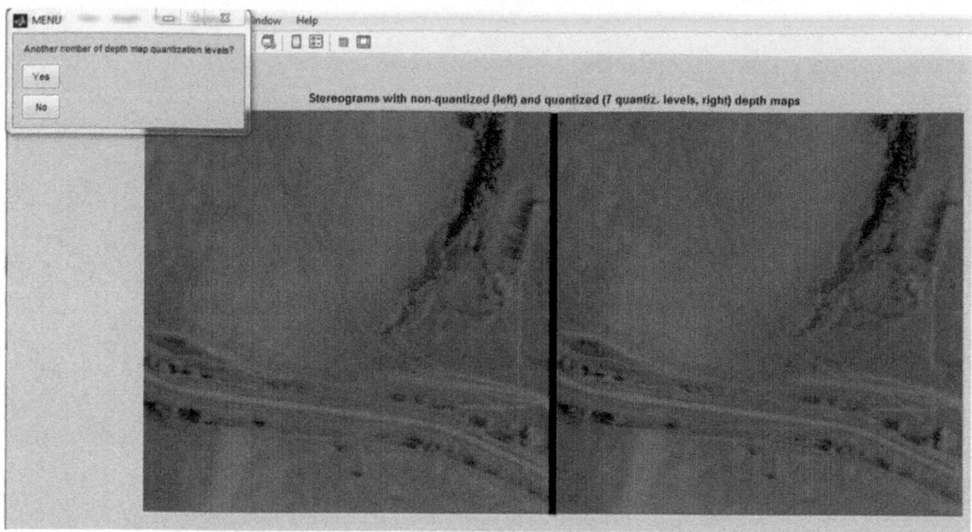

Figure 2.53. Quantization of depth map.

Quantization of UV components

This exercise is intended for verification of redundancy of color stereoscopic images in terms of colors. Specifically, the program which supports it generates and displays stereoscopic images, one of which is reproduced with saturation of color and coarse quantization of image U and V components. RGB components of this image are reconstructed from its YUV components according to the equations:

$$R = Y - s[V]_Q;$$
$$G = Y + s[V]_Q/2 + s[U]_Q/6;$$
$$B = Y - s[U]_Q;$$

where s is color saturation factor ($0 \leqslant s \leqslant 1$) and $[U]_Q$ and $[V]_Q$ are U and V components quantized to Q levels. The case $s = 0$ corresponds to full color saturation, when the color image is replaced by a colorless gray scale image ($R = G = B = Y$); in the case $s = 1$ the image is reproduced in its full colors. The program first prompts the user to choose a test pair of stereoscopic images, for which options are offered of either using two pre-prepared stereo-pairs or using an arbitrary stereo-pair from the image data set, and then displays the images side by side and prompts setting the color saturation factor s, the number of quantization levels Q for image U and V components, and choosing the image to be subjected to color saturation and quantization, the left or the right one. Finally, displayed for visual evaluation is the stereo-pair, in which the chosen image is color saturated and quantized, as illustrated in figure 2.54.

By changing the saturation and the number of quantization levels of image U and V components, one can determine the lowest saturation parameter and the lowest number of quantization levels, for which 3D and color sensation remain satisfactory.

Figure 2.54. Quantization of UV components of color stereo images. Stereo images are displayed side by side. In order to see the scene in 3D, one should slightly squint the eyes to make the left eye see the right image and the right eye see the left one.

Questions for self-testing

1. In which image areas are false contours most annoying and in which are they least annoying and visible?
2. Is your vision sensitivity threshold the same for stimuli of all sizes and for all background levels?
3. Why are 256 gray levels chosen as a standard for image quantized representation?
4. What would be your recommendation regarding setting pixel gray level quantization range?
5. Is uniform quantization optimal for quantization of image gray levels?
6. Does Max–Lloyd quantization always substantially reduce quantization artifacts? Does it improve the image visual quality?
7. What would be your recommendation regarding setting intensity of additive noise that would be sufficient to hide quantization false contours?
8. From your experiments, do you think that there is a value of the parameter *P* for *P*th law quantization of image transform coefficients that would be sufficiently appropriate for the majority of images?
9. What artifacts are seen in coarsely quantized color images with component-wise quantization of image RGB components? Is there any difference with quantization of YUV-components?
10. What is your evaluation of the number of quantization levels of stereo images depth map required for preservation of the 3D sensation without visible quantization artifacts?

11. What is your evaluation of the degree of color saturation and of the number of quantization levels U and V components of stereo images required for satisfactory preservation of 3D and color sensation?

2.4 Image compression

2.4.1 Introduction

As was mentioned, image representation in the form of arrays of samples taken at nodes of uniform rectangular sampling lattices is the most frequently used method of image discretization. It is also standard for image displays, which means that any imaging system and image processing should ultimately produce sampled images for display according to this standard. However, the sampled representation of images is, as a rule, very redundant in terms of the amount of data needed to produce images of admissible quality. The reason is that image samples should be taken densely enough to secure a good reproduction of object edges, though edges usually occupy only a small fraction of the image area. This redundancy amounts to tens and, for some images, even hundreds of times. The same refers to video data represented as sets of video frames taken with a uniform time intervals. In addition to this, scalar quantization of pixel gray levels also requires an excessive number of quantization levels in order to secure invisibility of quantization artifacts, such as false contours, to which the most vulnerable are exactly those excessive image samples from non-edgy image areas.

All this means that, for image data storage and transmission, the standard sampled image representation can be substantially compressed. The compression is the third step of image digitization usually conducted as a supplemental image processing applied to the 'primary' sampled and quantized image representation.

Basically, there are two groups of image compression methods: predictive and transform.

In *predictive compression methods,* differences between the gray level of each pixel and its predicted estimate found as a weighted sum over pixels that surround the given one on the sampling lattice are computed and then subjected to scalar quantization. The method, in which the 'prediction' and computing differences is performed in the course of image row-wise/column-wise scanning is called *differential pulse code modulation (DPCM)*. In DPCM, a difference between the current pixel gray level and its value predicted from previously scanned neighboring pixels is quantized and then encoded for transmission or storage. In 1D DPCM, the predicted value is gray level of the pixel preceding the given one on the scanning row weighted by the correlation coefficient between gray levels of two adjacent pixels. In 2D DPCM, a weighted average over pixels nearest to the given one in the previous scanning row and the previous pixel in the given row is used as a predicted value. DPCM is historically the earliest data compression method. Nowadays it is used solely for 'interframe' coding of video sequences. However, the method is very instructive for understanding basic principles of data compression.

In transform image compression, it is image transform coefficients that undergo scalar quantization. The compression efficiency of the transform compression methods roots in the energy compaction capability of transforms (see section 2.2.1). In principle, transform compression can be applied image frame-wise or block-wise. In frame-wise compression, the image frame as a whole is transformed, transform coefficients with sufficiently low energy are truncated and the remaining ones are quantized using the optimized non-uniform quantization. In block-wise compression, the image is split into non-overlapping blocks of relatively small size and transforms are applied to individual blocks separately. For every block, low energy block transform coefficients are truncated and the remaining ones are optimally quantized.

Applying transforms block-wise is well suited to image spatial inhomogeneity, and transform coefficient quantization can be better optimized if it is performed individually for transform spectra of image blocks. The size of blocks is determined by the degree of image inhomogeneity and, in principle, can vary within an image frame: it should be as large as possible provided image remains 'homogeneous' within the block. Among compressing transforms, DCT proved to be the best one and it is put as the basis of the modern image and video compression standards JPEG and MPEG.

The set of exercises 'Image compression' is intended for experimentation in predictive and transform image compression. 1D and 2D DPCM and block-wise transform coding in DCT domain are implemented (figure 2.55).

Predictive coding

Two exercises are offered in this section: 'Prediction errors', and 'DPCM coding' (figure 2.56)

Exercise 'Prediction errors' is intended for experimental evaluation and comparison of distribution histograms and standard deviations of predictive errors in the case of 1D and 2D prediction for different images chosen by the user from either pre-prepared images or from an image data set. These histograms are key parameters for optimization of prediction error quantization. The program displays chosen test images and their

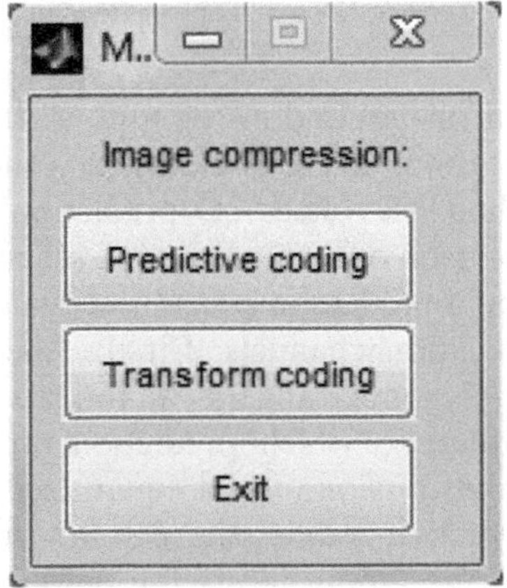

Figure 2.55. Image compression: start menu.

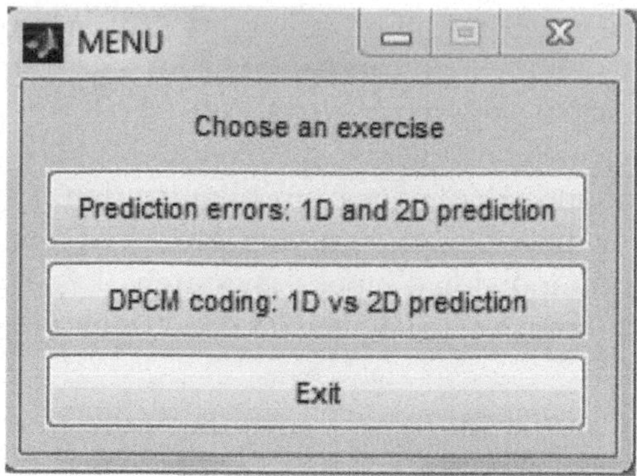

Figure 2.56. Predictive coding: start menu.

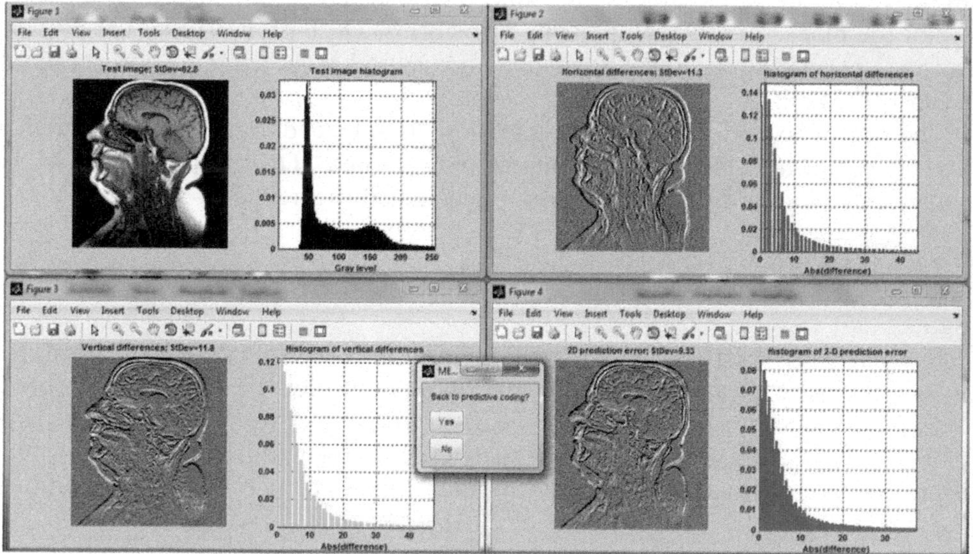

Figure 2.57. Prediction errors, 1D and 2D prediction: an example of the result.

histograms, prediction error images and histograms of absolute values of prediction errors. An example of results obtained in this exercise is shown in figure 2.57.

In exercise 'DPCM coding: 1D versus 2D prediction', DPCM with 1D and 2D predictions is run for comparison of their prediction efficiency for different images in terms of standard deviation of prediction errors and evaluation of their immunity to impulse noise in communication channels. Firstly, the program prompts setting parameters of the exercise: dynamic range of quantization of prediction errors, i.e. minimal and maximal values, to which prediction errors will be bounded, and probability of error in transmission of the quantized prediction error. In this implementation of the predictive coding, the *P*th law quantization of magnitudes of prediction errors is used. So, upon setting the parameters, the program runs an optimization procedure for determining an optimal value of the parameter *P*, which

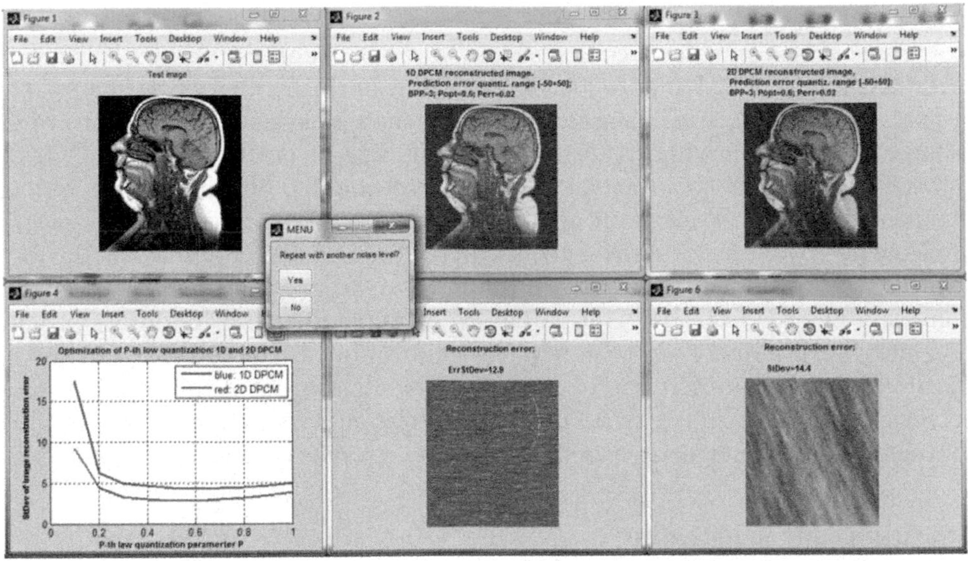

Figure 2.58. 'DPCM coding, 1D versus 2D prediction': an example of the results.

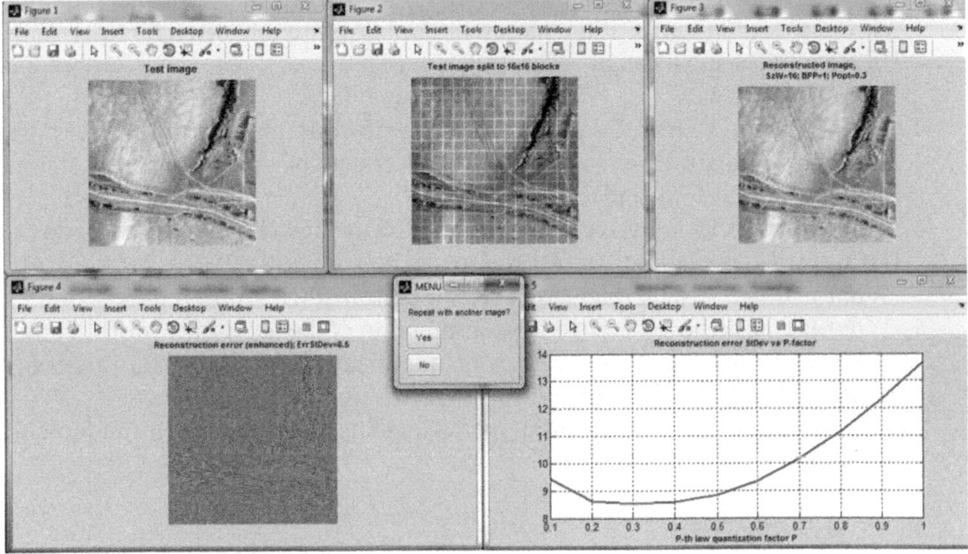

Figure 2.59. Transform coding: an example of the results.

minimizes mean square image reconstruction error for the chosen test image. The results of the optimization, quantization error standard deviations are plotted versus parameter P of Pth low quantization. Finally, 1D DPCM and 2D DPCM coding and decoding are performed one after another with display of reconstructed images and prediction errors in real time of the running program. Figure 2.58 presents a sample of displayed results of this exercise.

Transform coding

For the exercise 'Transform coding', block-wise DCT domain image compression method is implemented and its efficiency in terms of the number of bits per pixel it requires and mean square image reconstruction error is evaluated. Parameters of the exercise the user is prompted to set are: (i) the size of blocks (in pixels), (ii) the fraction of transform coefficients left for quantization and (iii) the number of their quantization levels. Truncation of DCT spectral coefficients of image blocks is implemented by means of zeroing coefficients outside of a spectral mask in the form of a pie sector whose area is a chosen (by the user) fraction of the block area. The number of bits per pixel (BBP) for the chosen set of parameters is found as a product of binary logarithm of the number of quantization levels and the fraction of transform coefficients left for quantization. Nonlinear quantization of retained coefficients is implemented as a Pth law quantization with parameter P optimized for each particular image. An example of displayed results is presented in figure 2.59.

Questions for self-testing

1. Why are sampled images compressible?
2. What is your estimate, how much are standard deviations of DPCM prediction errors lower than those of the corresponding images, and how much can one expect to win in terms of the required number of quantization levels?
3. Is 2D DPCM substantially more efficient in terms of image data compression than 1D DPCM?
4. Are 1D and 2D DPCM equally vulnerable to communication channel noise?
5. What is the main difference between the effects of communication channel noise in 1D DPCM and 2D DPCM?
6. What would be your recommendation regarding choosing block size for DCT transform coding for a given particular image?
7. What artifacts are characteristic for block transform compression?
8. What factor is more decisive for compression efficiency of transform coding: the number of transform coefficient quantization levels or the fraction of transform coefficients retained for quantization?
9. Do predictive and transform image coding share any common fundamental principle?

IOP Publishing

Leonid P Yaroslavsky

Chapter 3

Digital image formation and computational imaging

3.1 Introduction

This chapter is devoted to computational image formation from numerical data, or computational imaging. Apparently, the earliest examples of the computational imaging are computed tomography and digital holography. In computed tomography, discrete numerical data of object slice projections obtained under a set of angles is converted into a set of samples of a slice image over a regular square sampling grid suited for conventional image displays. In digital holography, samples of electronically recorded optical or other types of holograms of real objects are used for numerical reconstruction of images of the objects. Nowadays, thanks to remarkable progress in computer power and capacity, computational imaging is used for solving imaging problems in many new areas, where imaging was regarded as not feasible not long ago.

The set of exercises unified by the title 'Digital image formation and computational imaging' is listed in the start menu (figure 3.1).

3.2 Image recovery from sparse irregularly sampled data. Recovery of images with occlusions

As was mentioned in section 'Image irregular and random sampling', there are many practical situations, when images are sampled in an irregular fashion, whereas the standard for image displays and for image processing software is a representation of images by their samples taken over regular square sampling grids. Therefore, a problem exists of converting sets of arbitrarily taken image samples into the standard sampled representation.

A simple and intuitive method of such a conversion was presented in section 'Image irregular and random sampling' in the exercise 'Reconstruction of sparsely sampled images by means of interpolation of nearest neighbors'. This is, however,

doi:10.1088/978-0-7503-1233-2ch3

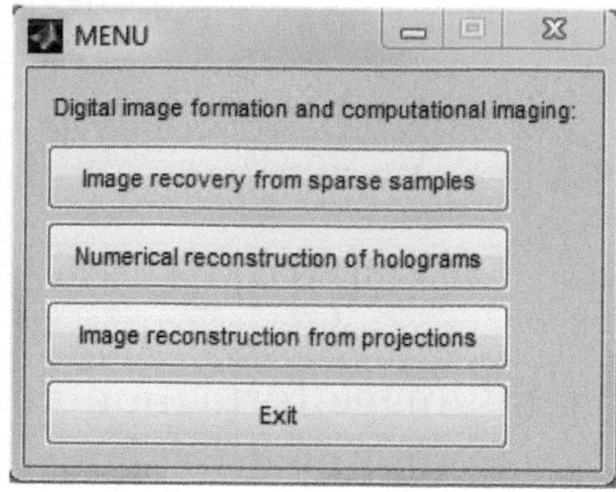

Figure 3.1. Digital image formation and computational imaging: start menu.

not the best possible solution. Exercises 'Image recovery from sparse samples' in this section demonstrate an ultimate solution of this problem.

In an assumption that the quality of image reconstruction is evaluated in terms of mean square recovery error, a framework for solving this problem is provided by the *discrete sampling theorem.* As was already mentioned in section 'Estimating image effective bandwidth', the discrete sampling theorem states that if K samples of the required N samples of a signal ($K < N$) are available, the signal can be approximated by its 'sparse' or band-limited, in a certain selected transform domain, copy, which has exactly K non-zero transform coefficients, and that mean square error of such an approximation is equal to the energy of signal $N - K$ neglected (i.e. zeroed) transform coefficients. The approximation error can be minimized by means of band limitation in a domain of a transform with the best, for the particular class of signals, energy compaction capability. In a special case of sparse, or band-limited, in a certain transform, signals, a precise reconstruction is possible. The type of the transform and the degree of band limitation are the *a priori* knowledge that one brings in to solve the problem of signal reconstruction from its arbitrarily taken samples.

Theoretically, reconstruction of N signal samples from its $K < N$ samples can be achieved by means of computing, from those available samples, K signal spectral coefficients in the chosen transform that are supposed to be non-zero, setting all $N - K$ other coefficients to zero and then performing inverse transform of the obtained zero pad spectrum. The task of computing from K samples of K non-zero spectral coefficients requires inversion of the transform matrix, which is, in the case of images of even small sizes, an extremely hard computational task. A practical option is using an iterative reconstruction algorithm that works alternatively in image and transforms domains and, at each iteration, inserts available pixels at their known positions in image domain and zeroes the chosen transform coefficients in the spectral domain.

Exercise 'Image recovery from sparse samples' provides an opportunity to gain a practical insight into the capability of the iterative image reconstruction from sparse samples. As a transform, DCT is used.

The exercise starts from choosing a test image and evaluation of its potential compressibility, i.e. from determining the area and shape of the part of its spectrum that allows reconstructing the image with the mean square error of the order of that of JPEG compression of this image. In this part, the exercise repeats the exercise 'JPEG image quality based estimating shapes and dimensions of effective image DCT spectra' in section 'Estimating image effective bandwidth'.

The choice of two spectrum shapes, rectangular and oval, is offered, and setting the spectrum shape area (in fraction of the total spectrum area) and shape aspect ratio (the ratio of the shape horizontal diameter to the vertical diameter) are prompted (figure 3.2). In addition to the prompt panel, displayed also are the chosen test image, its sparse DCT spectrum that contains DCT spectral coefficients, which reconstruct the image with the same mean square reconstruction error as that of image JPEG compression, border of the chosen spectral band-limitation mask and image band limitation reconstruction error. As a hint for setting the shape area, an estimate is offered (in the caption for the test image) of image spectrum sparsity at the level of the mean square reconstruction error of test image JPEG compression.

Upon setting spectrum shape parameters, three prompting panels are displayed, one after another, for choosing one of five types of sampling grids, sampling redundancy factor and object of sampling (figure 3.3).

When uniform sampling grid with jitter is chosen, the image is sampled in random positions placed uniformly between nodes of the regular sparse square sampling grid with number of nodes equal to the square root of the chosen number of samples (the spectrum shape area times sampling redundancy factor). When random sampling grid is chosen, the selected number of samples is placed randomly and uniformly over the image area. Spiral sampling grid originates from the center of the test image area and then covers the area. It is an example of sampling grids with non-uniform

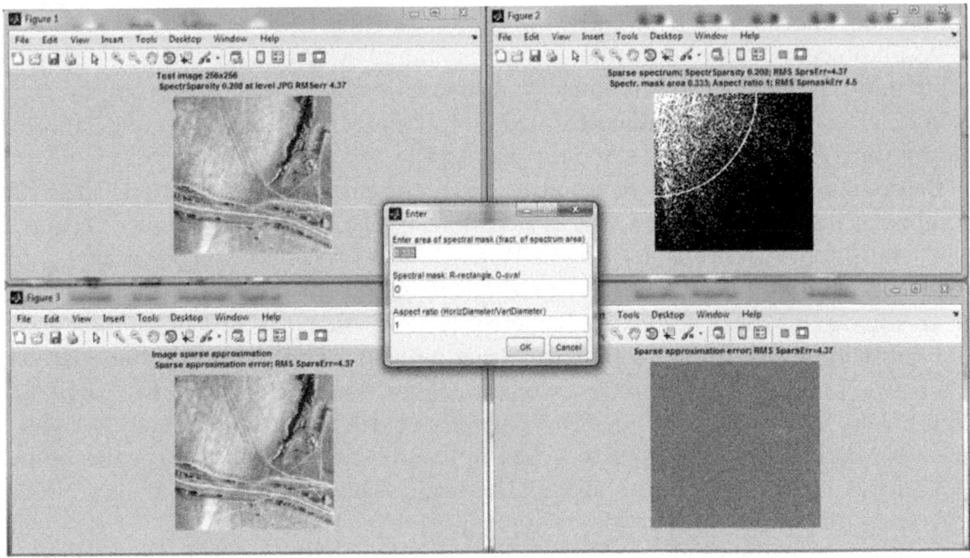

Figure 3.2. Image recovery from sparse samples: setting spectrum band limitation parameters.

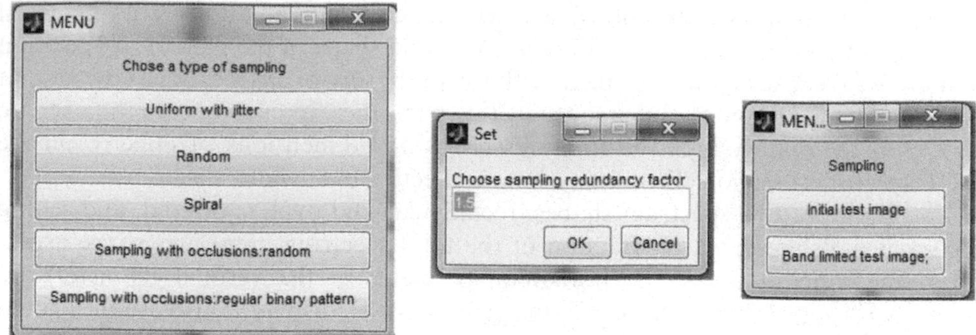

Figure 3.3. Image recovery from sparse samples: menu and setting parameters panels.

density of nodes: the density decreases from the center to periphery. The process of spiral sampling grid formation is displayed in real time. In addition, an option of uniform sampling with occlusion is offered. Sampling with occlusions is implemented in two versions: (i) occlusions are positioned randomly and uniformly over the image area and (ii) occlusions are deterministic binary patterns.

The sampling redundancy factor determines the required number of image samples, or image sampling rate, as a multiplying factor to the spectrum shape area. Theoretically, according to the discrete sampling theorem, the minimal required number of image samples is equal to the area of the spectrum shape, i.e., theoretically, the sampling redundancy factor may be equal to one. However, in this case the iterative reconstruction algorithm converges quite slowly, and too many iterations are needed for image reconstruction with a sufficiently low reconstruction error. The iteration convergence accelerates considerably if the number of image samples exceeds the area of the spectrum shape by about 25–75%, i.e. the sampling redundancy factor should be chosen in the range 1.25–1.75.

As an object of sampling, either initial test image or test image 'blurred' using the band limiting filter, whose frequency response is the chosen spectrum shape, is offered. The latter case implements image pre-filtering required by the sampling theory for avoiding aliasing sampling artifacts.

Before starting the iterative reconstruction, the program prompts one to set the number of iterations. The process of iterations is displayed in real time. Displayed are: band-limited test image, sampled image, reconstructed image, image sparse DCT spectrum and border of the band-limiting spectrum shape, two graphs of root mean square (RMS) of reconstruction error (one, in blue, for 90% of smallest errors and another, in red, for the total reconstruction error) and, in a color map 'jet', the reconstruction error, i.e. the difference between initial test and reconstructed images (figure 3.4). Small and large reconstruction errors are counted separately because it turns out that the majority of errors are small and large errors are concentrated in a very few isolated places in the image. The error values are given in units of image gray scale quantization interval.

Captions to images indicate the relative area of the band-limiting spectral shape, RMS error of image band limitation using this spectral shape, the type of the

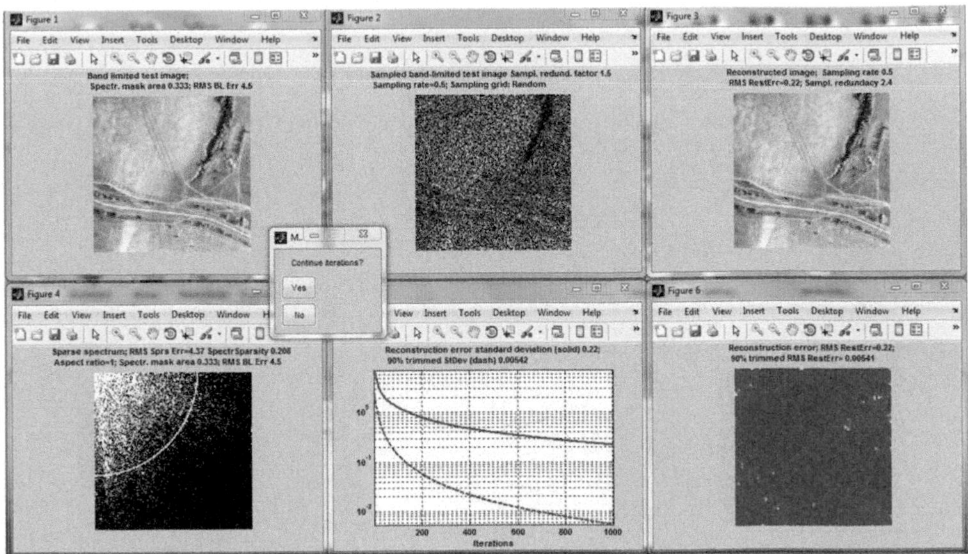

Figure 3.4. Image recovery from sparse samples, random sampling grid: an example of the final display.

sampling grid, sampling rate, the chosen sampling redundancy factor, RMS reconstruction error (separately for 90% of smallest errors and for all errors), and sampling redundancy found as the ratio of sampling rate to the spectrum sparsity (the relative number of image non-zero spectral coefficients, which reconstruct image with the same RMS error as that of JPEG compression).

In experiments with the same image, one can test all offered kinds of sampling grids and different sampling redundancy factors. An example of a final display of reconstruction results obtained for spiral sampling is presented in figure 3.5.

For experiments with occlusion in-painting, two types of occlusions are prepared: random, in the form of random stripes of 1×3 and 1×5 pixels and random squares of 3×3 and 5×5 pixels, and deterministic: a piece of printed text and radial chart (figure 3.6).

Examples of corresponding final displays are shown in figure 3.7 (squares 3×3) and figure 3.8 (printed text).

3.3 Numerical reconstruction of holograms

3.3.1 Introduction

Holograms are recorded amplitudes and phases of coherent radiation wavefronts emitted or reflected by physical objects. When a hologram is illuminated by the same source of coherent radiation that was used for its recording, it reconstructs the object wavefront. Object wavefronts are continuous signals. They can be recorded in digital form using standard procedures of sampling and quantization of radiation wavefront. Holograms recorded digitally can be reconstructed numerically in computers. The process of reconstruction of digital holograms imitates analog wave propagation from the plane, in which a digital hologram was recorded, to the object that

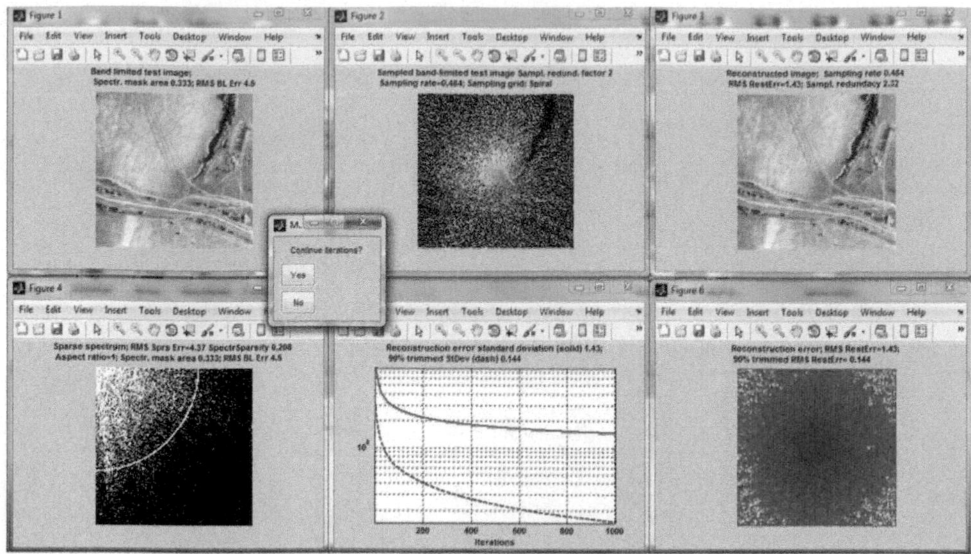

Figure 3.5. Image recovery from sparse samples: an example of the final display (spiral sampling grid).

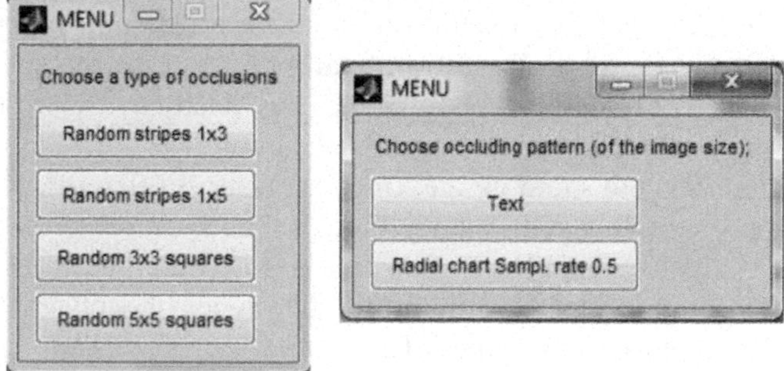

Figure 3.6. Image recovery from sparse samples: menus of types of occlusions.

generated the recorded wavefront. In other words, numerical reconstruction of holograms inverts analog wave propagation from the object to the hologram plane.

In what follows, by holograms we mean optical holograms. As physical radiation sensors are sensitive to only intensity of radiation, for recording optical holograms, the hologram recording sensor is illuminated by an 'object' light beam reflected from the object or passing through it and by a reference light beam. The two beams form a sinusoidal interference pattern with its amplitude and phase modulated of the object wavefront. This pattern is recorded by the hologram recording sensor.

Two complementing methods of hologram recording are used: 'off-axis' and 'on-axis' recording methods. In the 'off-axis' method, the reference beam is directed on the hologram under a certain angle with respect to the object beam, the angle being sufficiently large to enable separation of real and imagine images, which are reconstructed from the sinusoidal interference pattern. In this case, applying the

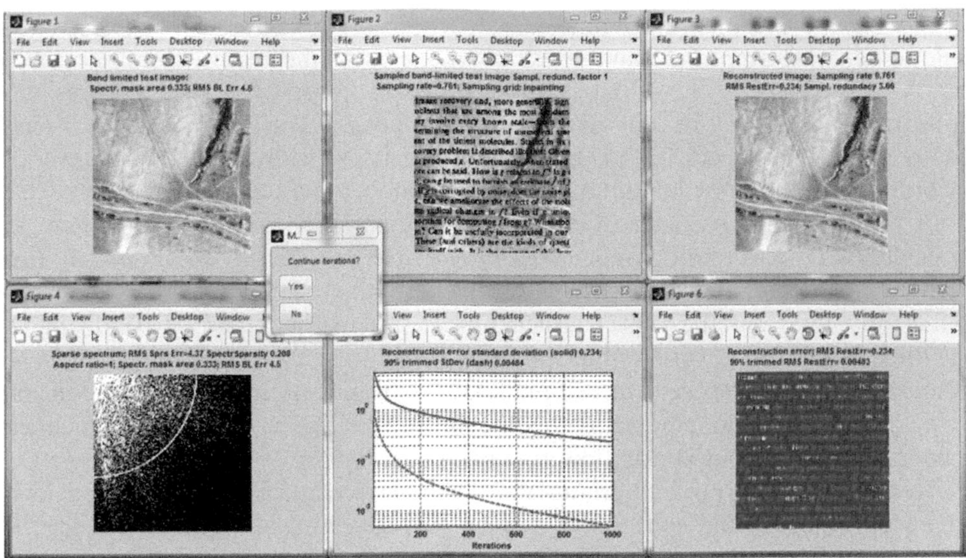

Figure 3.7. Image recovery from sparse samples: an example of the final display (occlusions: squares 3×3).

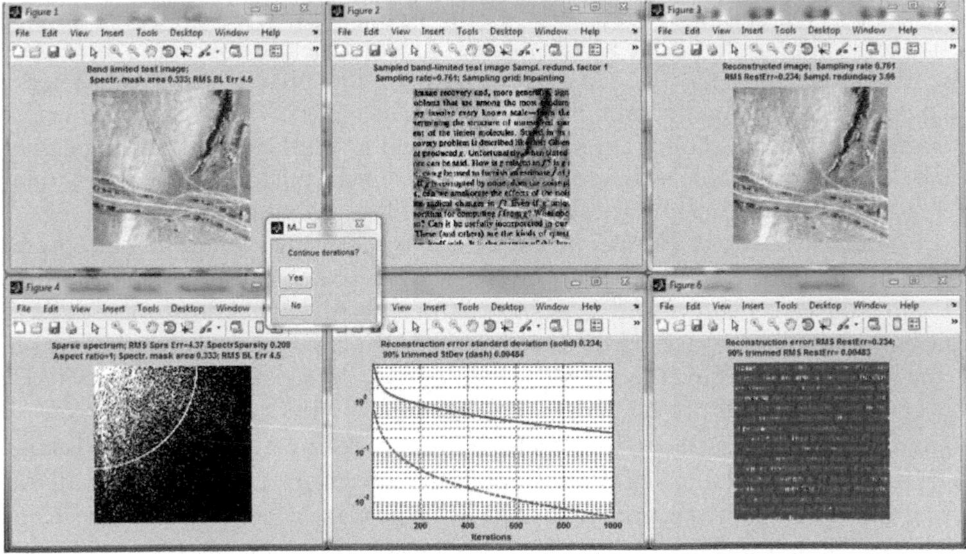

Figure 3.8. Image recovery from sparse samples: an example of the final display (occlusions: text).

'back propagation' transform directly to the recorded hologram is sufficient for hologram reconstruction.

While the 'off axis" method is suitable for both optical and numerical reconstruction of holograms, the 'on-axis' method is suitable only for numerical reconstruction. In the 'on-axis' recording method, the reference beam is collinear with the object beam. If the 'back propagation' transform is applied directly to the recorded hologram in this way hologram, real and imaginary object images overlay each other in the reconstructed image. In order to avoid this overlay, one needs to be able to separate amplitude and phase components in the recorded hologram. To enable this, 'on axis' holograms are recorded in three or four exposures with appropriate changing of the reference beam phase. The amplitude and phase components of the recorded wavefront are then numerically separated from those recordings and used for hologram reconstruction.

In terms of the character of object-to-hologram wave propagation, there are basically two types of holograms: *Fourier holograms* and *Fresnel holograms*. Fourier holograms are holograms recorded in the so called 'far diffraction zone', i.e. sufficiently far from the object, when object size in the plane perpendicular to the direction to hologram is sufficiently small, such that the wavefront shape at the hologram plane can be the regarded plane. Wave propagation to far diffraction zone is well described mathematically by the integral Fourier transform, which can numerically be computed using discrete Fourier transform.

Fresnel holograms are holograms recorded in the so called 'near diffraction zone', where deviation of the spherical wavefront from the plane cannot be neglected. Wave propagation to near diffraction zone can mathematically be described by integral Fresnel transform, which can numerically be computed using various forms of the discrete Fresnel transform.

Fresnel holograms are capable of focusing to different object planes at different distances. The algorithm for Fresnel hologram reconstruction contains a dimensionless distance parameter $\mu^2 = \lambda Z/\Delta f^2 N = \lambda Z/\Delta f S z_h$, that links physical parameters of holograms and of hologram sampling device: wavelength λ of the radiation, object-to-hologram distance Z, hologram sampling interval Δf (hologram recording camera pitch), the number of hologram samples N (in one dimension; total number of a square hologram is N^2) and the physical 1D dimension of the hologram $Sz_h = \Delta f N$.

For reconstruction of Fresnel holograms, two complementing discrete representation of the optical Fresnel transform exist, *canonical discrete Fresnel transform* (DFrT) and *convolutional discrete Fresnel transform*. These transforms differ in hologram sampling strategy. For the canonical DFrT, image sampling interval Δx in the object plane is equal to $1/\Delta f N$, where Δf is hologram sampling interval. For the convolutional DFrT, $\Delta x = \Delta f$. The canonical DFrT should be applied for hologram-to-object distances, for which the distance parameter of DFrTs μ^2 is larger than one, the convolutional DFrT is applicable, when $\mu^2 < 1$. Otherwise, aliasing artifacts appear in reconstruction images. When $\mu^2 = 1$, both transforms are identical. Canonical DFrT is implemented by the direct use of the fast Fourier transform; Convolutional DfrT is implemented as the FFT based convolution; hence the names of the algorithms.

Exercises in this section are designed to demonstrate numerical reconstruction of Fresnel holograms. Pressing the button 'Numerical reconstruction of holograms' in the start menu of this section opens a panel with a list of three exercises, as shown in figure 3.9.

The first exercise demonstrates numerical reconstruction of a simulated Fresnel hologram. The other two exercises demonstrate numerical reconstruction of real optical holograms.

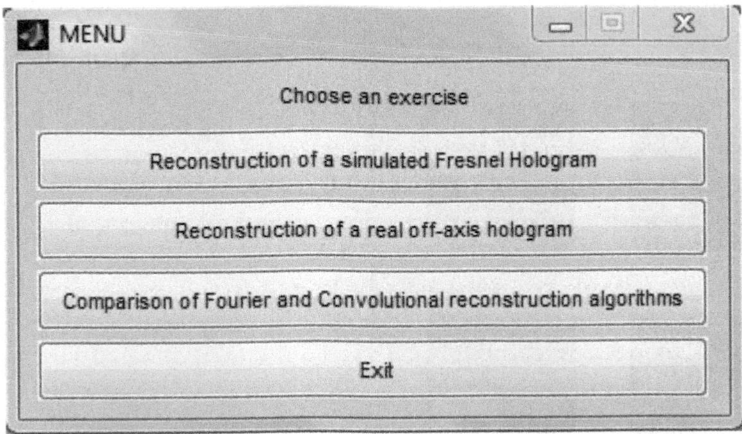

Figure 3.9. Numerical reconstruction of holograms: menu of exercises.

3.3.2 Reconstruction of a simulated Fresnel hologram

The exercise 'Reconstruction of a simulated Fresnel Hologram' simulates formation of an on-axis Fresnel hologram of four test images placed at different positions with respect to the hologram plane and reconstruction of images from the hologram. In the synthesis of holograms, a random phase is assigned to test images in order to imitate diffuse properties of objects' surfaces. At the start, the program displays test images and requests setting depth parameters for each of four test pictures (figure 3.10).

Then the program computes and displays a Fresnel hologram of those images in their different positions and demonstrates its reconstruction by means of 'focusing' inverse DFrT at different distances from the hologram plane. The results of the reconstruction are displayed in real time as a sequence of frames obtained for different values of the scene depth parameter. One of the displays is shown in figure 3.11.

3.3.3 Reconstruction of a real off-axis hologram

In the exercise 'Reconstruction of a real off-axis hologram', the program performs reconstruction of a real optical Fresnel hologram of a dice, using the canonical DFrT and, for comparison, its focal plane invariant version (FPI-DFrT). The experiment starts from displaying a test hologram and prompting the user to set the range of the distance parameter and step, with which it will be changed in the process of reconstruction for different scene depths (figure 3.12). Then the hologram reconstruction begins, and two reconstructed images are displayed in real time for reconstruction in the form of a movie: an image reconstructed using the canonical DFrT (figure 3.13, left image) and an image reconstructed using FPI-DFrT (figure 3.13, right image). In the caption to the images, current values of the distance parameter are indicated.

At negative values of the distance parameter, the image is reconstructed in (-1)th diffraction order to the left from the optical axis; for positive values, the image is

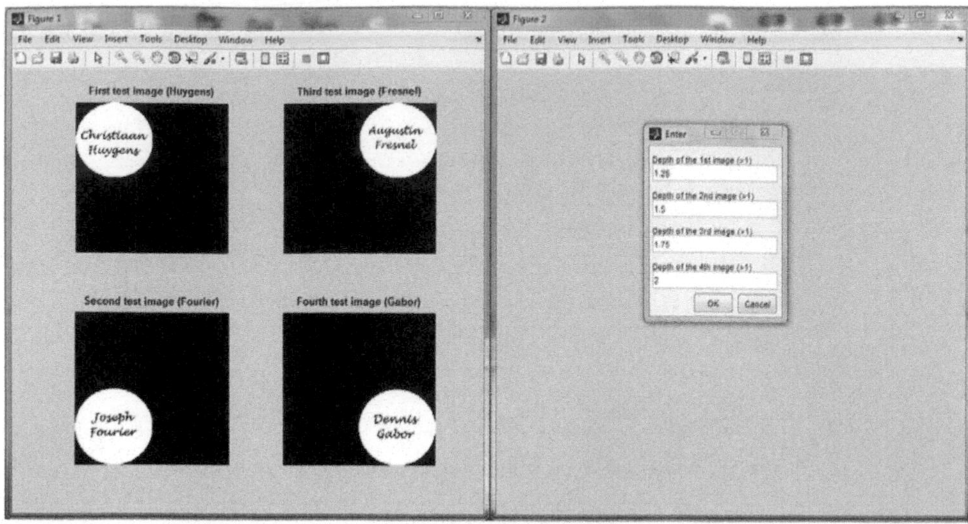

Figure 3.10. Reconstruction of a simulated Fresnel hologram: test images and a panel for setting depth parameters.

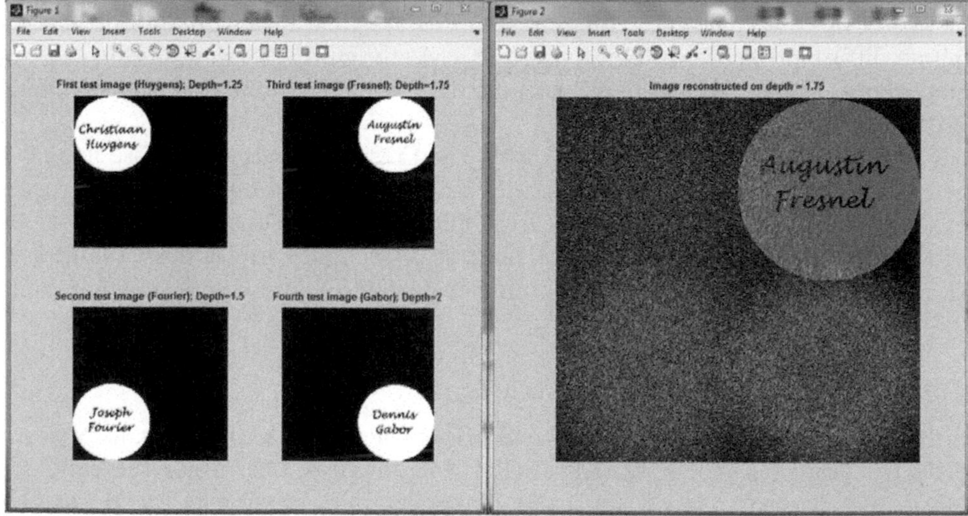

Figure 3.11. Reconstruction of a simulated Fresnel hologram: test images placed at different distances from the hologram (left) and results of reconstruction focused on one of the images (right).

reconstructed in (+1)th diffraction order to the right from the optical axis. The central spot in the reconstructed image corresponds to the zero-order diffraction. In the process of reconstruction, one can see gradual focusing to the reconstructed image and shifting positions of the reconstructed images and of the spot of

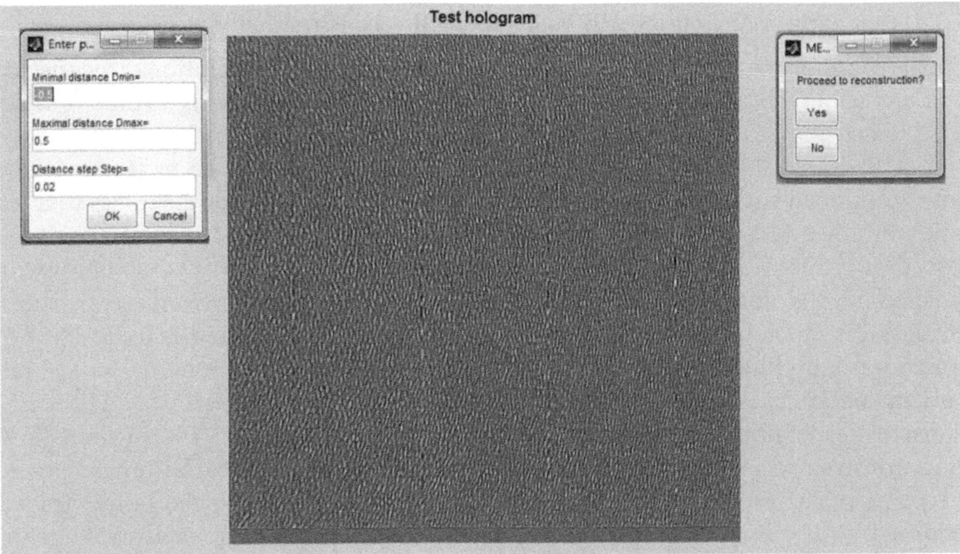

Figure 3.12. Reconstruction of a real off-axis hologram: a test hologram.

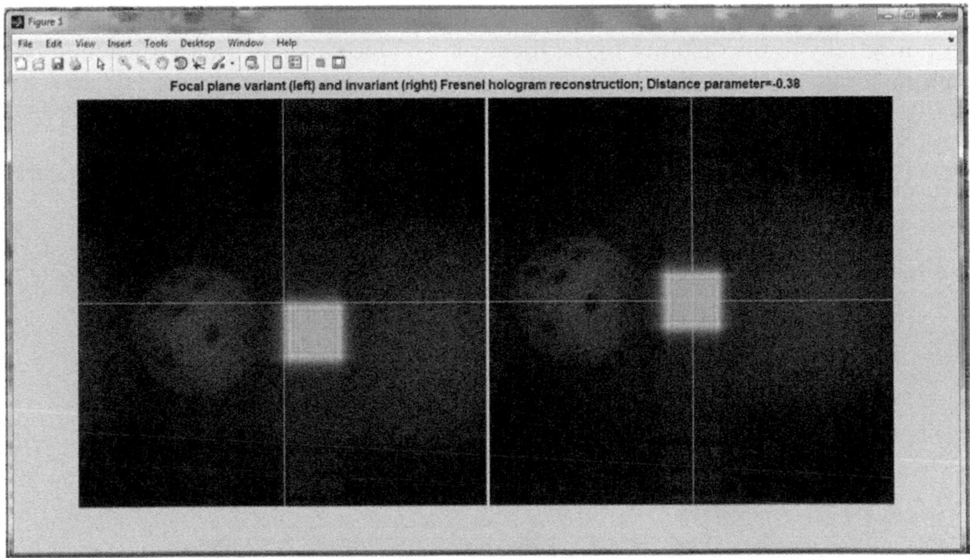

Figure 3.13. Reconstruction of a real off-axis hologram: focal plane variant (left) and focal plane invariant (right) reconstructions.

zero-order diffraction with respect to the optical axis for reconstruction by means of the canonical DFrT for different values of the distance parameter For reconstruction by means of FPI-DFrT, position of the reconstructed image of the zero-order diffraction spot are invariant to the distance parameter.

3.3.4 Comparison of Fourier and Convolutional reconstruction algorithms

The purpose of the exercise 'Comparison of Fourier and convolutional reconstruction algorithms' is a demonstration of hologram sampling aliasing artifacts, which arise, when application conditions for the reconstruction algorithms are violated, and of their elimination, when those conditions are obeyed. The program applies both mentioned canonical and convolutional DFrTs for different distances to a real hologram of a test object (two filaments crossed under 90° and a piece of a ruler, placed at different distances) and displays, frame by frame, corresponding reconstructed images along with a sketch of the test object (to the left from reconstructed images), on which reconstruction distance for each particular view is indicated by a horizontal line. Physical parameters of the hologram are: wavelength $\lambda = 458$ nm; camera pitch $\Delta f = 11$ µm, number of hologram samples $N \times N = 512 \times 512$. A particular example of displayed results is shown in figure 3.14. In the title of the reconstructed images, parameter Z indicates, in mm, physical distance between the plane of focusing the reconstruction and the plane in which the hologram was recorded, and μ^2 is the dimension-less distance parameter described in the Introduction to this section. Aliasing artifacts can be observed in the image reconstructed by the Fourier method (left image). The central of three reconstructed images demonstrates that aliasing artifacts can be eliminated if, for $\mu^2 < 1$ a μ^2th fraction of the hologram is used for restoration, i.e. when the hologram is cropped proportionally to the distance to the focus plane. One can also see that when $\mu^2 = 1$, both methods produce identical results.

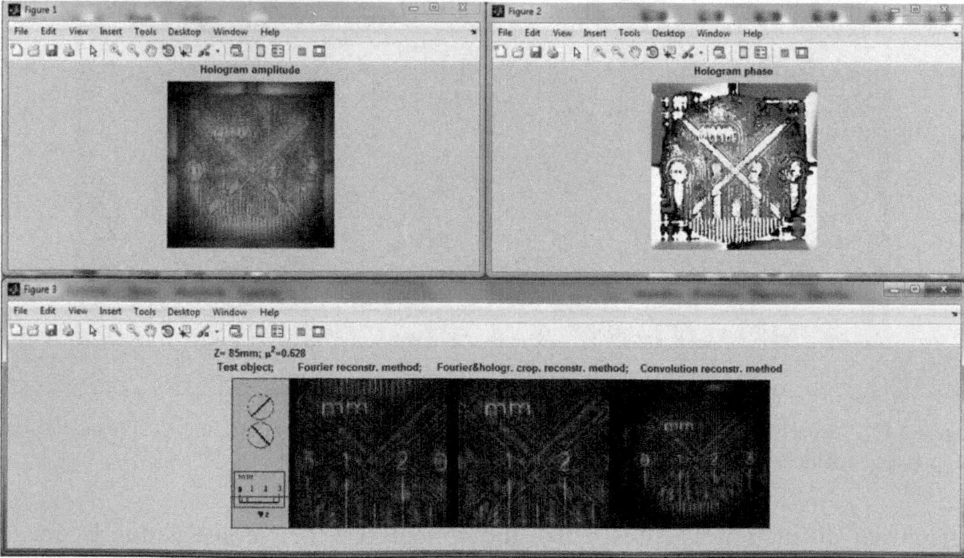

Figure 3.14. Comparison of convolutional and Fourier reconstruction algorithms: an intermediate frame that shows aliasing artifacts in the bottom left image. A sketch of the test object to the left from reconstructed images at the bottom image indicates, by means of a moving horizontal line, the distance, for which each particular view is obtained.

3.4 Image reconstruction from projections

Image numerical reconstruction from projections is obtaining images of body slices, which otherwise are not accessible for viewing, from sets of projections of the slices taken under different angles. This is how *computed tomography* works. There are various methods of acquiring projections of body slices. The simplest for understanding the principles of image reconstruction from projections is the method of '*parallel projections*', when the body is scanned by a plane beam of parallel radiation rays, which rotates around the body for obtaining projections of the body slice under different angles.

The exercise 'Image reconstruction from projections' is intended to demonstrate how parallel projections of images are generated and how reconstruction of images from their projections is performed using the reconstruction method known as the '*filtered back projection*' method. Generating image parallel projections taken under different angles is simulated through summation along column of images rotated by a sequence of angles from a start angle to an end angle with a step equal to the ratio of the angle range to the number of projections. The angular range and the number of projections are numerical parameters that the user is prompted to set after being asked to choose a test image. Figure 3.15 shows three successive displays that appear at the start.

After completion of computing projections of the chosen test image, image reconstruction by means of filtered back projection is initiated. Filtered back projection reconstruction consists in (i) computing derivatives of individual projections using '*ramp*' *filtering* (exercises in image differentiation using 'ramp' filtering are described in chapter 4, section 'Comparison of signal numerical differentiation and integration methods'), (ii) back projecting the differentiation result under the corresponding angle by means of column-wise replication of its samples arranged as an image row, (iii) rotation of the obtained 2D array of the back projected derivative by the given angle and (iv) accumulating the rotated back projected derivatives for all the angle range. For image rotation in both stages of the simulation, the

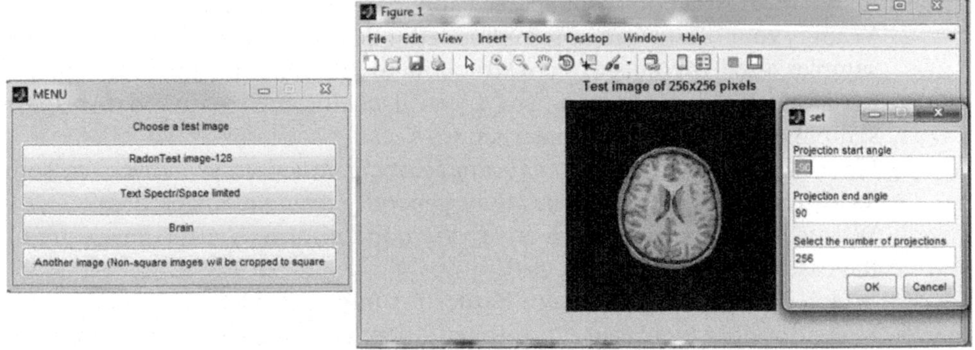

Figure 3.15. Image reconstruction from projections: start menu, chosen test image and a prompt for setting start and end angles of projections and the number of projections.

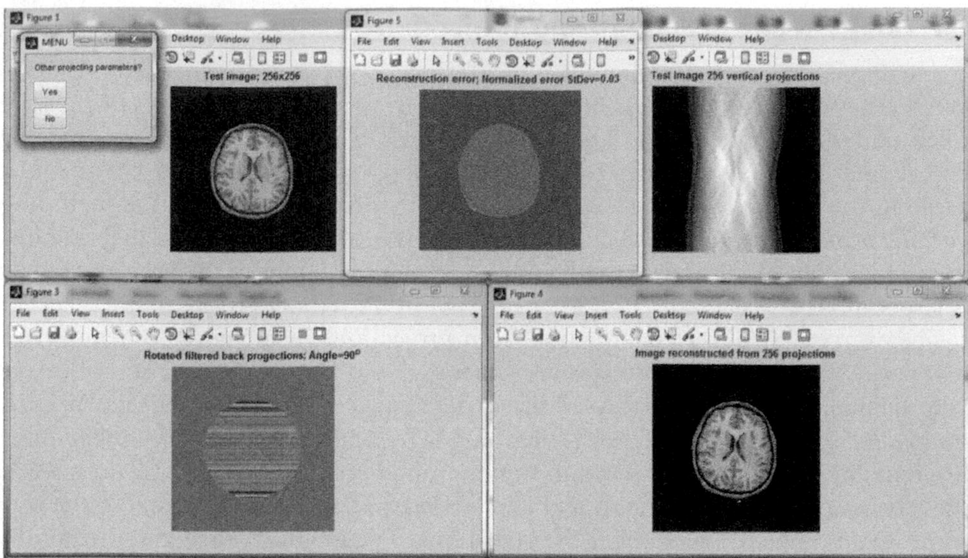

Figure 3.16. Image reconstruction from projections: an example of images displayed during the exercise.

three-step image rotation algorithm demonstrated in chapter 4, section 'Three step image rotation algorithm', is used.

The result of image reconstruction is displayed in real time. Figure 3.16 illustrates images displayed in the exercise.

The bottom left figure of the displayed image shows individual filtered back projections. The bottom right figure shows the process of accumulation of the filtered back projections for image reconstruction. Upon completion of the reconstruction, image reconstruction error is displayed and its standard deviation normalized to the image dynamic range is indicated in the title of the error image.

Questions for self-testing

1. From your experimental experience, which case of sparse sampling iterative image reconstruction from sparse samples converges faster?
2. What is your evaluation of sampling redundancy (the ratio of the number of samples used for image reconstruction to the minimal number equal to the number of image non-zero spectral coefficients) required for sparse sampling and iterative reconstruction?
3. How would you explain that image reconstruction is slower in some localized places within images than generally over the image area?
4. Why is image reconstruction error very non-uniform over the image area in the case of spiral sampling grid?
5. Which kinds of occlusions are harder for in-painting?
6. How do objects placed at different depths from the hologram affect reconstructed images of each other?

7. How do the inter-object cross-talk errors of image reconstruction from Fresnel holograms depend on inter-object distances?
8. What physical parameter of hologram off-axis recording scheme affects the separation of reconstructed images from the zero-order diffraction spot?
9. Why is image scale changing with the distance parameter in hologram reconstruction by the Fourier reconstruction algorithm?
10. How would you describe aliasing artifacts in reconstruction of Fresnel holograms using Fourier reconstruction algorithm for $\mu^2 < 1$?
11. How does the error of image reconstruction from projections depend on the number of projections?
12. Were errors of image reconstruction from projections more or less uniform for all tested images? If not, why might this be?

Leonid P Yaroslavsky

Chapter 4

Image resampling and building continuous image models

4.1 Introduction

Accurate and fast image resampling is a key operation in many digital image processing applications. Typical examples, to name a few, are multi-modality data fusion, image mosaicing, image reconstruction from projections, image reconstruction from holograms, image super-resolution from sequences of image frames, stabilization of videos distorted by turbulence, target location and tracking with sub-pixel accuracy.

Image re-sampling assumes reconstruction of a *continuous image model*, i.e. an approximation to the original non-sampled image, by means of interpolation of available image samples to obtain samples 'in-between' the available ones and subsequent resampling of the model. The most feasible interpolation methods are convolutional ones that implement interpolation by means of weighted summation of available samples. A number of convolutional interpolation methods are known, beginning from the simplest nearest neighbor and linear (bilinear, for 2D case) interpolations to more accurate cubic (bicubic, for 2D case) and higher order spline methods. The ultimately accurate method of convolutional interpolation of sampled data is the *discrete sinc interpolation* (*sincd-interpolation*), which secures virtually perfect interpolation with no interpolation errors except those caused by round-off calculation errors.

This chapter offers exercises in image resampling using perfect image discrete sinc-interpolation and its comparison with other known numerical interpolation methods in terms of interpolation accuracy. The exercises are listed in the start menu shown in figure 4.1.

The first exercise illustrates the basic principle of the fast algorithm of signal/image discrete sinc-interpolation, that of signal/imager sub-sampling through successive signal/image fractional shifts. The second exercise demonstrates examples

doi:10.1088/978-0-7503-1233-2ch4

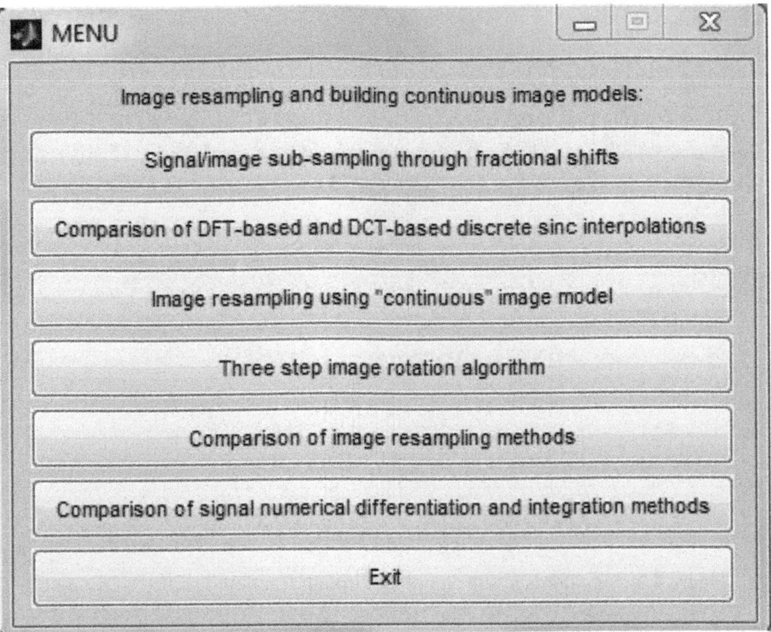

Figure 4.1. Image resampling and building continuous image models: start menu.

of image geometrical transformation by means of resampling numerical models of initial non-sampled images generated using discrete sinc-interpolated fractional shifts. The third exercise visualizes the work of the fast three step image rotation algorithm, also implemented through discrete sinc interpolated fractional shifts. The last two exercises are intended to demonstrate the superiority of the discrete sinc interpolation in comparison with other numerical interpolation methods in terms of the interpolation accuracy.

4.2 Signal/image sub-sampling through fractional shifts

This exercise demonstrates, using, as test signals, 1D signals and 2D images, the principle of image resampling with discrete sinc interpolation through successive fractional shifts. In the first part of the exercise, 1D interpolation, realizations of pseudo-random signals of 16 samples with uniform DFT spectrum are used as test signals. The program successively shifts initial test signal samples by $1/Lx$ fractions of the sampling interval, which defines the signal base band, where Lx is the signal subsampling rate that the user is prompted to specify. Interpolated values of the shifted signal samples are found by means of discrete sinc interpolation. The core feature of the discrete sinc interpolation, its signal spectrum preservation capability, is illustrated by displaying the DFT spectrum of the subsampled signal. The spectrum plot shows that the subsampled signal generated using discrete sinc interpolation is a band-limited signal with band-limitation defined by the subsampling rate and that the uniform spectrum of the initial signal within the limited bandwidth is preserved without any distortions. An example of the display is shown in figure 4.2.

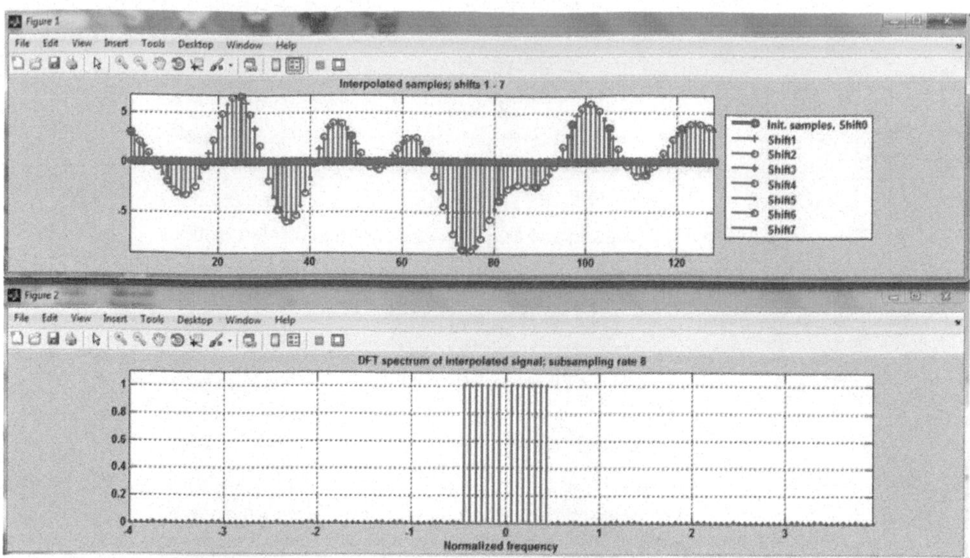

Figure 4.2. Signal/image sub-sampling through fractional shifts: 1-D signal.

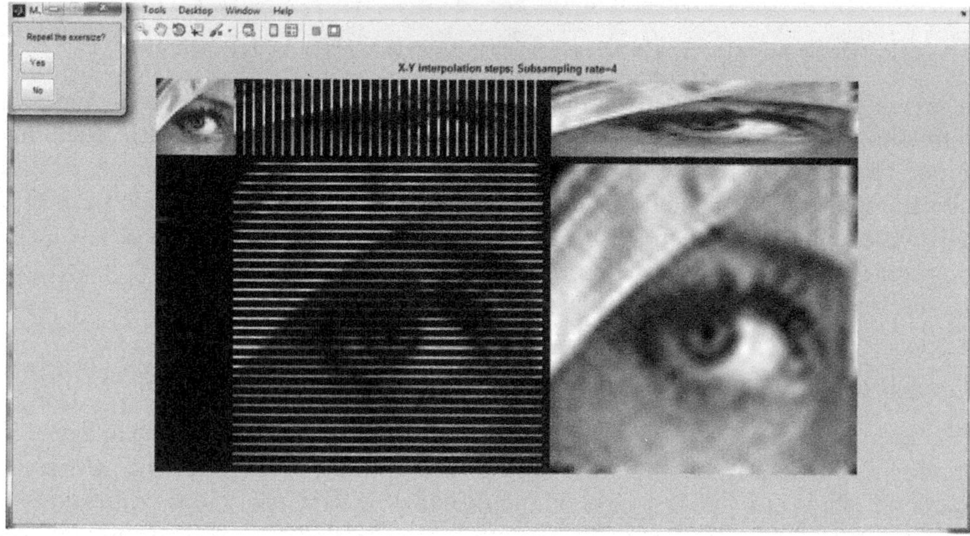

Figure 4.3. Signal/image subsampling through fractional shifts: 2D signal. Upper part, from left to right: initial test image, this image with zero pixels inserted in the image rows according to the subsampling rate and a result of row-wise interpolation that replaces the zero pixels. Bottom part: row-wise interpolated image with zero rows inserted between image rows according to the subsampling rate (left) and a resulting 2D interpolated image after column-wise interpolation of the row-wise interpolated image (right).

The second part of the exercise, 2D interpolation for image subsampling, is carried out in two steps, first over image rows and then over image columns. Both steps are displayed in real time. As test images, a prepared 32 × 32 pixel image 'Eye' and 32 × 32 pixel fragments of images that can be chosen by the user are used. Subsampling rate is also a user defined parameter. Figure 4.3 presents an example of displays of the exercise outcomes. It shows the initial test image and results obtained at all steps of its resampling.

4.3 Comparison of DFT-based and DCT-based discrete sinc interpolations

Discrete sinc interpolation, the perfect method of sampled data interpolation, is a convolutional interpolation method. Numerical convolution can be computed in two ways: (i) in signal domain by means of summation, for each sample of the interpolated signal, of the product of signal samples and samples of the discrete sinc-function, and (ii) in the domain of DFrT using *Fast Fourier transform* (FFT) by means of inverse FFT of the product of FFT of sampled signal and frequency response of the discrete sinc interpolator. The latter is, in the case of signal fractional shifts, illustrated in the exercise in the previous section, a complex exponent of required fractional shift. The interpolation discrete sinc-function has the same number of samples as that of the signal, say N. Therefore, the number of multiplication and summation operations per one output signal sample for computing convolution in signal domain is equal to N, whereas for computing convolution in the DFT domain it is, thanks to use of FFT, equal to log N, i.e. very substantially less.

An important practical issue of numerical convolution is how to treat signals at their borders, where convolution involves signal samples, which are outside their borders and are, therefore, unavailable. When convolution is computed in the domain of DFT using FFT, signal is automatically treated as periodical with period N, i.e. after sample number N follow again samples number one, number two and so on. Such a forcible periodical extension of signals is very unnatural: first and last signal samples, which in the initial non-sampled signal are very far from each other, are treated by DFT as adjacent. This, in the case of discrete sinc-interpolation, may cause heavy boundary effects at signal borders in the form of oscillations, because first and last signal samples may frequently have much different values, between which discrete sinc-interpolation tries to smoothly interpolate. This drawback of discrete sinc-interpolation can be very substantially overcome, if the signal, before its convolution in DFT domain with discrete sinc-function, is evenly extended outside its borders by means of mirror reflection at the borders, such that in the extended signal after its Nth samples follow again Nth signal sample, then its $(N-1)$ th sample and soon. Such an extension eliminates any potential signal gaps at the signal border. Obviously, this doubles the signal length, which requires that, for perfect discrete sinc-interpolation, the N-point discrete sinc-function must be padded with N zeros to the full $2N$ length, and DFT convolution should be carried out with $2N$ point signals. It turns out that such $2N$ point convolution of evenly extended signal with zero padded discrete sinc-function is reduced to inverse discrete cosine transform (DCT) of the product of DCT spectral coefficients of the initial not extended signal and DFT spectral coefficients of the zero padded discrete sinc-function. This method is called *discrete sinc-interpolation in DCT domain.*

Exercises in this section are designed to illustrate mentioned boundary effects characteristic for fast discrete sinc-interpolation in DFT domain and elimination of

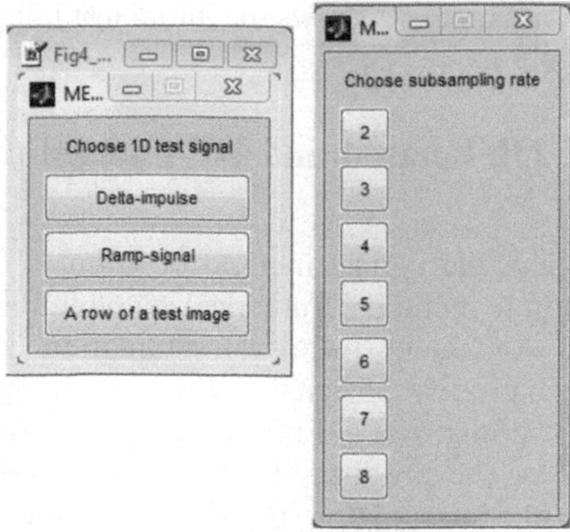

Figure 4.4. Comparison of DFT-based and DCT-based discrete sinc interpolations: 1D signals, start menus.

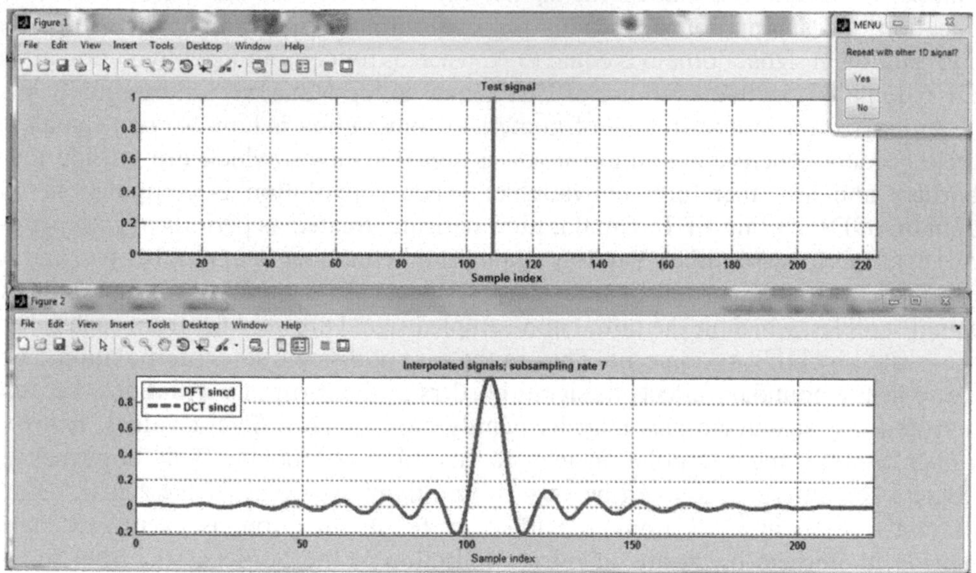

Figure 4.5. Comparison of DFT-based and DCT-based discrete sinc interpolations: delta-impulse.

them, when interpolation is implemented in DCT domain. At the program start, one should first choose between two options: working with 1D or with 2D signals. In the case of 1D signals, the choice is offered of three types of test signals and then of signal subsampling rate, i.e. of the number of intermediate signal samples to be placed after each of two initial signal samples (figure 4.4).

In the case of delta-impulse as a test signal, the program displays point spread functions of DFT and DCT based interpolators (figure 4.5) overlaid, for comparison, one on the other, from which one can see that the two point spread functions are identical and are the discrete sinc-function.

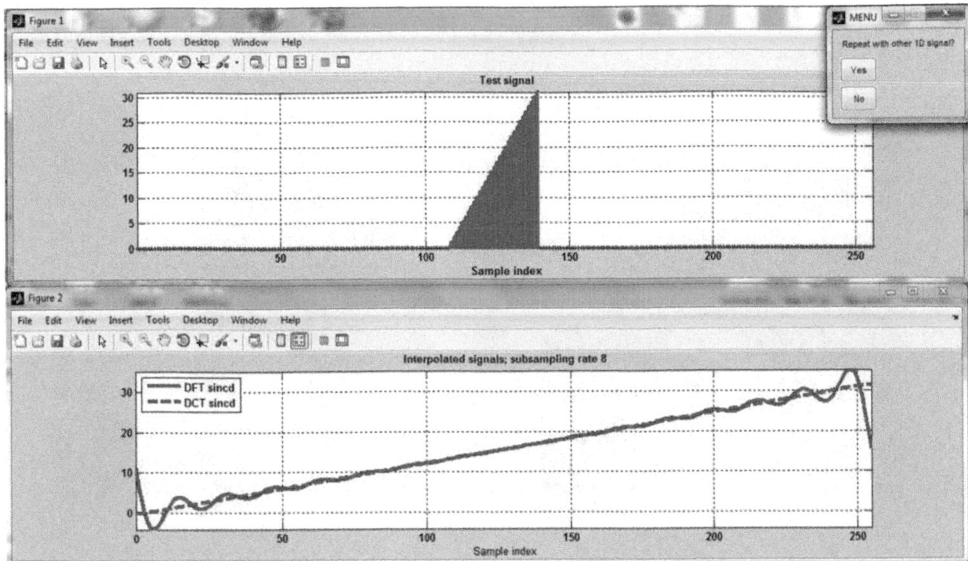

Figure 4.6. Comparison of DFT-based and DCT-based discrete sinc interpolations: ramp-signal.

When a ramp-signal is chosen as a test signal, interpolation results for the two interpolators are also displayed overlaid one on the other to visually demonstrate heavy oscillations on signal borders in the case of DFT based interpolator and their absence in the case of DCT based one (figure 4.6).

The last option of a test signal, a user chosen row of an image from the image data base, provides an opportunity to check what may happen on borders of rows of real images.

For 2D signals, two options are offered: a prepared fragment of image 'Camera man', or the possibility of taking any 32 × 32 pixel fragment of any image from the image database. The user is also prompted to choose a subsampling rate, as in the previous exercise. Upon making the choices, the program displays side by side for comparison two results of subsampling, i.e. magnification, of the selected test image by DFT and by DCT based interpolators (figure 4.7).

4.4 Image resampling using 'continuous' image models

This set of exercises is intended to illustrate some possible applications of 'continuous' image models created by means of image subsampling using discrete sinc-interpolation. The list of exercises in using image "continuous" models is presented in the start menu shown in figure 4.8.

In each exercise the user is prompted to select a test image and an image subsampling rate for creating a 'continuous' image model. The larger the subsampling rate, the more accurate, i.e. closer to the initial not sampled image, is the obtained continuous image model, which is then used for image resampling required by the particular task.

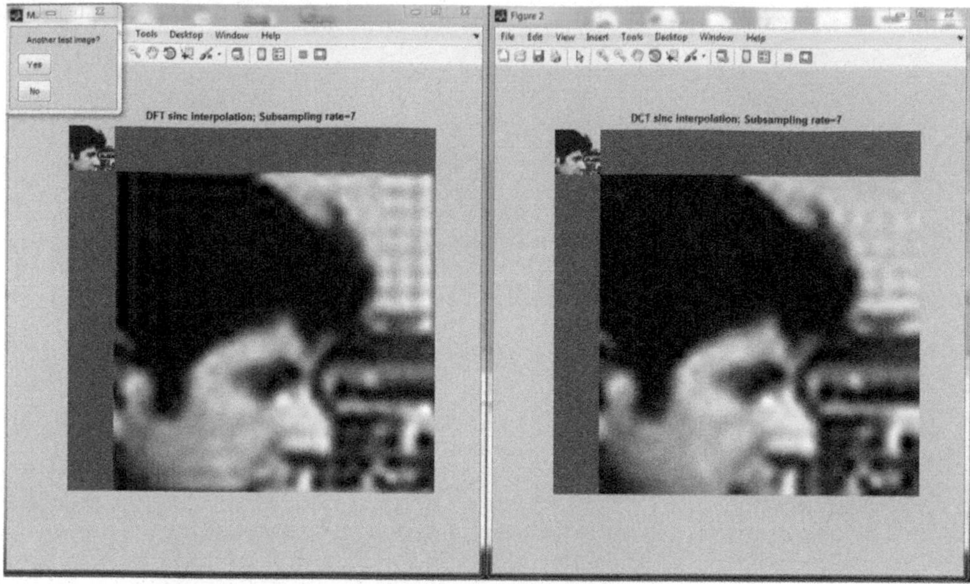

Figure 4.7. Comparison of DFT-based and DCT-based discrete sinc interpolations: ramp-signal: camera man.

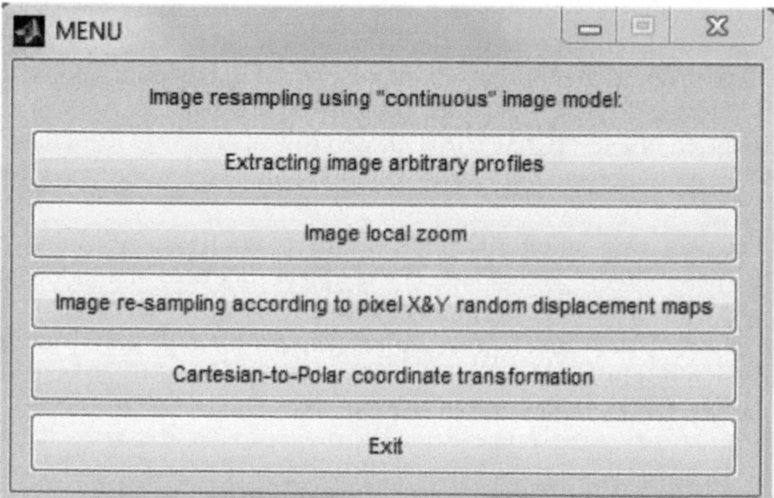

Figure 4.8. Image resampling using 'continuous' image model: start menu.

4.4.1 Extracting image arbitrary profiles

The exercise starts from loading a test image from the image data base and then the user is prompted first to choose sub-sampling rate for building 'continuous' image model and the required number of samples along this profile (figure 4.9), after which a 'continuous' image model is generated by image subsampling in two passes, first in horizontal and then in vertical coordinates as is demonstrated in the exercise in

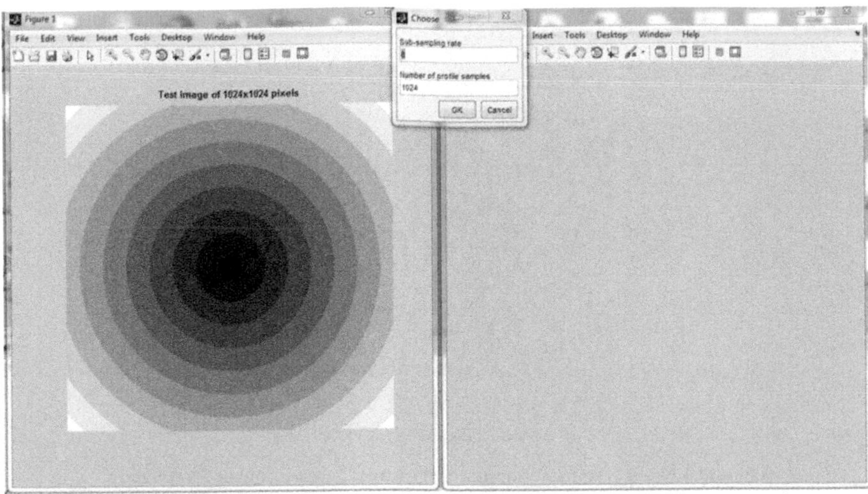

Figure 4.9. Extracting image arbitrary profiles: setting parameters.

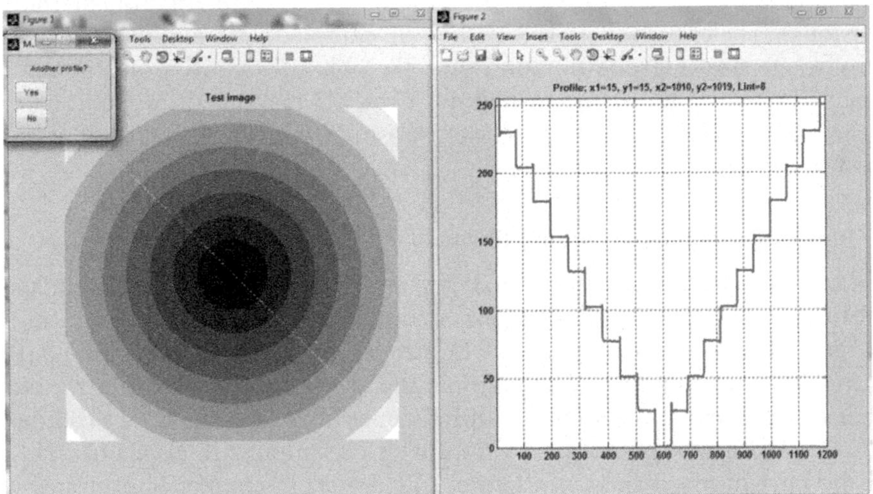

Figure 4.10. Extracting image arbitrary profiles: final display.

section 4.2. Once this is done, the user is asked to indicate on the displayed test image using the cursor the left and then the right end points of the required profile, after which image is resampled along the chosen profile line in the chosen number of sampling points with rounding up coordinates of profile points on the new dense sampling grid. The obtained profile is plotted as illustrated in figure 4.10.

4.4.2 Image local zoom

For experimenting in image local zoom, the user, upon choosing a test image from the image database, is prompted to specify a zoom factor as a rational number

Figure 4.11. Image local zooming-in of user selected image fragments.

L/*M* and then to indicate on the displayed test image by a cursor a center of the desired image fragment (fragment dimensions are a 1/8th fraction of the image dimensions). The chosen fragment is then up-sampled with a step 1/L using DFT based discrete sinc-interpolation and then the obtained 'continuous model' of the fragment is down-sampled with a step *M*. The *L*/*M*-magnified fragment is inserted into the chosen test image at the chosen position and displayed as illustrated in figure 4.11.

4.4.3 Image re-sampling according to random pixel *X*/*Y* displacement maps

In this exercise, two options are offered: generating individual resampled images and generating a sequence of resampled images displayed as a real-time video. *X*/*Y* pixel displacement maps are generated as 2D arrays, isomorphic to images, of pseudo-random correlated numbers. The map parameters: image sub-sampling factor, the number of map 'spots' per image *X* and *Y* dimensions and maximal pixel displacement (maximal height of the maps, in number of sampling intervals) should be set using the pop-up menu shown in figure 4.12. Later, in chapter 6, exercises will be provided that demonstrate how one can generate such pseudo-random maps. Image sub-sampling factor defines the test image zooming for creating its 'continuous model', which is re-sampled according to generated pixel *X*/*Y* displacement maps. An example of the obtained result is shown in figure 4.12.

If the second option (generating a video of a sequence of resamgepled images) is chosen, the program, upon setting the resampling map parameters, generates and displays in real time a sequence of 100 frames with resampled images for different realizations of pseudo-random re-sampling maps.

4.4.4 Cartesian-to-polar coordinate conversion

At the start of this exercise, the user is prompted, in addition to choosing a test image, to set the image sub-sampling rate and the number of samples over the radial

Figure 4.12. Image re-sampling according to random pixel X and Y displacement maps: parameter menu, test image, displacement maps and re-sampled image.

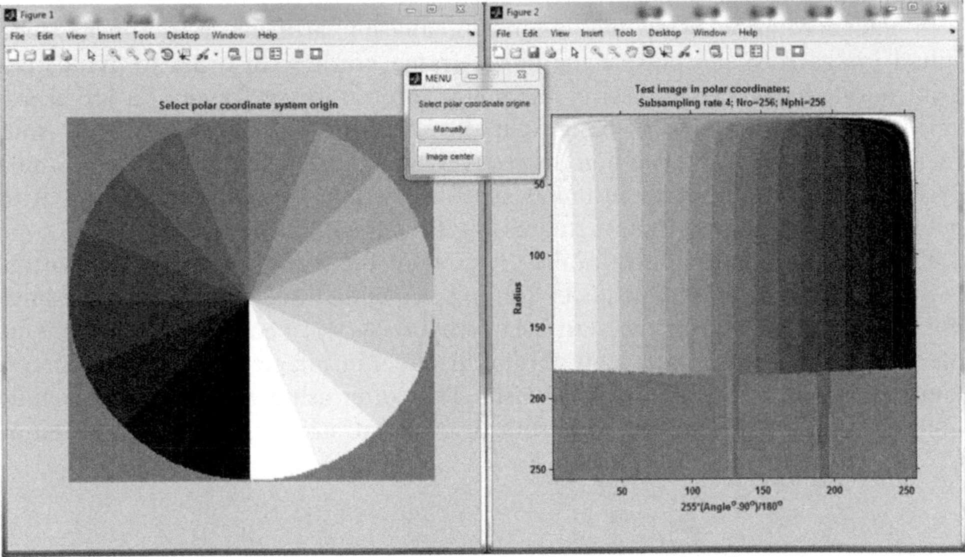

Figure 4.13. Cartesian-to-polar coordinates conversion: prompt for choosing position of the center of polar coordinate system, test image (left) and converted image.

and angular coordinates of the polar coordinate system, to choose a center of the polar coordinate system either manually, using a cursor, or to set it in the test image center. The test image is then sub-sampled with the chosen sub-sampling rate and the obtained 'continuous model' is re-sampled in a polar coordinate system. The result is displayed as illustrated in figure 4.13.

4.5 Three step image rotation algorithm

Image rotation is a very frequent operation in many image processing applications. Of course, it can be implemented through re-sampling of 'continuous' image models as in the above described exercises. After all, having at hand a 'continuous' image model, one can perform any image geometrical transformation. However, 'continuous' image models generated by means of image sub-sampling (zooming-in) are not ultimately accurate approximations to non-sampled images. Their accuracy depends on the subsampling rate: the higher the subsampling rate, the better the accuracy of the subsequent resampling. Therefore, higher interpolation accuracy requires higher memory buffer for storage of sub-sampled images.

For image rotation, there exists an alternative fast algorithm, the one that enables performing image rotation virtually without interpolation errors. This is the so-called *three step rotation algorithm*. It implements image rotation through three successive image 'shearings': say, at first in the horizontal direction, then in the vertical direction and finally again in the horizontal direction. In the horizontal (vertical) shearing, each image row is shifted by a value, which depends on the rotation angle and is also proportional to the row (column) number, counted from the rotation center. For shearing of image rows and columns, the *discrete sinc-interpolation fractional shift algorithm* (see exercise 4.1. 'Signal/image sub-sampling through fractional shifts') is perfectly suited.

In image rotation using this algorithm, aliasing artifacts may appear, when shifted image rows get outside the image frame borders. In order to avoid these artifacts one has either to inscribe the image into an image frame of a larger size, which creates 'safety zones', or to split the rotation angle into sufficiently small fractions and carry out rotation successively by those fractional angles. Similar aliasing artifacts may occur in image spectral domain as well, because, when the image is rotated, its spectrum is rotated by the same angle as well.

The present exercise illustrates the principle of the three-step rotation algorithm as well as possible aliasing artifacts. For experiments, three options for choosing a test image are offered in the start menu (figure 4.14). The first two options are intended for vivid illustration of aliasing artifacts in image and in image spectral domains and of the method to avoid them. They offer using, as test images, pseudo-random images with uniform spectrum of different sizes inscribed into an empty

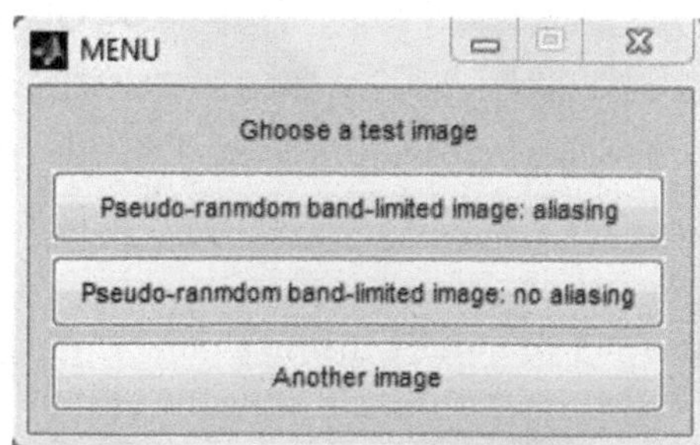

Figure 4.14. Three-step image rotation algorithm: start menu.

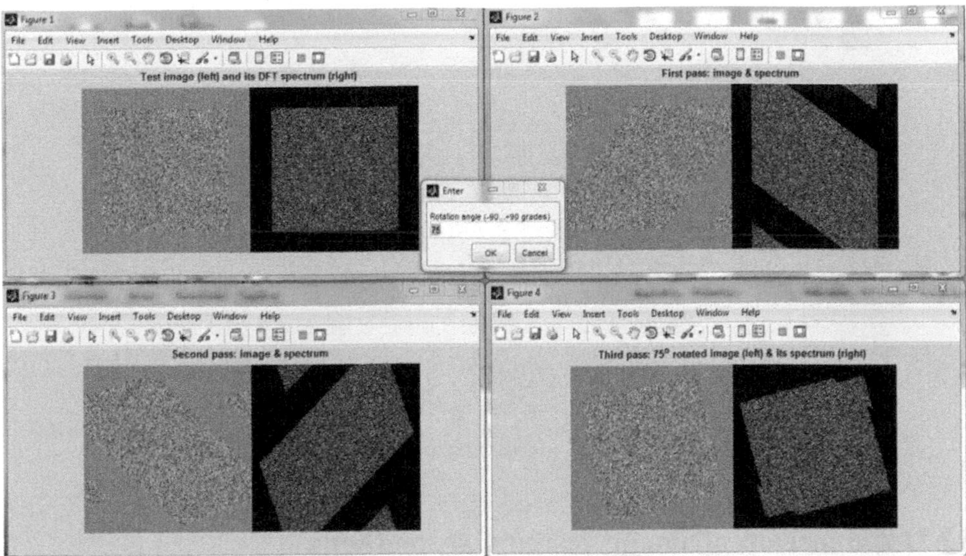

Figure 4.15. Three-step image rotation algorithm: rotation aliasing in image and spectral domains.

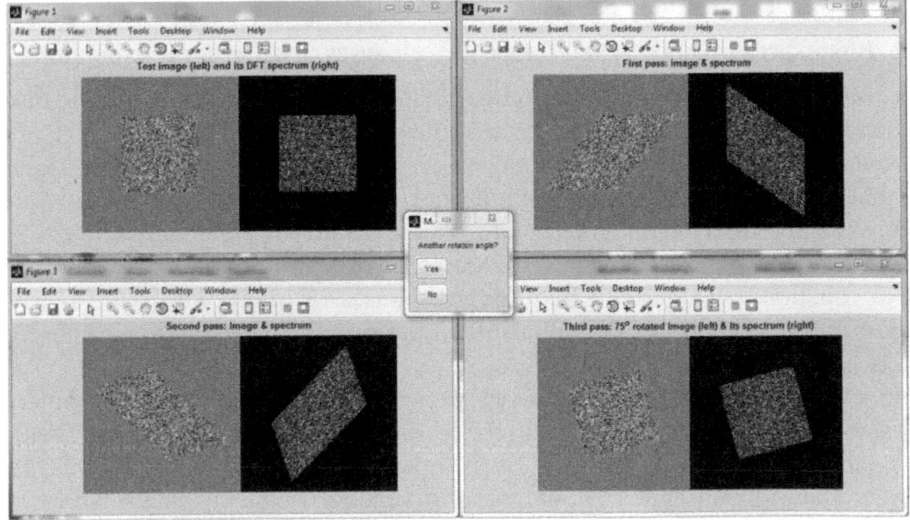

Figure 4.16. Three-step image rotation exercise: no rotation aliasing.

image frame of a larger size, one image with 'safety zone' insufficient for avoiding aliasing and another with a sufficient 'safety zone'. Spectra of these images are similarly limited. The user can also choose an option of experimenting with any other image from the image data set.

Once a test image is chosen and the user has set the rotation angle (in grades), results of all three steps (sheared/rotated images and sheared/rotated spectra) of image rotation are displayed, as is shown in figures 4.15 and 4.16.

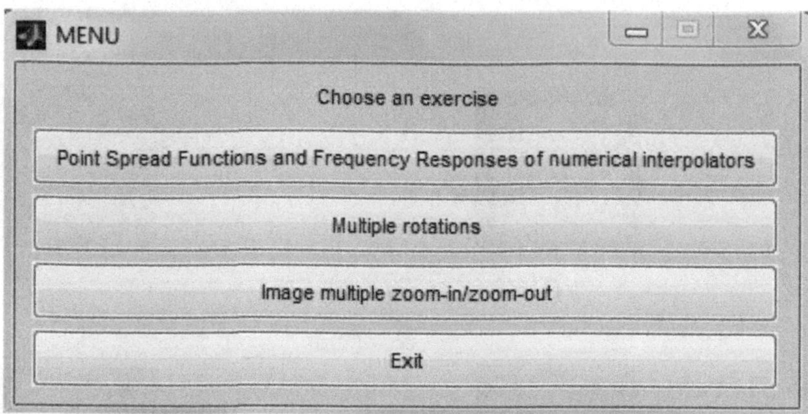

Figure 4.17. Comparison of image resampling methods: start menu.

4.6 Comparison of image resampling methods

For comparison of image resampling methods and demonstrating possible interpolation distortions, three exercises listed in figure 4.17 are offered.

4.6.1 Point spread functions and frequency responses of different interpolators

This exercise is intended solely for comparison of point spread functions and discrete frequency responses of regular nearest neighbor (nn), linear (lin) and spline interpolators from MATLAB® signal processing and image processing toolboxes and that of the discrete sinc-interpolator, and, in particular, to show that frequency response of the discrete sinc-interpolator is flat within the baseband defined by the sampling rate, whereas frequency responses of other interpolators are not. Point spread functions and discrete frequency responses of interpolators are useful for analysis and interpretation of results of their performance comparison in subsequent exercises.

Note that the sample of the frequency response of the discrete sinc-interpolator at the signal baseband border is equal to 0.5, and not to 1, i.e. the highest frequency component of signals is halved. Such 'spectrum shaping' is a recommended modification of the discrete sinc-interpolation made with the purpose of accelerating the discrete sinc-function decay to zero. Figure 4.18 shows a display generated by the program.

4.6.2 Multiple rotations of a test image

This exercise demonstrates losses that may happen in output images due to insufficiently accurate interpolation performed using regular nearest neighbor, bilinear and bicubic interpolators from MATLAB® tool boxes and image preservation capability of the discrete sinc interpolator. For experiments, one can choose either multiple rotations of an image or rotation, in ten steps by 360° of a pseudo-random

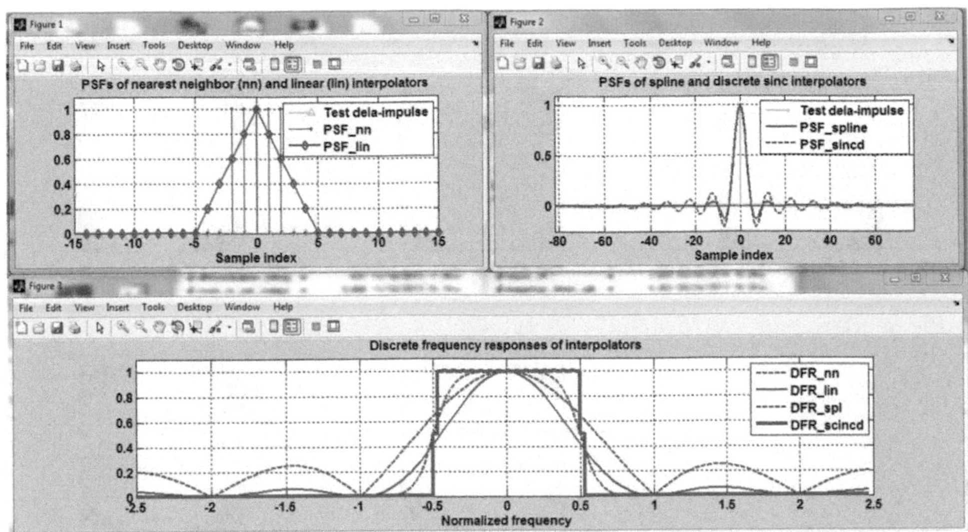

Figure 4.18. Point spread functions and discrete frequency responses (DFRs) of different interpolators. Interval [−0.5 0.5] in plots of discrete frequency responses is the signal baseband defined by its sampling rate.

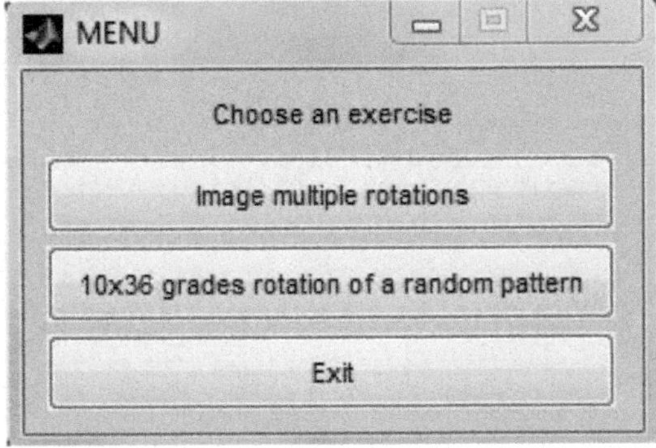

Figure 4.19. Multiple rotations of a test image: start menu.

pattern with uniform DFT spectrum within a square of 0.7 of the base band dimensions (figure 4.19).

In all experiments, test images are subjected to rotations by multiples of 360°, meaning that, ideally, after such rotations, the image must not change. The exercise provides an opportunity to verify that this virtually is, to a certain degree, true only for the discrete sinc-interpolation.

For multiple rotation of an image, numerical parameters that the user is prompted to set are the number of multiples of 360° rotations and the number of rotation steps per 360° (see menu panels in figure 4.20). The program visualizes in real time of computations rotated images and, after completion of rotations, offers to show rotation errors (differences between initial and rotated images) and their DFT spectra (see menu in figure 4.21). The latter are important for understanding the interpolation algorithms that distort signal spectra. In the titles of rotation error

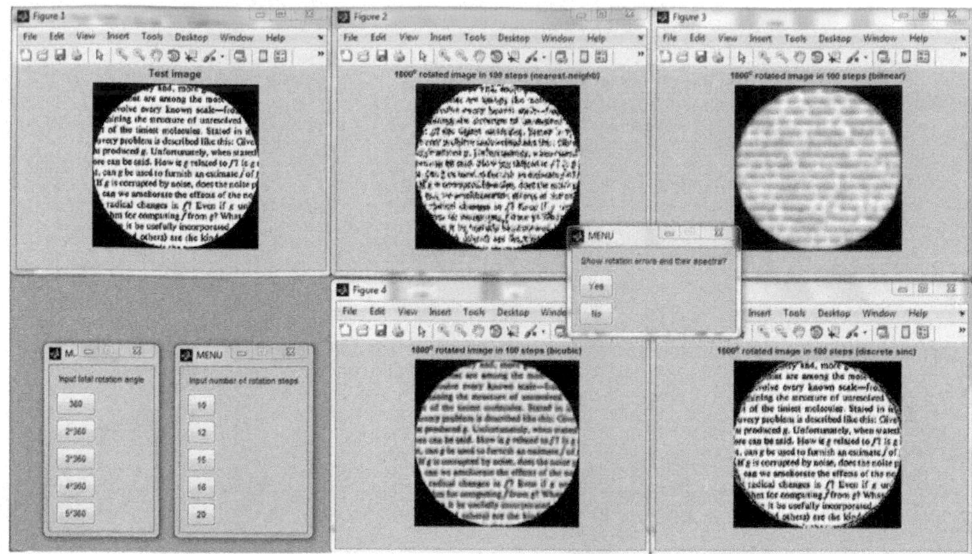

Figure 4.20. Exercise 'Multiple rotations of a test image': test image 'Text', results of its multiple rotations using nearest neighbor, bilinear, bicubic and discrete sinc-interpolations and relevel menu panels.

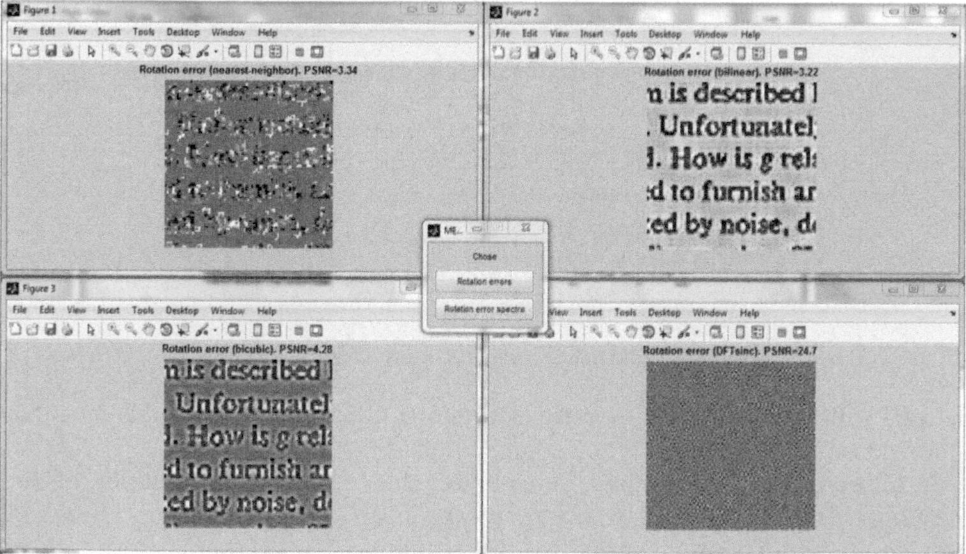

Figure 4.21. Multiple rotations of a test image 'Text': rotation errors.

images, peak signal-to-noise ratios (PSNR) of errors, i.e. ratios of image range 255 to standard deviation of errors, are indicated. Note that PSNR of rotation error for discrete sinc interpolation is always the highest. However, the error is not zero because, as was mentioned in section 4.6.1, discrete sinc-interpolation halves the highest frequency component of signals for accelerating the discrete sinc-function decay to zero.

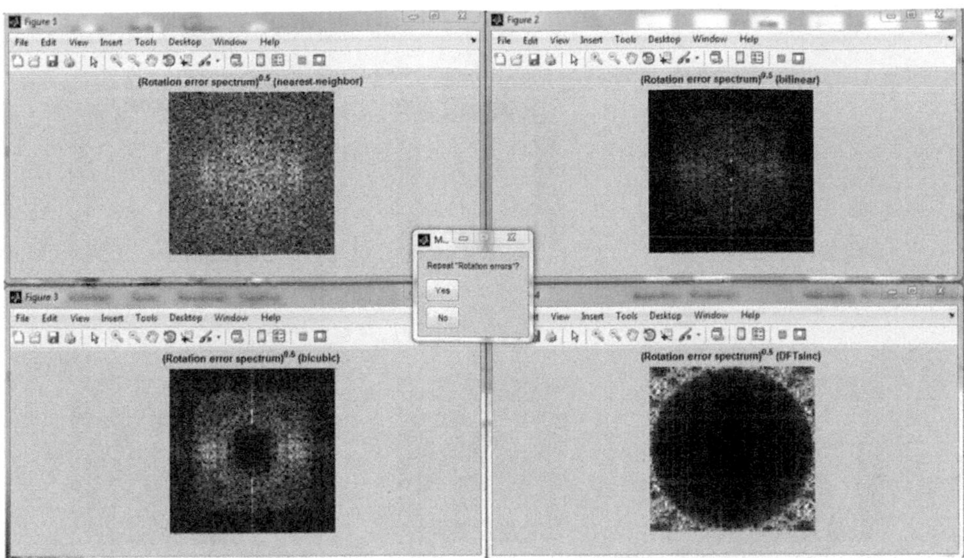

Figure 4.22. Multiple rotations of a test image 'Text': rotation error DFT spectra.

Figure 4.20–4.22 illustrate the exercise. In particular, figure 4.21 convincingly confirms the above described nature of the rotation error for the discrete sinc-interpolation.

If the option of 10×36 grades rotation of a random pattern is chosen, the test pattern is rotated by 360° in 10 steps, and the rotation experiment is repeated several times, set by the user, with different realizations of pseudo-random patterns and with accumulating the rotation error power spectrum for obtaining its sufficiently good statistical estimate. The accumulated error spectra are displayed at each iteration. A final result is illustrated in figure 4.23.

4.6.3 Image multiple zoom-in/zoom-out

Image multiple zoom-in/zoom-out provides a further opportunity for comparison of performance of bilinear, bicubic and discrete sinc interpolators. In this exercise, a test image chosen by the user from the suggested options is repeatedly subjected to zooming-in/zooming-out with a user defined zoom-in/zoom-out factor and the number of cycles (figure 4.24).

At each zoom-in/zoom-out cycle, the resulting images are displayed in real time of processing sequentially for three interpolation methods, bilinear, bicubic and discrete sinc-interpolations After completion of iterations for each of the interpolation methods, a 3 second pause is introduced to allow visual evaluation of the result. Figure 4.25 shows an example a result of 25 cycles of image zoom-in/zoom-out with bilinear interpolation.

At the end, a test image and three results of its iterative zoom-in/zoom-out and their DFT spectra are displayed for visual evaluation (figure 4.26).

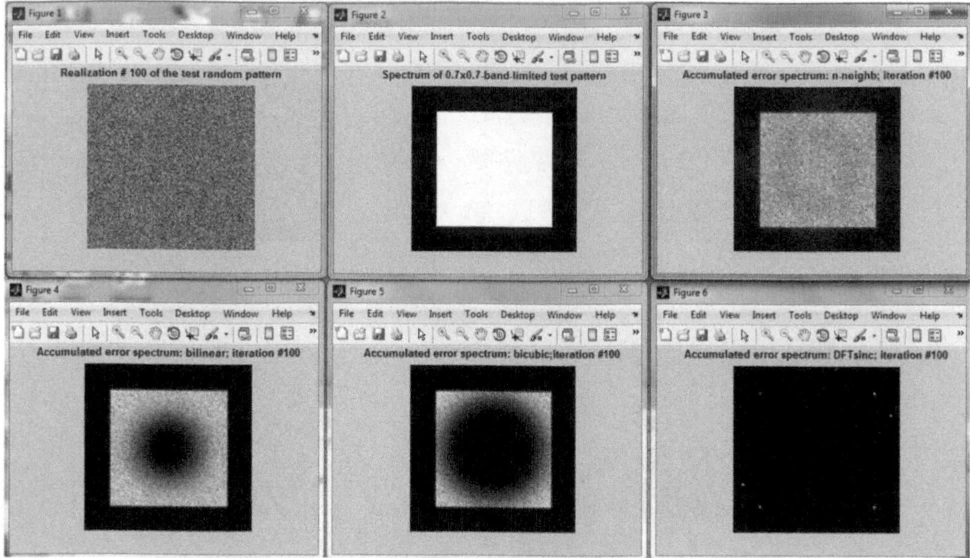

Figure 4.23. Rotation error spectra: pseudo-random test image with uniform DFT spectrum.

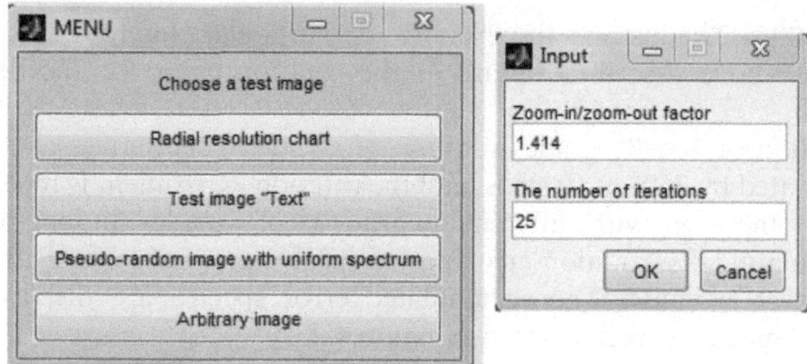

Figure 4.24. Image iterative zoom-in/zoom-out: start menu and panel for setting parameters.

4.7 Comparison of signal numerical differentiation and integration methods

Differentiation and integration are operation defined for analog signal: derivative is a limit of the ratio of signal increment to increment of its argument, and integral is a limit of the sum of signal point values times increment of signal argument, when the latter tends to zero. Numerical differentiation and integration methods are supposed to imitate these operations on the computer by operating with signal samples. Therefore, they, by necessity, assume one or another method of creating, from signal samples, their continuous models. Differentiation and integration methods that are traditional for computational mathematics assume signal expansion into Taylor series in the vicinity of signal samples, whereas sampling theory demands discrete

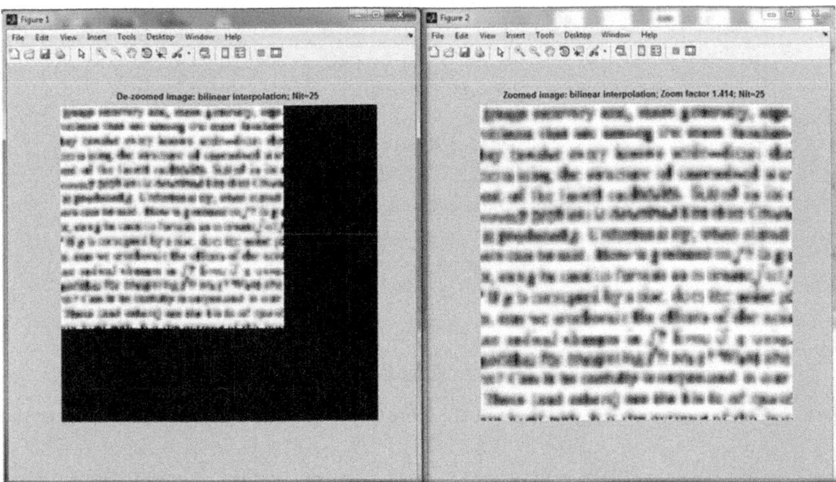

Figure 4.25. Image iterative zoom-in/zoom-out: zoomed and de-zoomed images after 25th cycle (the case of bilinear interpolation).

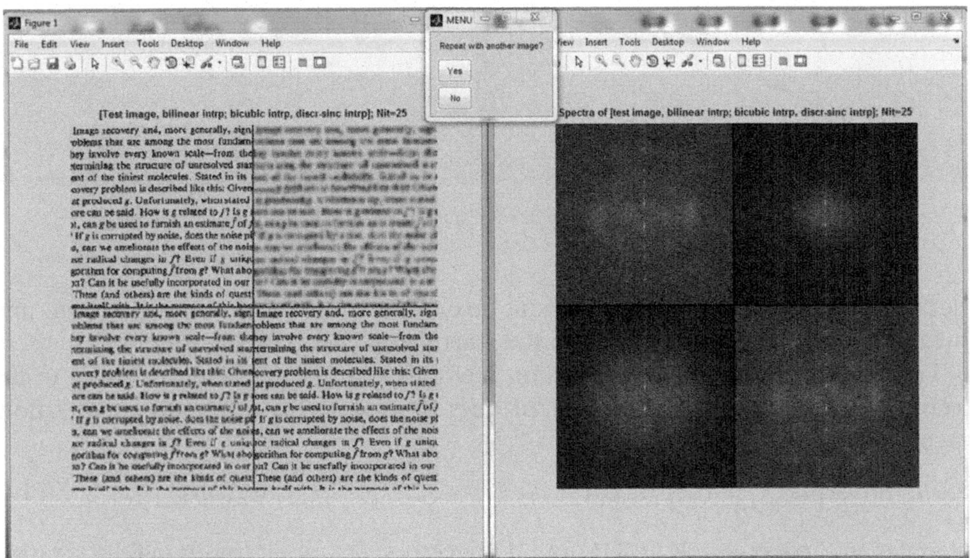

Figure 4.26. Image multiple zoom-in/zoom-out: test image, results of its 25 times repeated zooming and de-zooming using three interpolation methods (bilinear, bicubic and discrete sinc-interpolation) and their corresponding DFT spectra.

sinc-interpolation. The latter is realized in DFT/DCT based differentiation and integration methods.

In the group of exercises presented in this section, one can compare performance of traditional numerical signal differentiation and integration methods and DFT/DCT based methods, which assume, implicitly, signal discrete sinc-interpolation and

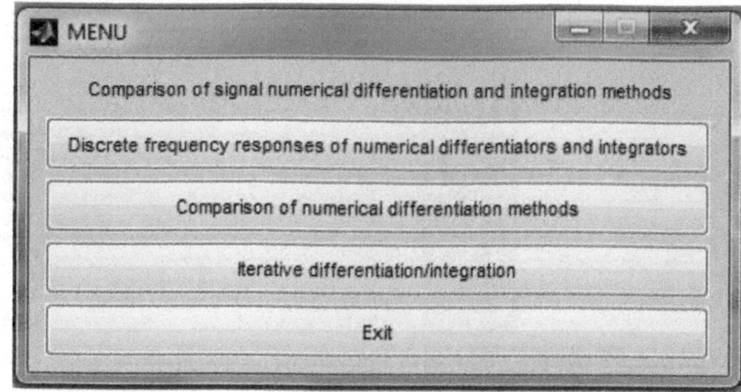

Figure 4.27. Comparison of signal numerical differentiation and integration methods: start menu.

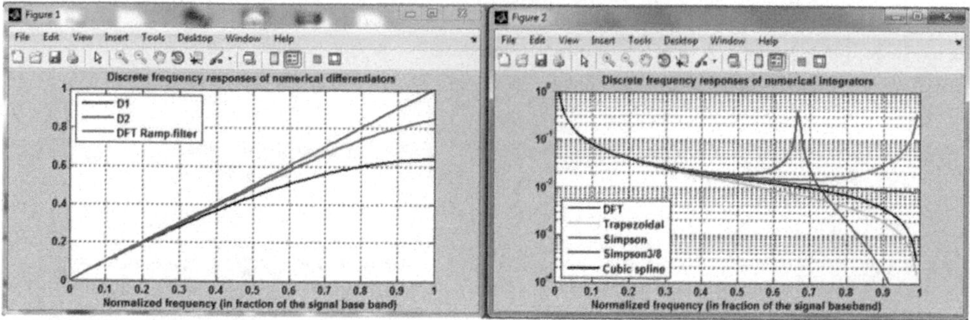

Figure 4.28. Discrete frequency responses of numerical differentiators and integrators.

therefore secure perfect interpolation error free numerical differentiation and integration. Three exercises listed in the start menu (figure 4.27) are offered.

Traditional numerical differentiation methods that are chosen for testing in the exercises are the most commonly used ones that, in terms of digital convolution, have point spread functions:

$$h_n^{\text{diff}(1)} = [-0.5,\ 0,\ 0.5] \quad \text{and} \quad h_n^{\text{diff}(2)} = [-1/12,\ 8/12,\ 0,\ -8/12,\ 1/12]. \tag{4.1}$$

We refer to these methods as ‘D1’ and ‘D2’ methods. Among traditional integration methods, the most commonly used ‘trapezoidal’ integration method is chosen for testing and comparison.

4.7.1 Discrete frequency responses of numerical differentiators and integrators

The first exercise in this section is an introductory one. It demonstrates discrete frequency responses of numerical differentiation (D1, D2 and DFT/DCT based ‘ramp-filter’) and integration (trapezoidal, Simpson, 3/8 Simpson, cubic spline and DFT/DCT-based) methods (figure 4.28) in order to provide a base for further comparison of the methods and interpretation of comparison results.

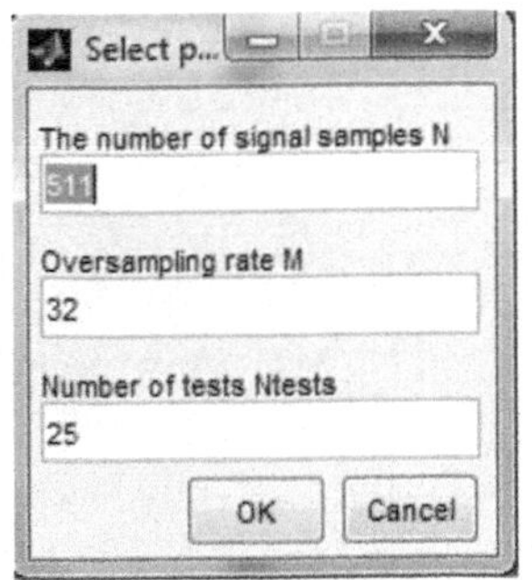

Figure 4.29. Comparison of numerical differentiation methods: menu panels for setting the differentiation model parameters.

4.7.2 Comparison of numerical differentiation methods

In this exercise, the accuracy of signal differentiation using D1, D2 differentiation methods and of the DCT/DFT based differentiation methods are tested by means of computer simulation of differentiation of analog signals.

In order to investigate the dependence of differentiation accuracy on the signal bandwidth, computer generated pseudo-random signals with uniform DFT spectra within different bandwidth in fractions (1/8, ¼, 3/8, ½, 5/8, ¾, 7/8, 1) of the signal baseband are used as test signals in the exercise. Test signals of a user defined length are generated highly oversampled with a purpose of imitating non-sampled (continuous) signals; the oversampling rate is also a user defined parameter (figure 4.29).

Realizations of these oversampled signals are first band limited according to one of eight above-mentioned fractions of the signal baseband, and their 'ideal' derivatives are computed using the *ramp-filter* (the filter with linearly increasing frequency response in DFT domain) that imitates the analogue differentiating. After that, the realizations of the 'ideal' derivative and of initial oversampled signals are down-sampled with the chosen oversampling rate, and obtained down-sampled signals are subjected to differentiation using the above-mentioned traditional methods chosen for testing as well as using, for comparison, DFT and DCT based differentiators. The ideal sampled derivative is used as a benchmark for computing differentiation errors as sample-by-sample differences between it and the results of the differentiators under the comparison. This procedure is repeated several times using different realizations of pseudo-random test signals, and squared differentiation errors are accumulated in order to obtain sufficiently good statistical estimates of standard deviations of sample-by-sample differentiation errors. The number of realizations is a user defined parameter as well (figure 4.29).

This procedure can be performed in two versions: without and with an 'apodization mask' (figure 4.29). The 'apodization mask' is a window function that is applied as a multiplier to realizations of test signals before differentiation. It is equal to one everywhere except a certain number of samples in the vicinity of signal boards, where it gradually decays from one to zero. The purpose of the using of the 'apodization mask' is reducing boundary effect errors of the differentiation algorithms.

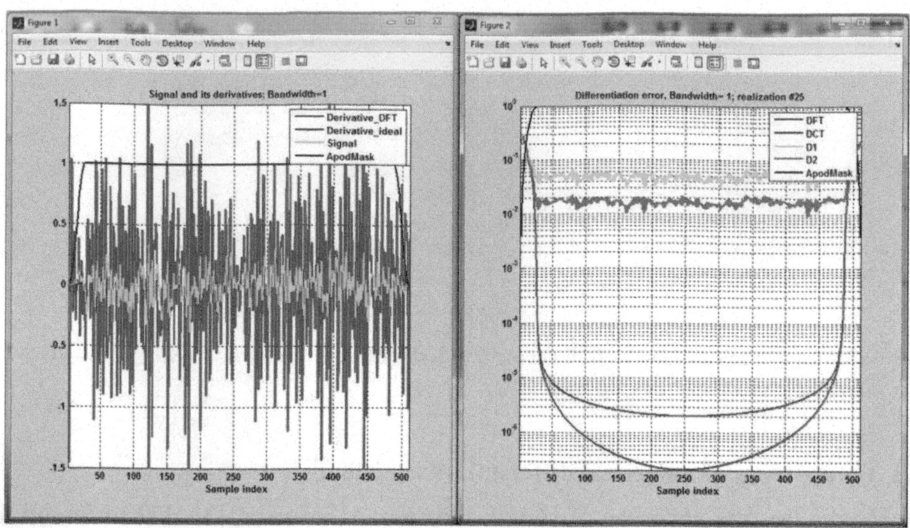

Figure 4.30. Comparison of numerical differentiation methods: plots of a realization of test signal, its derivatives and differentiation errors accumulated over 25 realizations.

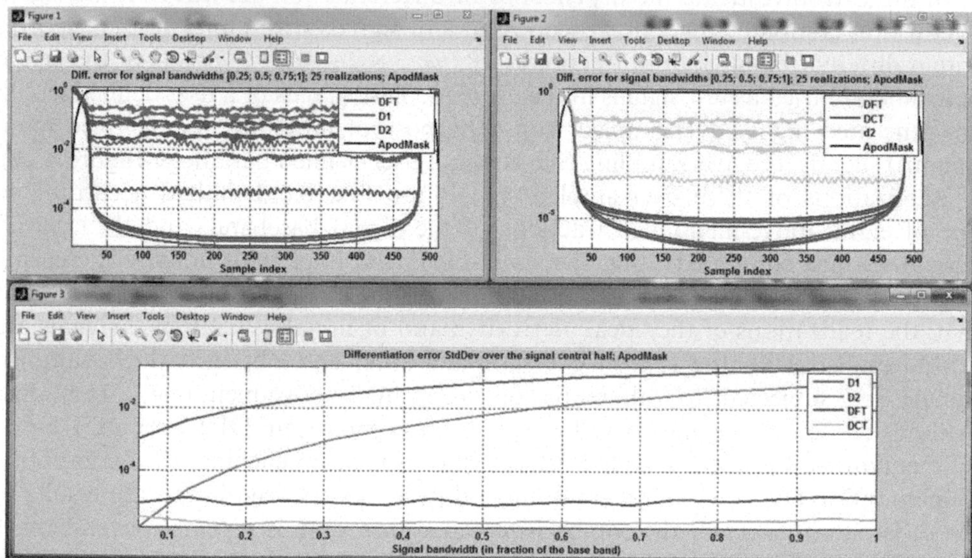

Figure 4.31. Comparison of numerical differentiation methods: the final display.

For each realization of test signals, the program displays, in one figure, plots of realizations of test signals, their ideal and obtained by DFT-method derivatives, and, in another figure, plots of estimates of standard deviations of sample-by-sample differentiation errors for all tested methods, the estimates being accumulated over the iteration steps (figure 4.30).

After completion of evaluating differentiation errors for all realizations of signals of all bandwidths, the program displays final estimates of standard deviations of

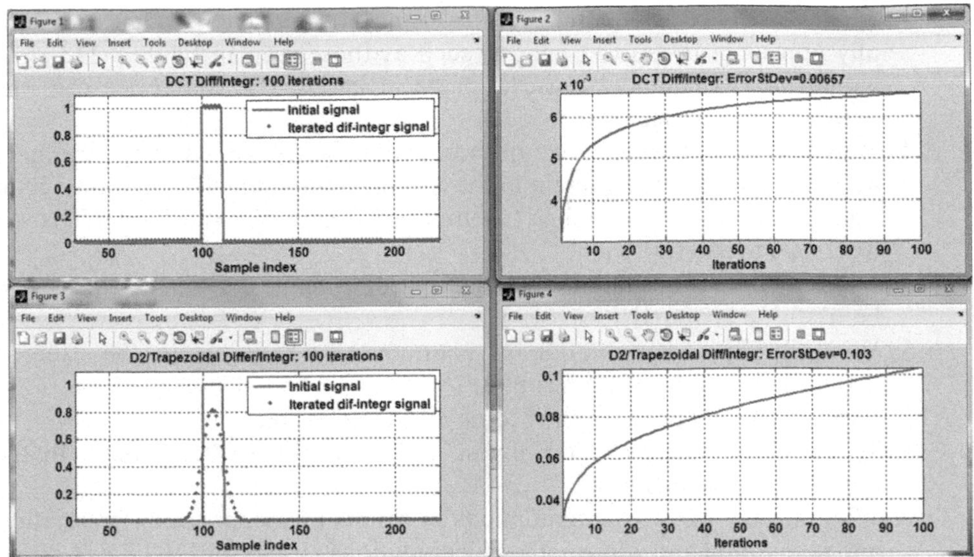

Figure 4.32. Iterative differentiation/integration: final display.

sample-wise errors, as is shown in figure 4.31 in two upper panels as well as plots of standard deviations of differentiation errors averaged over all signal samples with an exclusion of 1/8 of them at left and right signal borders (for excluding boundary effect errors) versus test signal bandwidths (figure 4.31, bottom panel).

4.7.3 Iterative differentiation/integration

The last exercise in this section performs simultaneous testing of both differentiation and integration methods through repetitive successive differentiation and integration of a test signal in the form of a rectangular impulse. Ideally, signals should not be changed by such processing. The exercise is intended to show that this is the case only when signal derivatives and integrals are computed by DFT/DCT based algorithms, whereas conventional numerical differentiation and integration algorithms after multiple repeated applications result in considerable signal blur. Implemented for comparison are D2 differentiation and trapezoidal integration methods and the DCT based differentiation and integration methods. The number of differentiation/integration cycles is a user defined parameter. All steps are visualized by plots of initial and processed test signals and of signal reproduction root mean square error as a function of the number of iterations (figure 4.32).

Questions for self-testing

1. Why is image interpolation needed for extracting image signal arbitrary profiles?
2. In what application might it be useful and computationally efficient to generate subsampled (zoomed-in) images to use as 'continuous' models of non-sampled images?

3. Have you noticed oscillations in the vicinity of image edges that occasionally appear in resampled images, such as those seen in figure 4.11? How would you explain the cause of these artifacts? At what price can one prevent these artifacts?
4. Why are no oscillations seen on borders of the magnified image in figure 4.11, whereas they are present in the left image in figure 4.7, even though in both cases image subsampling (zooming-in) is carried out using DFT based discrete sinc-interpolation?
5. In what applications might Cartesian-to-polar image coordinate conversion be useful or required?
6. What is your interpretation of rotation error spectra in the exercise 'Multiple rotations of a test image'?
7. Explain aliasing artifacts in spectra of rotated images.
8. What is your interpretation of test image spectra in the exercise 'Image iterative zoom-in/zoom-out'?
9. What are the expected degradations of results of numerical differentiation and integration and why are these degradations absent for DFT/DCT based algorithms?
10. Why does DFT-based differentiation result in large differentiation errors in the vicinity of signal borders when no apodization mask is used, and in what respect does application of apodization mask improve performance of DFT-based differentiation?
11. Why does the DCT-based differentiator perform better than the DFT-based one, even when apodization mask is used for the latter?
12. What conclusions regarding practical limitations of applicability of different numerical differentiators and integrators can be made from results of their comparison?
13. What do frequency responses of numerical integrators tell regarding artifacts one can expect in applying for signal integration Simpson and 3/8 Simpson integration methods?
14. Is it possible to further improve the image interpolation accuracy beyond that achieved by the discrete sinc-interpolation?

Leonid P Yaroslavsky

Chapter 5

Image and noise statistical characterization and diagnostics

5.1 Introduction

The set of exercises 'Image and noise statistical characterization and diagnostics' is aimed at assisting studying concepts and methods of statistical characterization of images and noises, which are usually present in image signals and distort them. Statistical characterization means measuring and using parameters and characteristics that do not specify concrete pixels or images, but rather refer to properties common to groups of pixels or images, which enables solving processing optimization problems for those groups. A large variety of statistical parameters and characteristics exists. Selected in this chapter are the most frequently used ones listed in the main menu presented in figure 5.1.

5.2 Image histograms

Histograms are one of the primary statistical characteristics of images. For achromatic images, *histograms of pixel gray levels* are used, which show how frequently different gray levels occur in a particular image. For color images, corresponding characteristics are histograms of image R, G and B components and *color triangle histograms*. The latter show how frequently the vector of RGB components of image pixels intersects different places within the color triangle that spans unit vectors of the 3D RGB coordinate system. In this section, exercises are provided for studying histograms of both achromatic and color images (figure 5.2).

5.2.1 Histograms of achromatic images

In this section, histograms of pixel gray levels are studied. One should distinguish global histograms measured over the entire image frame and *local histograms* that are measured over a certain, most commonly, spatial neighborhood of each pixel. Later in section 5.4 some other types of neighborhoods will be discussed and

doi:10.1088/978-0-7503-1233-2ch5

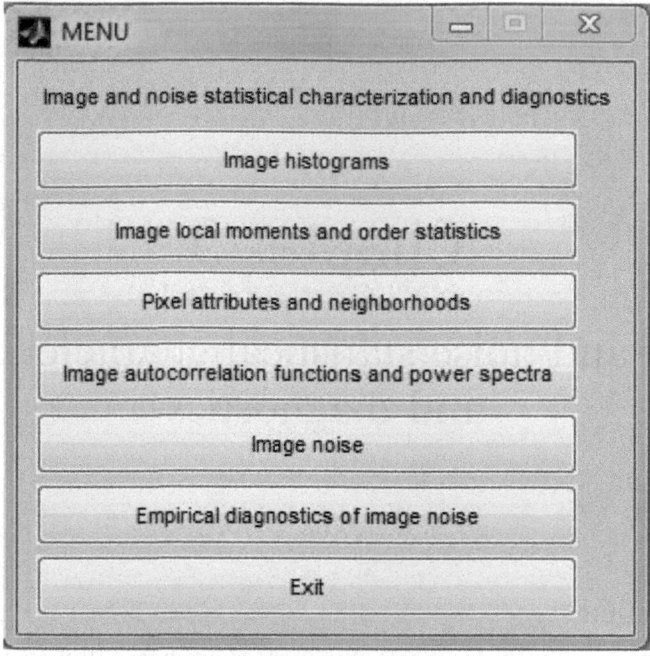

Figure 5.1. Image and noise statistical characterization and diagnostics: main menu.

Figure 5.2. Image histograms: start menu.

experimented with. Exercises in chapter 8 ('Methods of image perfecting') and chapter 9 ('Methods of image enhancement'), demonstrate that local image histograms computed for other types of pixel neighborhoods are also important for implementing image non-linear filters.

The exercise enables comparing global (frame-wise) histograms for different images as well as evaluating the variability of image local histograms within images. For conducting the exercise, three options are offered for selecting a test image: two pre-prepared images, a face image and a texture image, and any other image from the user's image data set.

Once a test image is chosen, the image and its global histogram are displayed and the user is prompted to set horizontal and vertical dimensions of a rectangular

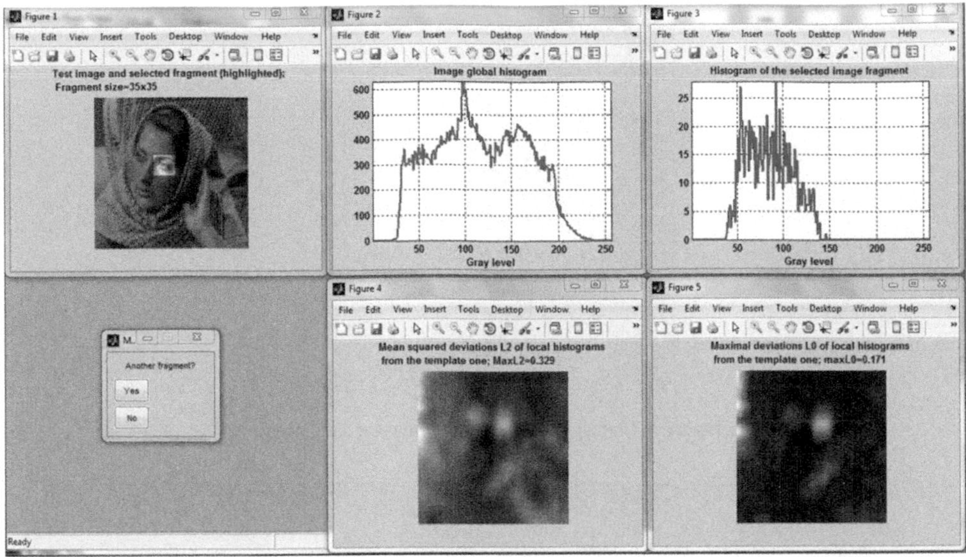

Figure 5.3. Histograms of achromatic images: image global and local histograms and 'maps' of deviations of image local histograms over 35 × 35 pixel windows from the local histogram of the highlighted fragment.

window for measuring the local histogram of the image fragment within the chosen window and, using the cursor, a position of the window center. The variability of local histograms is demonstrated by means of visualizing mean square deviations and maximal deviations of image local histograms from the local histogram of the chosen image fragment. These pixel-wise deviations are displayed as images homomorphic with the chosen test image; their numerical measures, maximal mean square and maximum of maximal deviations over the entire image, are given in the titles of the figures. One can use this numerical measure for evaluation of variability of local histograms in different test images. Plotted are also image global histogram and histogram of the selected reference image fragment. Figure 5.3 illustrates outcomes of this exercise.

5.2.2 Histograms of color images

Two types of color image histograms are studied in this section: RGB histograms and color triangle histograms (figure 5.4).

RGB histograms are individual histograms of R, G and B components of color images. Upon choosing a test color image, this image is displayed and histograms of its R, G and B components are plotted (figure 5.5).

Color triangle histograms are 2D functions. Their arguments are coordinates X, Y of points within a color triangle that spans unit vectors of the 3D RGB coordinate system. A color triangle histogram is computed from gray levels R, G and B of color image components by pixel-wise summation of the number of occurrences that the color vector with components (R, G and B) intersects the color triangle at the point with coordinates X and Y. Color triangle histograms do not depend on lengths of color vectors with R, G and B components of image pixels, i.e. on intensities of their

Figure 5.4. Histograms of color images: start menu.

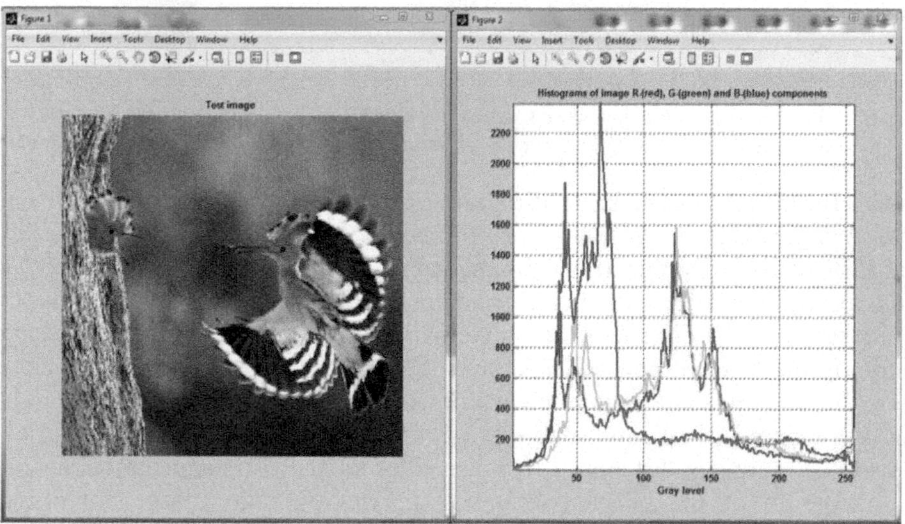

Figure 5.5. Histograms of color images: RGB-histograms.

R, G and B components. They rather depend solely on spatial angles of the color vectors in the 3D RGB coordinate system. Color triangle histograms of a pure red image, pure green or pure blue images are delta-functions at the R, G or B corners of the color triangle, correspondingly. The color triangle histogram of an achromatic image is a delta-function at the center of the color triangle.

Upon choosing a test image, it is displayed in one panel and its color triangle histogram is computed and displayed next to it in another panel side by side, for reference, with a color triangle (figure 5.6).

5.3 Image local moments and order statistics

Local histograms of achromatic images are arrays of 256 numbers computed, i.e. they are vectorial statistical parameters. More compact statistical descriptors are

Figure 5.6. Image histograms: test image, color triangle and image color triangle histogram.

scalar histogram parameters, its moments, such as mean value and standard deviation. Yet another alternative to histograms are the so-called *order statistics*, pixel array gray levels sorted in an ascending order into a sequence called a *variational row*.

The variational row spans from minimal gray level in the array, and this is the first term of the variational row, to the gray level maximum, the last term of the row. The length of the variational row is equal to the number of pixels in the array. The term in the middle of the variational row is the so-called *median*: it is a gray level, for which the numbers of pixels of lower and of higher gray values are equal. The median is known as an estimate of mean value over the array that is robust to outliers.

The exercise 'Image local moments and order statistics' is intended for visualizing these parameters for different test images. Upon choosing a test image, it is displayed and the user is prompted to set vertical and horizontal dimensions of a rectangular window for computing local means, local medians, local standard deviations, local maxima, local minima and local maxima minus minima (*local range*) in a running window, which are then computed and displayed in separate panels as grey scale images homomorphic to the test image, as is exemplified in figure 5.7.

5.4 Pixel attributes and neighborhoods

All pixels in images can be characterized by certain attributes that can be used in the design of image processing filters. The obvious primary pixel attributes are pixel coordinates in image arrays and pixel gray levels. There are also many other attributes, less obvious but nevertheless proved to be useful. The exercise 'Pixel attributes and neighborhoods' is intended for studying pixel attributes associated

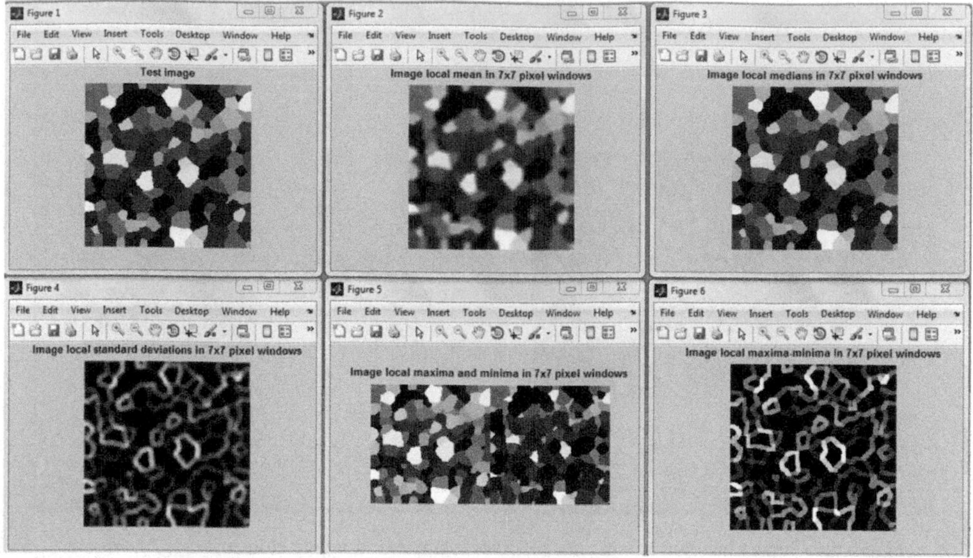

Figure 5.7. Image local moments and order statistics: local means, medians, standard deviations, maxima, minima and local ranges.

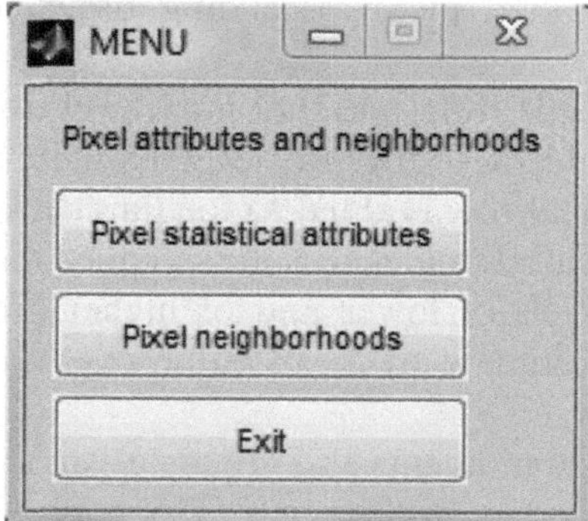

Figure 5.8. Pixel attributes and neighborhoods: start menu.

with image histograms and for studying pixel neighborhoods as groups of pixels unified in terms of their certain attributes (figure 5.8).

5.4.1 Pixel statistical attributes

Pixel statistical attributes associated with image histograms are *pixel cardinality* and *pixel rank*. Pixel cardinality is the number of pixels in the pixel array that have the same gray level as the given pixel. Pixel rank is an index of the pixel in the variational row, i.e. the number of pixels in the array that have lower gray levels than the gray level of this pixel. Pixel cardinalities and ranks can be computed globally over the entire image frame or locally in a moving window.

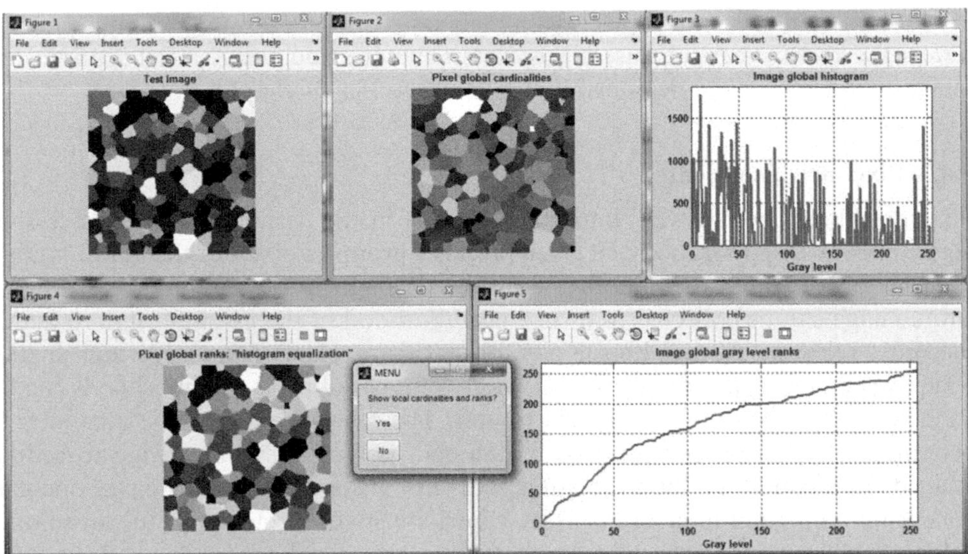

Figure 5.9. Pixel statistical attributes: pixel global cardinalities and ranks.

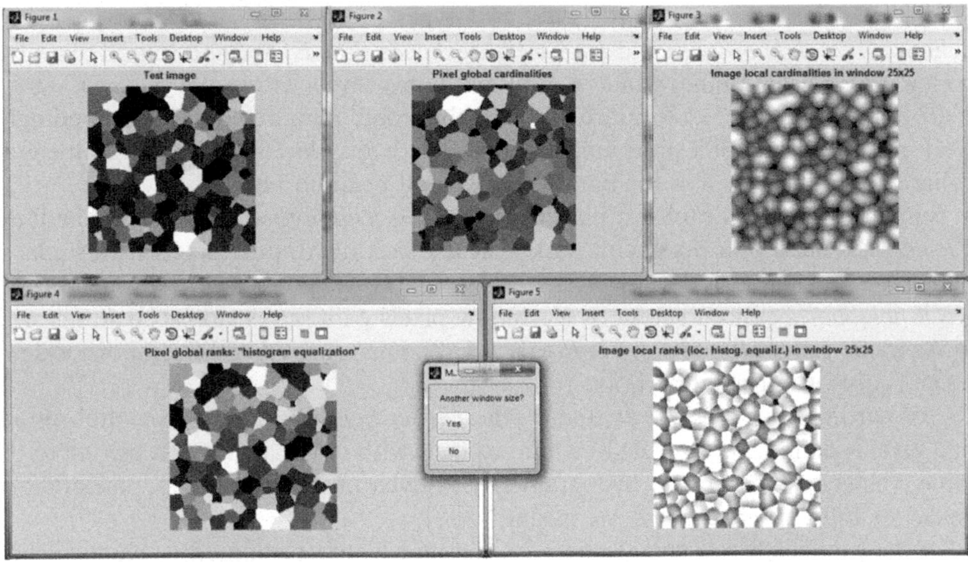

Figure 5.10. Pixel statistical attributes: pixels global and local cardinalities.

As test images, two prepared images or any other image in the image data set can be used. After choosing and loading a test image, this image is displayed and its global histogram, cardinalities and ranks are computed and displayed, the latter in a form of images homomorphic to the test image. After that, the user is prompted to choose an option of computing and displaying local pixel attributes in a running window and to set, for this purpose, vertical and horizontal dimensions of the window. Figures 5.9 and 5.10 present examples of outcomes of the exercise.

Note that replacement of pixels with their rank is a processing method known as *histogram equalization*. The use of histogram equalization and its modifications for image enhancement are demonstrated in the exercises of chapter 9.

5.4.2 Pixel neighborhoods

Pixel neighborhood is a very important concept in the design of image processing algorithms. A neighborhood of a given pixel is a group of pixels of the image unified in terms of a certain attribute of the pixel. Although in principle pixels from the entire image can be collected to form a neighborhood of the given pixel, in practice the most relevant are neighborhoods formed from pixels from a certain spatial window centered at the given pixel. A variety of types of pixel neighborhoods can be defined in terms of different pixel attributes. The relevance of specific attributes is determined by the processing task, by the end user *a priori* knowledge regarding imaged objects and by the processing goal. For instance, in many cases one can believe that a certain number of pixels, which are spatially closest to the given one, belong to the same object and, as such, form a pixel neighborhood called the pixel *spatial neighborhood*. More sophisticated are neighborhoods built on the base of other pixel attributes such as pixel gray levels, rank and cardinalities.

For gray levels as pixel attributes, two types of so-called *V-neighborhoods* are defined: *EV-neighborhoods* and *KNV-neighborhoods*. The *EV*-neighborhood of a pixel with a gray level V unifies window pixels with gray levels within the range $[V - \varepsilon V_-, V + \varepsilon V_+]$, where $\{\varepsilon V_-, \varepsilon V_+\}$ are the neighborhood parameters. Correspondingly, *KNV*-neighborhood of a pixel unifies K pixels with gray levels most close to the gray value V of that pixel. K is the parameter of *KNV*-neighborhood.

Similarly, for pixel ranks as pixel attributes, *R-neighborhoods* can be defined: the *ER-neighborhood* of a pixel with rank R as a subset of window pixels with ranks in the range $[R - \varepsilon R_-, R + \varepsilon R_+]$ with $(\varepsilon R_-, \varepsilon R_+\}$ as neighborhood parameters and *KNR-neighborhood* as a subset of K window pixels with ranks closest to R, i.e. with ranks in the range $[R - (K - 1)/2, R + (K - 1)/2]$. Obviously, *KNR*-neighborhood is a special case of *ER*-neighborhood.

For cardinalities as pixel attributes, the *cluster neighborhood* (Cl-neighborhood) of a pixel is defined as a subset of window pixels with cardinalities that belong to the same cluster of the window histogram as the given pixel. By clusters, consolidated peaks, or hills, of histograms are meant.

In the exercise 'Pixel neighborhoods', the user is first prompted to choose either one of two prepared test images or an arbitrary image from the image data set and then to set the horizontal and vertical dimensions of an image fragment, which will be used for collecting and visualizing neighborhoods of the fragment central pixel. Then the user has to specify, using a cursor, a center of an image fragment to work with. The chosen fragment and its gray level histogram are displayed and a list of types of neighborhoods pops up (figure 5.11).

Upon specifying the neighborhood type, the chosen neighborhood of the fragment central pixel is displayed in the bottom right panel with pixels not belonging to the neighborhood shown in black. In addition, borders of the neighborhood

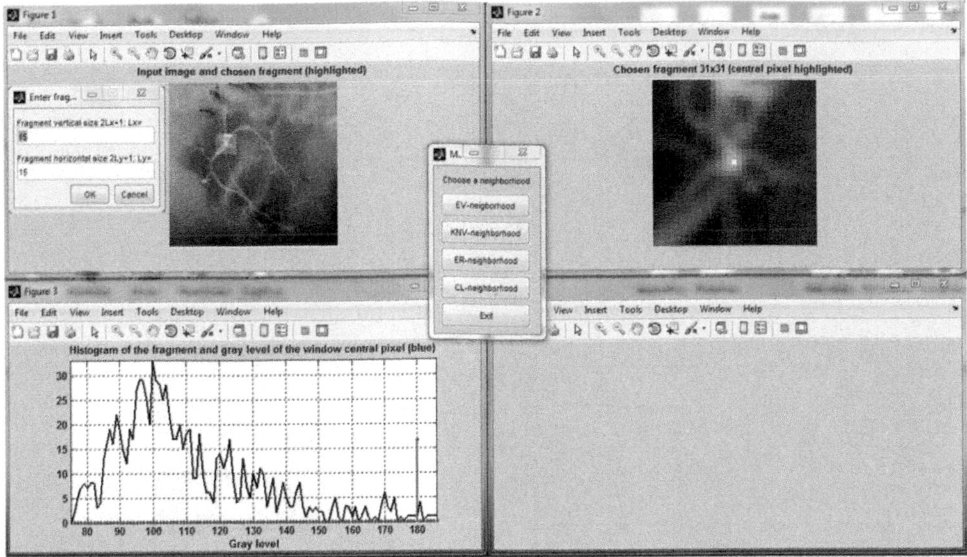

Figure 5.11. Pixel neighborhoods: test image, menu for setting window dimensions, chosen fragment and menu of neighborhoods.

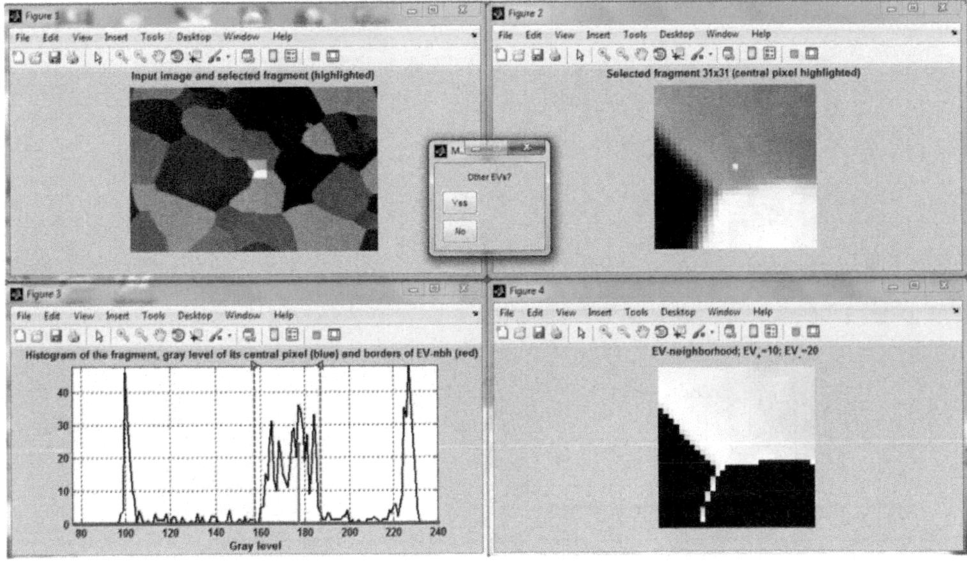

Figure 5.12. Pixel neighborhoods: EV-neighborhood.

are indicated on plots of the fragment histogram (for V- and Cl-neighborhoods) or of the fragment variational row (for R-neighborhoods), as illustrated in figures 5.12–5.15.

In the case of the Cl-neighborhood, the user is also prompted to set, using a cursor on the plot of the fragment histogram, left and right borders of the histogram cluster, to which fragment the central pixel is believed to belong.

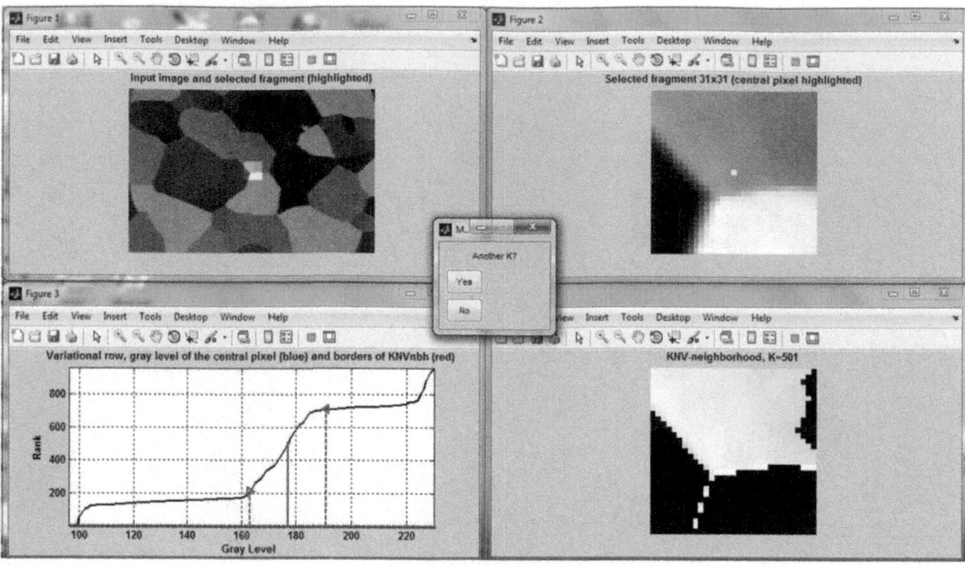

Figure 5.13. Pixel neighborhoods: *KNV*-neighborhood.

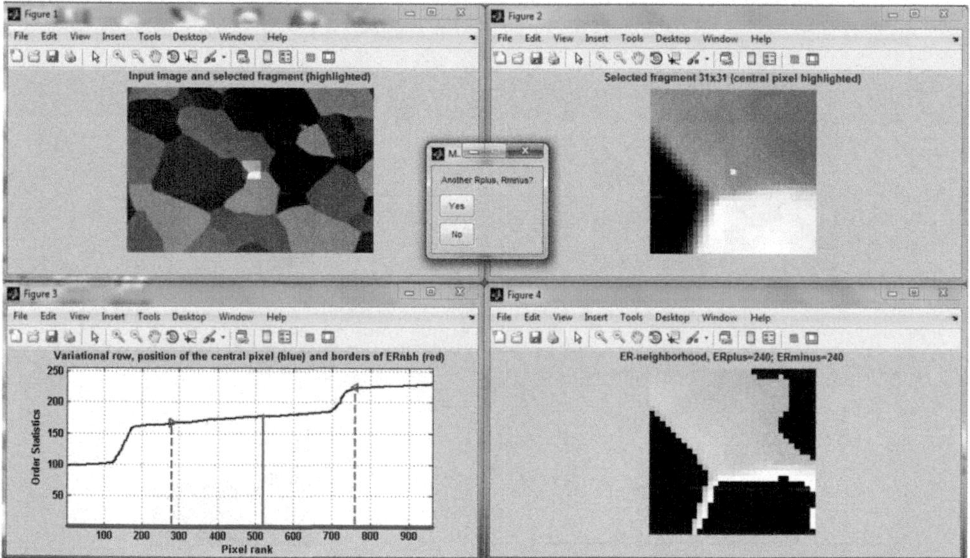

Figure 5.14. Pixel neighborhoods: *ER*-neighborhood.

5.5 Image autocorrelation functions and power spectra

Image autocorrelation functions and power spectra are complementing each other as image statistical characteristics that carry information on the spatial interdependence of pixel gray levels. The most common feature of images is that image autocorrelation functions decay relatively slowly with the distance over which pixel

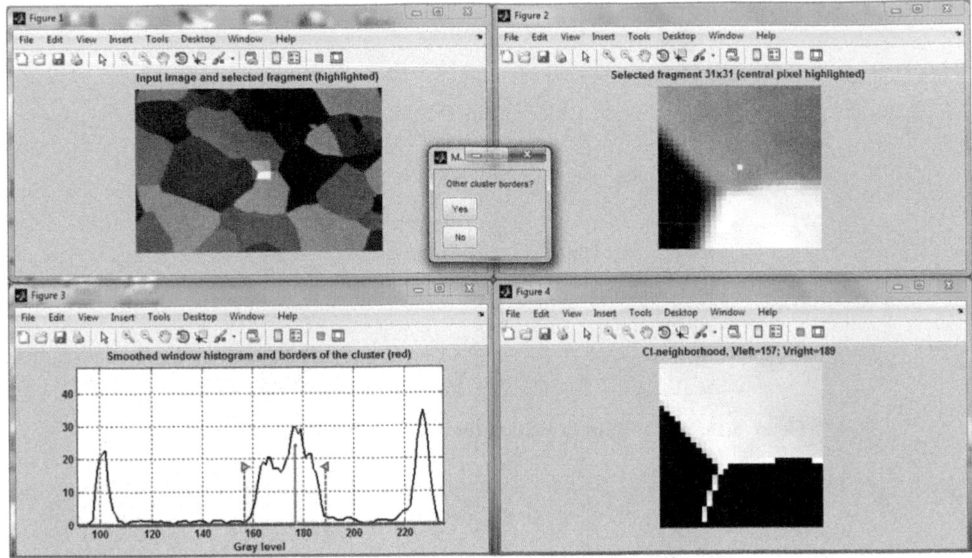

Figure 5.15. Pixel neighborhoods: Cl-neighborhood.

correlations are measured, and image power spectra in some bases, such as those of DFT, DCT and Walsh Transforms, decay considerably rapidly with spectral coefficient indices. The latter is a manifestation of the transform energy compaction capabilities studied in the exercises of chapter 2. The speed of the decay and the shapes of autocorrelation functions and power spectra are in a certain way associated with kind of 'average' size and shape of objects in images. The set of exercises 'Image autocorrelation functions and power spectra' (figure 5.16) are intended for studying these features and associations.

5.5.1 Image autocorrelation functions

In the exercise 'Image autocorrelation functions', the user can choose as test images either three prepared images (an artificial computer generated piece-wise constant image, a microscopic image of blood cells and an air photograph) or one of the images from the image database. Once a test image is chosen, the program displays, in the form of images, 2D arrays of image autocorrelation functions and, as an option, the same uniformly quantized arrays in ten levels that represent ten levels of autocorrelation function magnitude (figure 5.17).

In the latter case quantized autocorrelation functions are displayed to better visualize autocorrelation function level lines, color coded using a MATLAB® color map 'jet'.

5.5.2 Image power spectra

In this exercise, DCT image global and local spectra of test images are measured and visualized. As test images, three images ('geometrical figures', 'angular step wedge' and 'camera man') are offered. Any other test image from the image data set can be

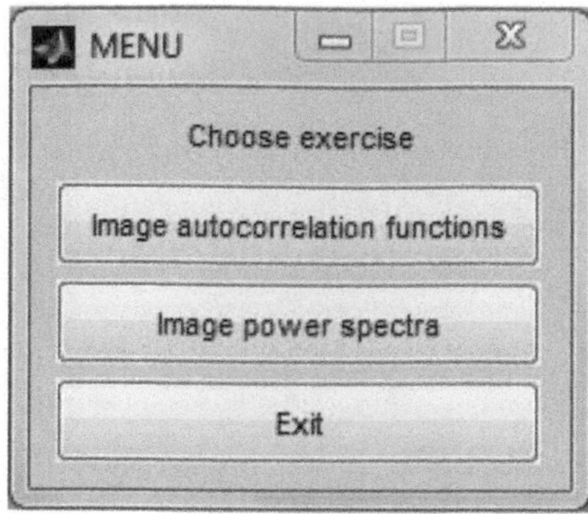

Figure 5.16. Image autocorrelation functions and spectra: start menu.

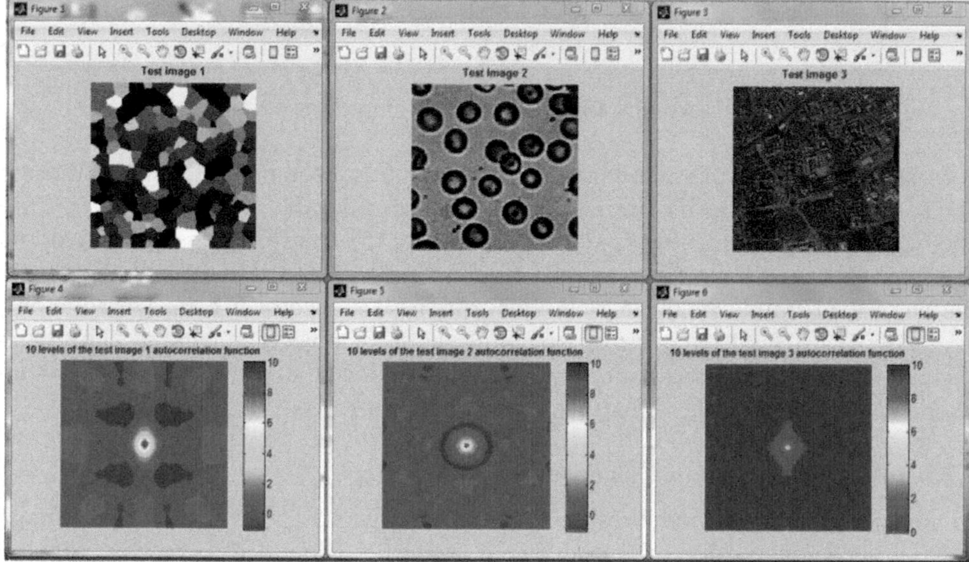

Figure 5.17. Image autocorrelation functions: test images and their correlation functions (shown color coded with color coding bar aside).

used as well. Magnitudes of global spectra are visualized raised to power 0.3 and color coded using a color map 'jet' in order to make visible low-intensity high-frequency image spectral components (figure 5.18). Local spectra are shown for image blocks (figure 5.19). Block vertical and horizontal dimensions are to be set by the user.

5.6 Image noise

Image noise is a very important factor that may substantially hamper image usage. One of the primary image processing tasks is image cleaning from noise. In order

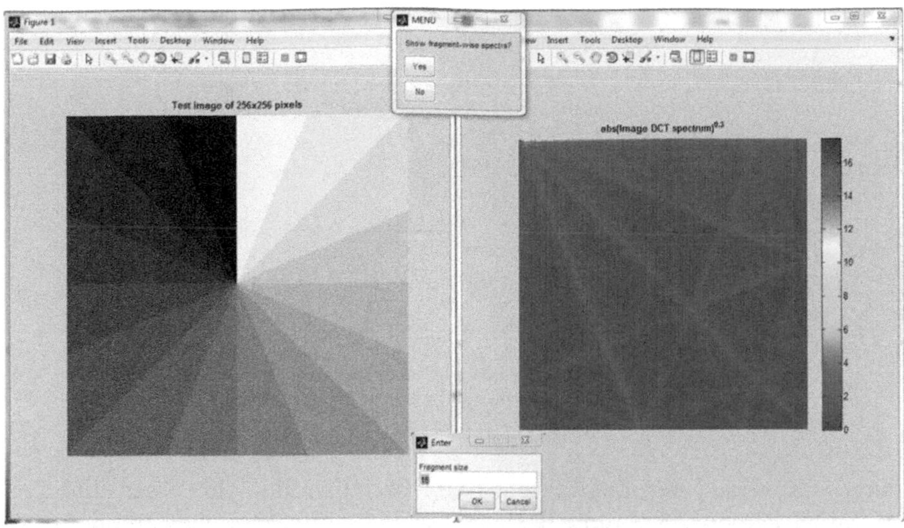

Figure 5.18. Image power spectra: test image (left panel), its global DCT spectrum shown as a color coded image with color coding bar to the side (right panel) and pop-up menus.

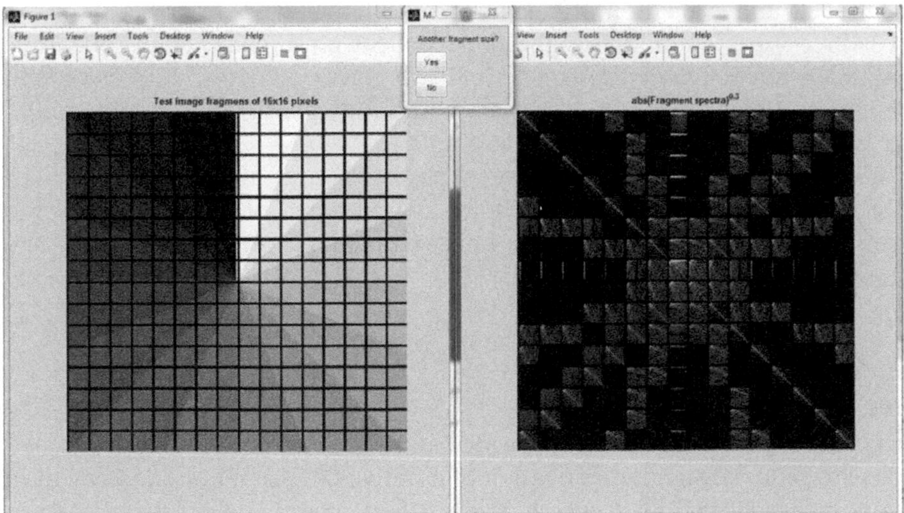

Figure 5.19. Image power spectra: DCT spectra (right panel) of corresponding fragments of the test image (left panel).

to enable the image denoising, one should know numerical parameters that can sufficiently well characterize the noise component of the image signal and its influence on image 'readability'. Though contamination of image signals by noise may be caused by different factors, such as quantum fluctuations of radiation used for imaging, thermal fluctuations of electrical current in image sensors, failures in communication systems used for transmitting image signals, mechanical instabilities

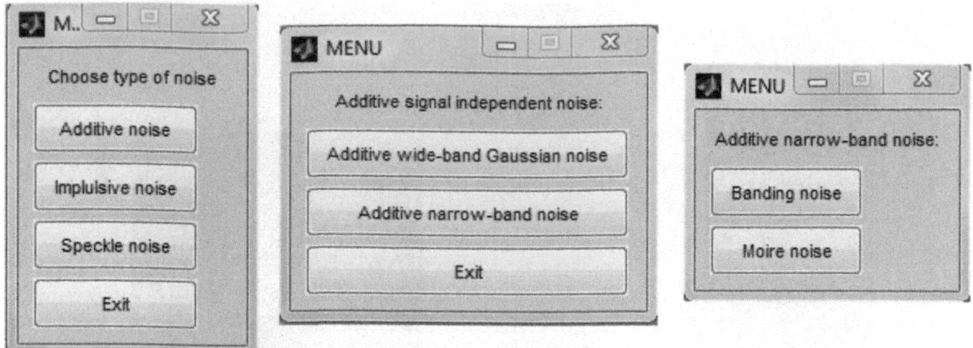

Figure 5.20. Image noises: menus of types of noises.

in image scanners, variations of sensitivity of individual photo sensitive cells in photographic cameras, etc, three basic mathematical noise models are in most cases sufficient for developing noise cleaning methods: *additive signal independent noise*, *impulsive signal independent noise* and *signal dependent noise*.

The set of exercises 'Image noise' is intended for demonstration of these typical noise models and evaluation of 'visibility' of different types of noise. Implemented are (i) three types of additive signal independent noise: wide band (uncorrelated) signal independent *normal white noise* and two types of narrow band noise, *banding noise* and *moiré noise*, (ii) impulsive noise and (iii) *speckle noise* (figure 5.20). The latter is an example of signal dependent noise.

For exercises of this group, three prepared test images are offered, 'Circular step wedge', 'Aerial photo' and 'Space photo' as well as an option of using any other image from the image data set. A test image has to be chosen once the type of noise is chosen.

5.6.1 Additive noise

Additive wide band Gaussian noise

Upon choosing the option 'Additive wide band Gaussian noise' and a test image, the user has to set noise standard deviation of additive Gaussian noise in units of image dynamic range 0–255, after which original and noised images are displayed for visual evaluation in two panels side by side, as shown in figure 5.21. The experiment can be repeated with another level of noise.

Additive narrow band noise: banding noise and moiré noise

As was mentioned, experiments with visibility of two types of additive narrow band noise are offered: banding noise and moiré noise. The banding noise is implemented in its simplest form: image rows are distorted by adding to all pixels of each row a zero mean random value uniformly distributed in the banding noise range specified by the user (in gray levels).

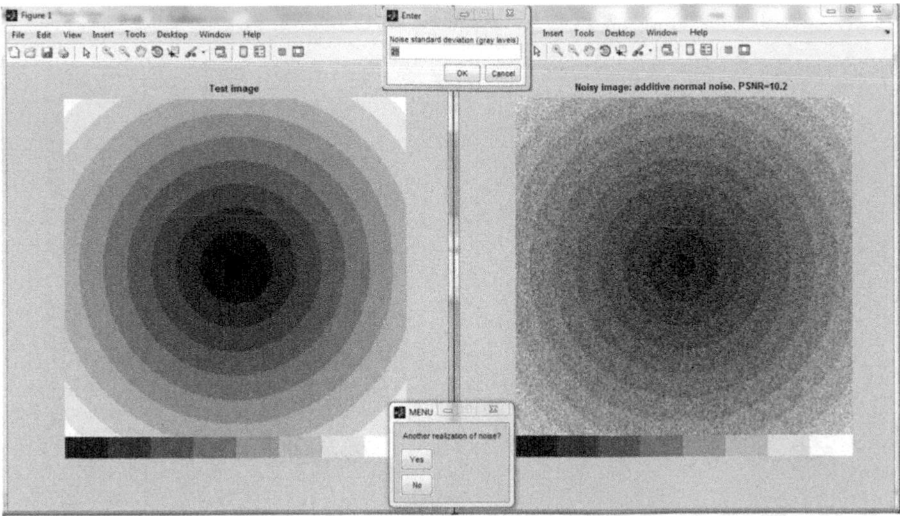

Figure 5.21. Additive wide band Gaussian noise: test image (left panel) and this image with added wide band normal noise (right panel).

Moiré noise is a type of additive noise with relatively small numbers of isolated spectral components. In the exercise, it is simulated by means of generating, in random positions in the DCT domain, a number specified by the user of moiré noise spectral components with random intensities and maximal intensity also specified by the user.

The program visualizes the chosen test image alongside this image with added realization of noise of the chosen type, banding or moiré one, and offers an option of choosing another realization of noise, as is illustrated in, correspondingly, figures 5.22 and 5.23.

5.6.2 Impulsive noise

Impulsive noise causes the replacement of gray levels of individual pixels, randomly selected with some probability called the probability of error, by a random value taken from the image dynamic range 0–255. In the exercise 'Impulsive noise', upon choosing a test image and specifying the probability of error, the program displays the image distorted by the impulsive noise with the chosen probability; this can be repeated with different realizations of noise on the same test image. An example of the display is shown in figure 5.24.

5.6.3 Speckle noise

Speckle noise is an image distortion characteristic for imaging using coherent radiation, such as holographic, synthetic aperture radar and ultrasound imaging. In distinction from noise in conventional incoherent imaging systems, such as photography, speckle noise originates not from random quantum fluctuations of radiation or from thermal fluctuations of sensor array current, but rather from such

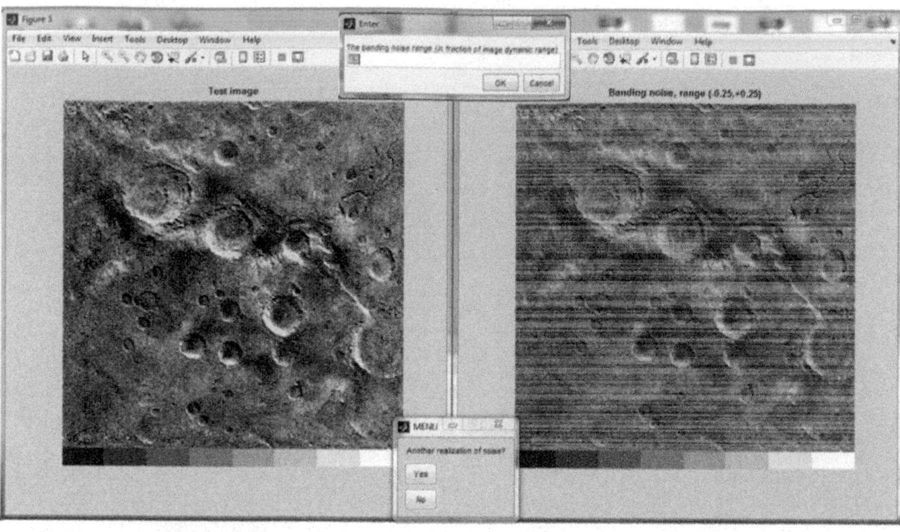

Figure 5.22. Additive narrow band banding noise: test image (left panel) and this image distorted by banding noise (right panel). Courtesy of NASA.

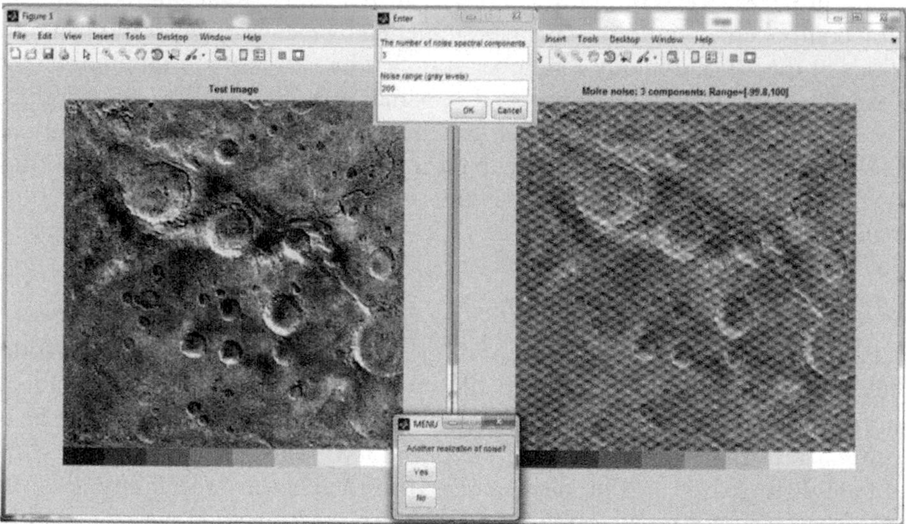

Figure 5.23. Additive narrow band moiré noise: test image (left panel) and this image distorted by banding noise (right panel). Courtesy of NASA.

signal distortions in radiation recording devices as limitation of their resolving power, limitation of the recoded signal dynamic range or signal quantization. Chaotic character of speckle noise is associated with chaotic character of object reflectance or transmittance phase component due to roughness of their surface or with other factors that affect phase variations of coherent radiation reflected or transmitted by objects.

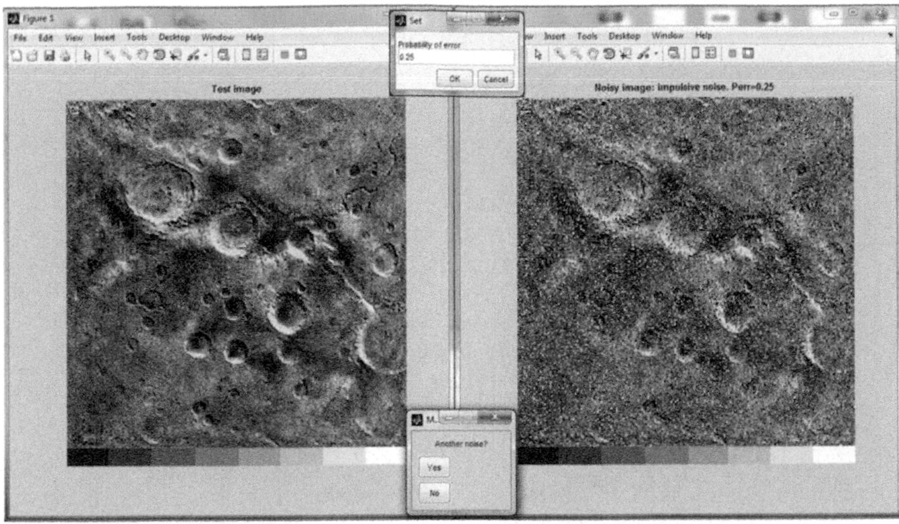

Figure 5.24. Image noise: a test image (left panel) and this image distorted by impulsive noise (right panel). Courtesy of NASA.

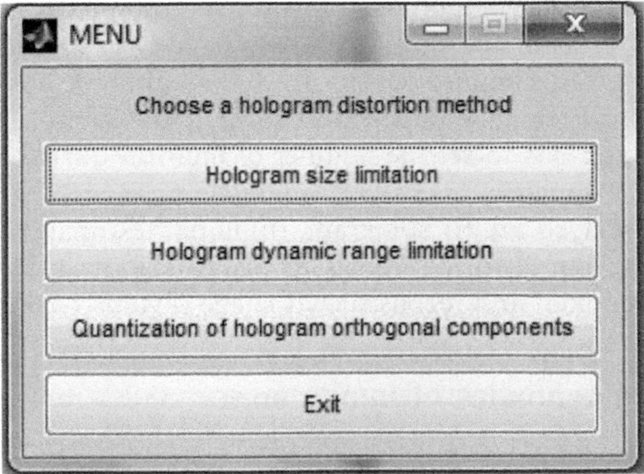

Figure 5.25. Image noise: speckle noise, start menu.

The program that imitates speckle noise simulates recording Fourier holograms with signal recording distortions listed in the start menu that pops up after the test image is chosen (figure 5.25).

As a test image, a circular step wedge image is offered; the user also has an option of choosing another test image from the image data set. Test images specify imaged object intensity. The image intensity component is supplemented, by the simulation program, with a pseudo-random uncorrelated phase component uniformly distributed between $(-\pi, \pi)$ that imitates the object surface roughness.

For limitation of the hologram size, the user has to specify a fraction (between 0 and 1) of the whole hologram area retained for image reconstruction.

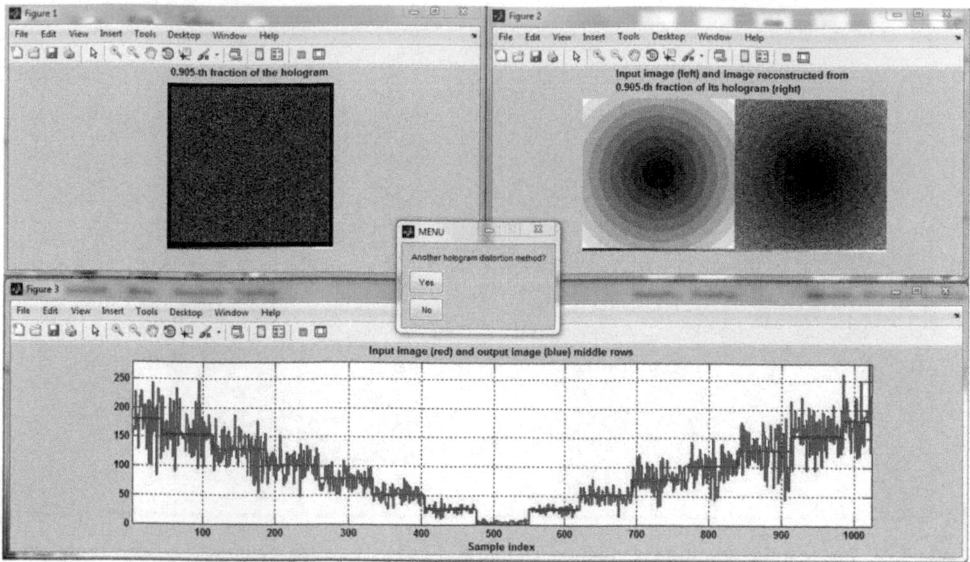

Figure 5.26. Image noise: speckle noise due to limitation of the hologram size.

For the dynamic range limitation, the user is prompted to specify hologram dynamic range in terms of the ratio (from two to five) of the hologram recording device dynamic range to standard deviation σ of hologram orthogonal components, i.e. of real and imaginary components of the hologram. For the hologram quantization, the user has to set the number of uniform quantization levels in the dynamic range of $[-4\sigma, 4\sigma]$.

In each case displayed are (i) hologram, (ii) initial test image and a result of its reconstruction from the distorted hologram placed side by side, and (iii) plots of middle rows of the initial and reconstructed image (figures 5.26–5.28).

5.7 Empirical diagnostics of image noise

For adjustment of image denoising algorithms, numerical data on statistical parameters of noise in image signals are needed. Sometimes these data are available in certificates of imaging systems provided by system producers. When they are not, as frequently happens in applications, one needs to extract the necessary data from available images. This is quite a tricky problem, a kind of a vicious circle: in order to measure statistical parameters of noise present in images, one needs to separate noise from signals, but, for this separation, knowledge of noise statistical parameters is required.

The way out of this vicious circle is to not separate noise from signals but rather to separate their statistical characteristics. In a number of cases the latter is possible with the help of quite simple means. The core idea is to measure those statistical characteristics of image distorted by noise, in which the presence of noise exhibits itself as an easily detected anomaly. The set of exercises 'Empirical diagnostics of image noise' illustrates this approach on examples of empirical evaluation of

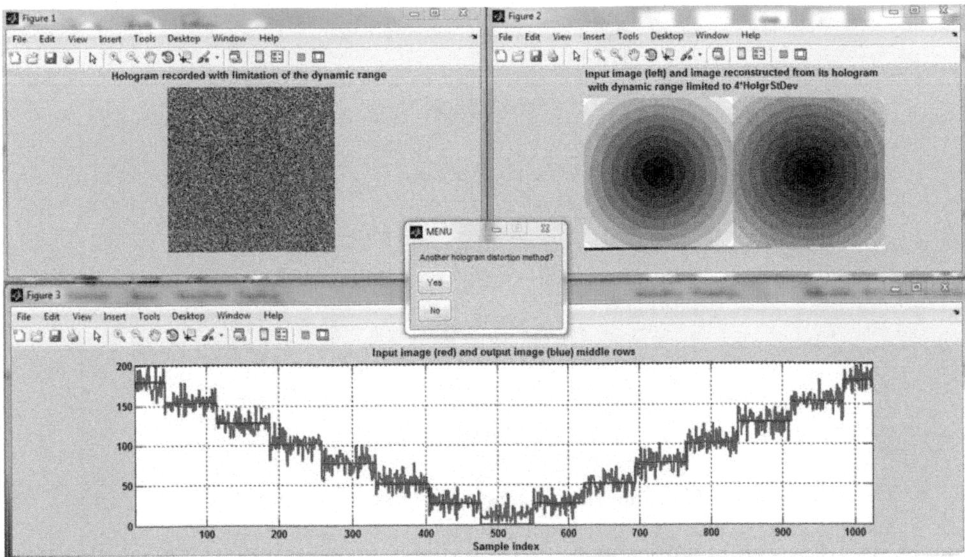

Figure 5.27. Image noise: speckle noise due to limitation of the hologram dynamic range.

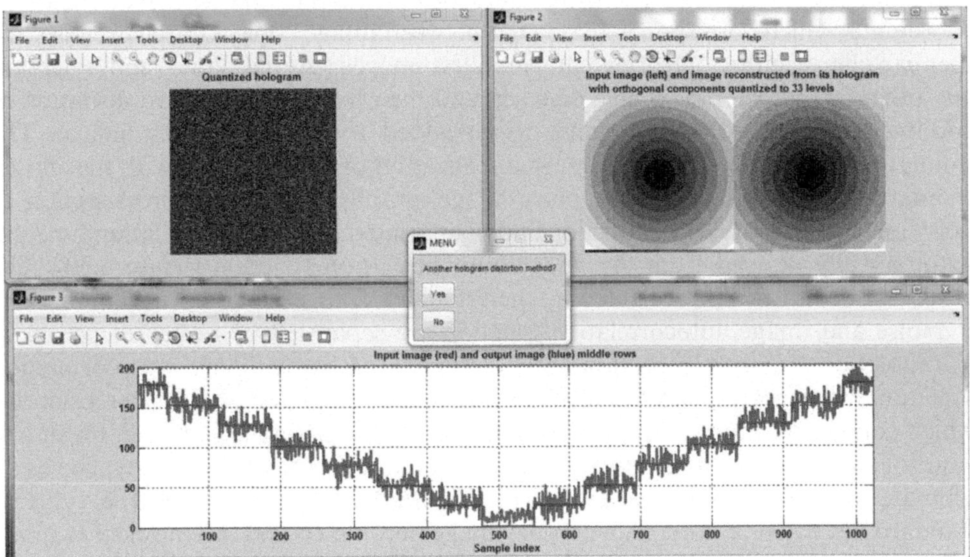

Figure 5.28. Image noise: speckle noise due to quantization of hologram orthogonal components.

standard deviation of additive uncorrelated (wide band) noise, of the frequencies and intensities of moiré noise components and of banding noise parameters in images. These options are listed in the start menu shown in figure 5.29.

5.7.1 Wide band noise

Additive wide band (uncorrelated) noise is statistically fully characterized by its standard deviation. For automated measurement of the noise standard deviation in

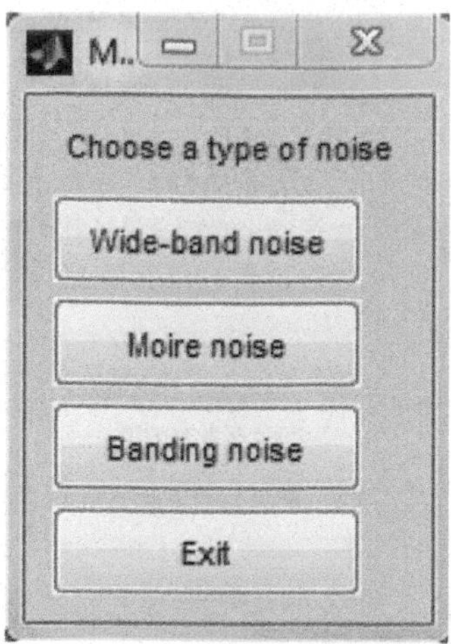

Figure 5.29. Empirical diagnostics of image noise: start menu.

images, it is frequently sufficient to measure noisy image autocorrelation functions. The presence in the image signal of additive uncorrelated noise exhibits itself in a sharp anomalous peak in the image autocorrelation function at the origin of its coordinate, which corresponds to no shift between image copies. In the exercise, the user can choose either one of two prepared test images ('Aerial photo' and 'Face') or any other image from the image data set, and then has to set standard deviation of additive uncorrelated normal noise to be added to the chosen test image. The simulation program adds to the image a realization of normal noise with the chosen standard deviation, displays the noisy image, graphs of a central cross-section of noisy image autocorrelation function and of estimated noise autocorrelation function automatically derived from the image autocorrelation function (figure 5.30). The latter is a delta function weighted by the estimate of noise standard deviation.

Noise and image autocorrelation function are separated by means of parabolic extrapolation of samples with indices 2 and 3 of noisy image autocorrelation function, which correspond to shifts by 2 and 3 sampling intervals, to its first sample, which corresponds to no shift. The square root of the difference between the actual value of autocorrelation function first sample and its extrapolated value is taken as an estimate of additive noise variance. Titles in the figure indicate the true value of standard deviation of noise added to the image (left panel) and its empirical estimate (right panel). The experiment can be repeated with another realization of noise.

5.7.2 Moiré noise

The characteristic indication of the presence in images of moiré noise is the presence of more or less isolated anomalously large sharp peaks in the image DFT or DCT power spectra. These peaks can be quite easily detected in the difference between the actual image spectrum and its sufficiently well smoothed copy, in which the noise peaks are suppressed. This principle is implemented and illustrated in the exercise. The program first displays two prepared test images with a real (not simulated)

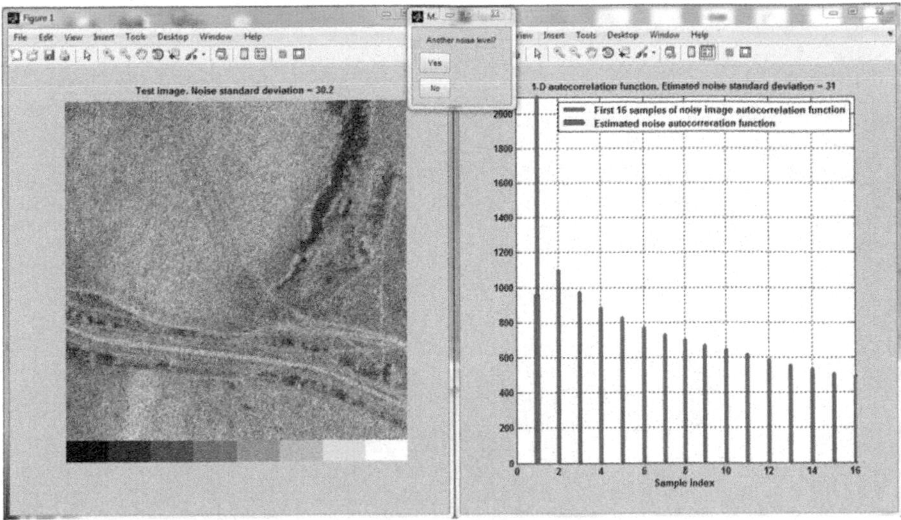

Figure 5.30. Empirical diagnostics of image noise: estimation of additive normal noise standard deviation.

moiré noise and prompts the user to choose one of these images or to download another image from the user's image database. Once a test image is chosen, it is displayed for viewing along with, in another figure window, DFT row-wise power spectrum of the chosen test image averaged over all image rows. Then the user is prompted to initiate detecting moiré noise peak and then to set a threshold for detecting anomalous peaks in the displayed spectrum, assuming that those peaks might be spectral components of moiré noise (figure 5.31).

The recommended range of the detection threshold is [0.01–0.1]. It is used by the program for detecting violations of 'monotonicity' of the spectrum decay with frequency index. The detection is carried out by means of comparing differences between intensities of spectral components with adjacent indices with this threshold in the course of their analysis from low-frequency to high-frequency components. At frequencies where violations of monotonicity are detected, the spectrum intensity is replaced by its value at the previous frequency index. In this way, a smoothed spectrum is formed. It is plotted in the upper subplot of the figure along with a plot of the initial spectrum; the difference between the initial and smoothed spectra represents estimates of spectrum of the supposed moiré noise. This is plotted for visual evaluation in the bottom subplot of the figure (figure 5.32). The user is then prompted either to choose another detection threshold or to choose another test image or to finish the exercise.

In the exercises of chapter 8 one will see how these estimates can be used for filtering out moiré noise.

5.7.3 Banding noise

As has been mentioned, in images distorted by banding noise gray values of all pixels of each individual image row are biased by the same random value. Therefore, diagnostics of banding noise assumes determination of these random additions to

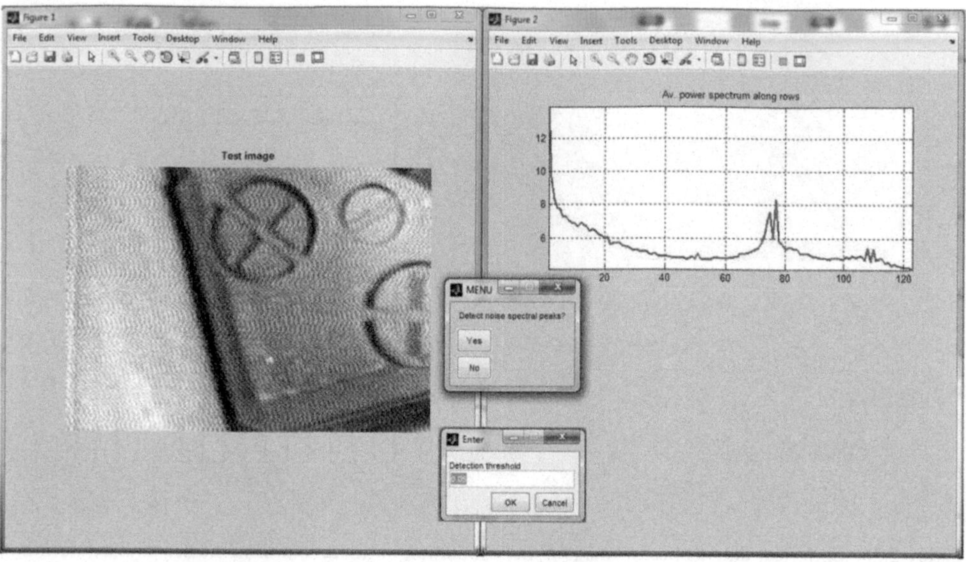

Figure 5.31. Moiré noise: test image and its averaged row-wise noise spectrum.

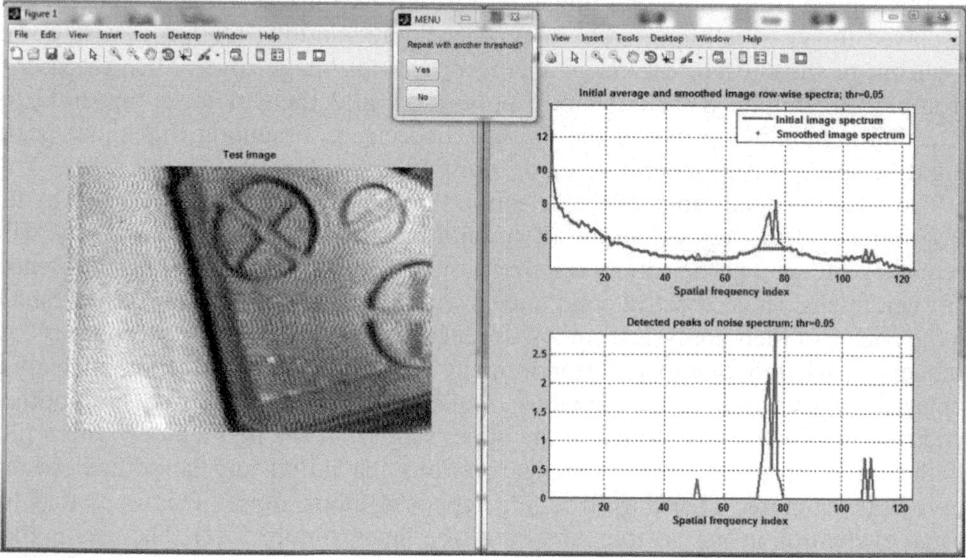

Figure 5.32. Moiré noise: noise spectral peaks detected.

image rows. This can be done with the assumption that mean values of individual image rows normally, in the absence of banding noise, do not change considerably from row to row, i.e. image row mean values regarded as a function of row indices are sufficiently smooth functions. This implies that smoothing the sequence of means of image rows contaminated with banding noise may provide a reasonably good estimate of the noiseless sequence and the difference between both will be a good estimate of values that distort image rows. This idea is implemented in the program

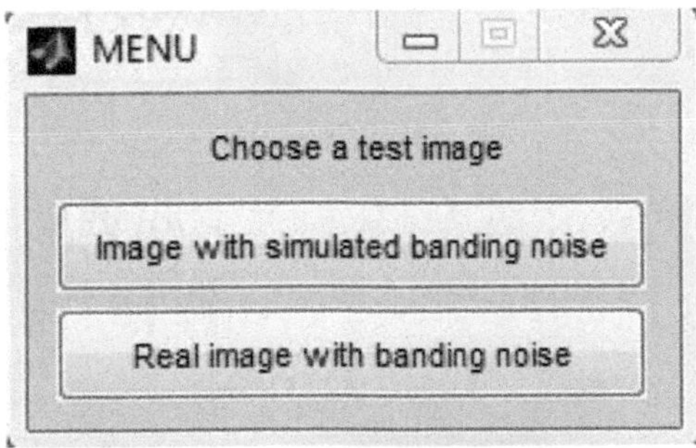

Figure 5.33. Bending noise: start menu.

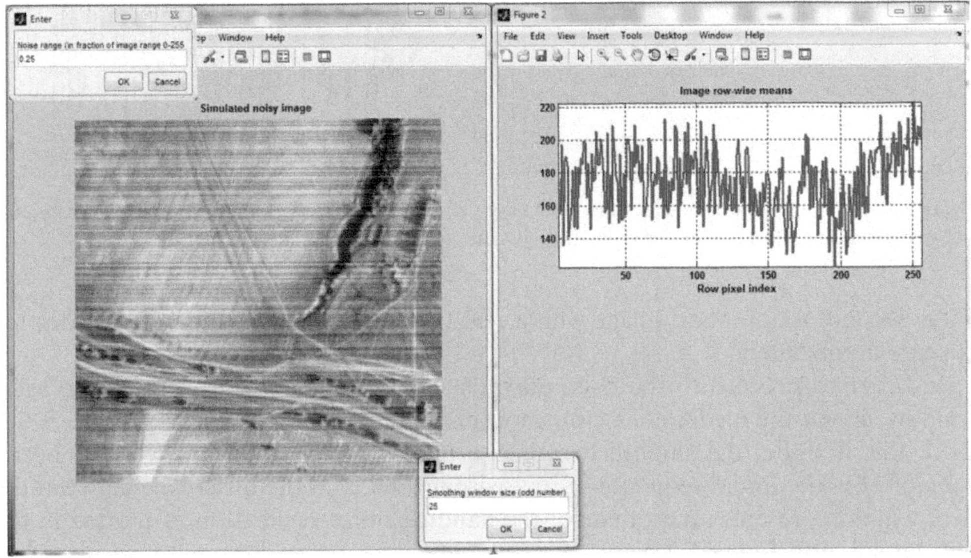

Figure 5.34. Banding noise: simulated noisy test image (left panel) and its row-wise means (right panel).

that supports the exercise. For smoothing row-wise means, median filtering is employed. The median filter works in a window sliding over the sequence under filtering and, in each window position, replaces the actual value of the window central sample by the median of the samples within the window. Window size is a filter parameter that is to be set by the user.

For experimentation, two options for choosing a test image are offered: either to download an arbitrary image from the image database and work with simulated banding noise or to use a prepared test image distorted by real banding noise, a sample image produced by an atomic force microscope (figure 5.33).

If the 'Image simulated banding noise' option is chosen, an image from the image data set has to be downloaded and used as the test image. It is displayed in one figure and the user is prompted to set the dynamic range of the banding noise (in a fraction of the image dynamic range 0–255), similarly to the exercise on banding noise in section 5.6.1. Then the chosen test image with a simulated banding noise is displayed and its row-wise means are plotted in another figure window versus row index (figure 5.34).

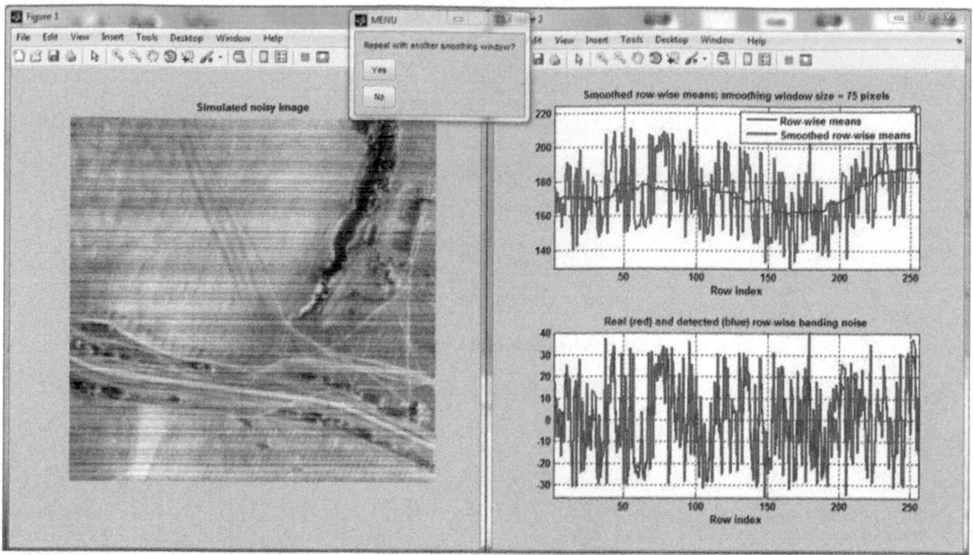

Figure 5.35. Banding noise: simulated noisy test image (left panel) and plots of image row-wise means (initial and smoothed) and plots of real and estimated row-wise values of banding noise (right panel).

If the second option of an image with a real banding noise is chosen, such a display appears immediately.

In order to proceed to the noise diagnostics, the user is then prompted to set a window size of the median filter for smoothing image row-wise means (figure 5.34). Once this is done, the smoothed row-wise means are plotted on the same upper subplot as is the initial sequence of row-wise means, and the difference between the two, which represents an estimate of the banding noise realization, is plotted in the bottom subplot (figure 5.35).

Questions for self-testing

1. What is the use of image histograms?
2. Are there images homogeneous in terms of local histograms? If yes, which types of images are?
3. Can one detect objects in images by means of comparing their histograms with image local histograms within fragments of the corresponding size?
4. Sometimes clusters (consolidated peaks, or 'hills') can be seen in image histograms. How they can be interpreted?
5. How would you interpret color triangle histograms of color images?
6. What distinctions if any have you found between local means and local medians?
7. What image local statistical characteristics can be used for detection of object borders (edge detection)?
8. What information about images is contained in differences between image local maxima and minima?

9. In what sense can local standard deviation and local maxima-minima difference be regarded as akin statistical characteristics?
10. How would you choose window size for image local statistical analysis?
11. How well, in your opinion, do different types of pixel neighborhood unify pixels that belong to the same object?
12. In addition to pixel gray levels and ranks, would you suggest any other pixel attributes as a base for forming pixel neighborhoods?
13. In your opinion, might displaying image local pixel attributes help in visual image analysis?
14. What are the common features of autocorrelation functions of different images?
15. What are common features of power DCT and DFT spectra of different images?
16. Have you appreciated any connections between shapes of image correlation functions and power spectra and shapes of objects present in images?
17. What features of images can be associated with variability of image local spectra? Is this variability characteristic for all types of images?
18. Where is energy compaction capability of transforms more pronounced, in global or in local spectra?
19. What numerical parameters of local spectra can be promising candidates for defining local spectra based pixel attributes?
20. In your opinion, what kind of noise, additive normal broadband, moiré noise, banding noise or impulsive noise, is more destructive for image readability assuming that all of them have the same standard deviation?
21. What kind of noise, additive, multiplicative or impulsive, is speckle noise caused by the limitation of imaging system resolving power or hologram size? What will be the answer to this question for speckle noise caused by other distortions of hologram recording devices?
22. Does the accuracy of empirical estimation of intensity of additive broadband noise depend on the image content?
23. Which is easier to detect, low-frequency or high-frequency moiré noise components?

IOP Publishing

Advanced Digital Imaging Laboratory Using MATLAB®

Leonid P Yaroslavsky

Chapter 6

Statistical image models and pattern formation

6.1 Introduction

Statistical image models are mathematical models for generating pseudo-random images with certain prescribed statistical properties. They are used in simulations of imaging systems and testing image processing algorithms, as well as for the synthesis of artificial images that imitate natural ones. The exercises in this chapter demonstrate an algorithmic approach to building statistical image models, according to which the models are built by means of certain (specific for each model) combinations of certain standard elementary operations applied in a certain order to a starting, or seed, image. Implemented here are the following models listed in the entrance menu (figure 6.1):

- *Point-wise nonlinearity (PWN) model*: seed images are subjected, pixel by pixel, to a point-wise nonlinear transformation specified by its amplitude transfer function.
- *Linear filter (LF) model*: seed images are subjected to a linear filtering with a certain prescribed filter point spread function or frequency response.
- *Point-wise nonlinearity and linear filter (PWN&LF) model*: assumes point-wise nonlinear transformation and linear filter in cascade, i.e. seed images are first subjected to a point-wise nonlinear transformation and then the result is fed to a linear filtering.
- *Linear filter and point-wise nonlinearity (LF&PWN) model*: assumes linear filtering and point-wise nonlinear transformation in cascade in the opposite order: seed images are first subjected to a linear filtering and then to a point-wise non-linear transformation.
- *Evolutionary models*: iterative, i.e. models with a feedback: at first iteration a seed image is subjected to a certain transformation specific for a particular model and then at other iterations, this transformation is applied to the image obtained at the previous iteration.

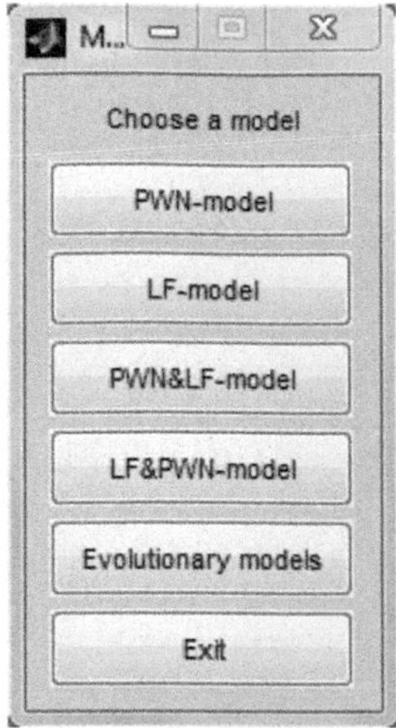

Figure 6.1. Statistical image models and pattern formation: start menu.

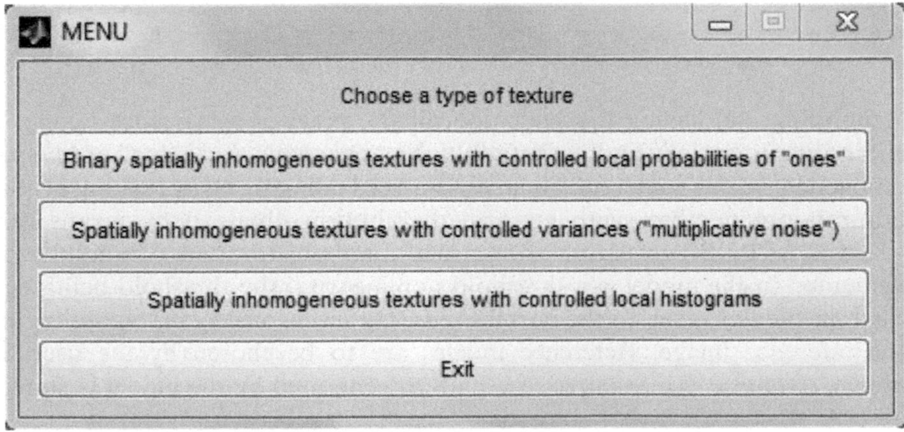

Figure 6.2. PWN-models: start menu.

6.2 PWN models

PWN models are the simplest ones in the family of the image statistical models and pattern generators. Using point-wise transformation, one can control probability histograms of output images, and this is the only image statistical parameter that can be directly controlled in this model. Three versions of PWN models implemented for exercises are listed in the menu shown in figure 6.2.

6.2.1 Binary spatially inhomogeneous texture with controlled local probabilities of 'one'

In this exercise one can generate binary pseudo-random images with probability of 'one' proportional, for each pixel, to normalized to the unity gray level of its

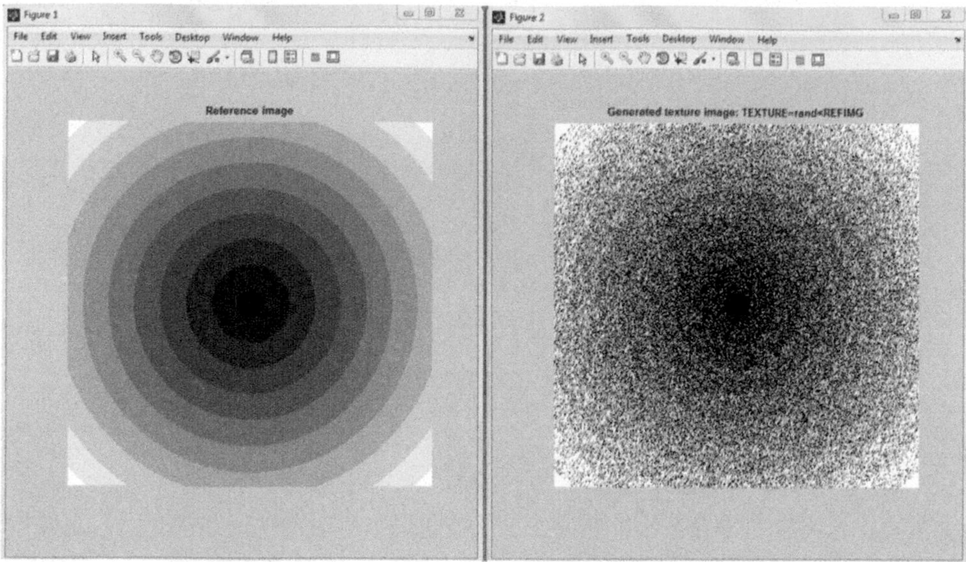

Figure 6.3. PWN model: reference image (left panel) and an example of a binary pseudo-random image with density of 'ones' (shown in white) controlled by the reference image (right panel).

corresponding, i.e. having the same coordinate, pixel of a reference image. The resulting images are, naturally, spatially inhomogeneous according to the spatial inhomogeneity of the reference images. As seed images, arrays of uncorrelated pseudo-random numbers with uniform distribution obtained by means of the standard MATLAB® generator of 'random' numbers are used. The nonlinearity implemented in the model is a threshold nonlinearity, the threshold being equal, for each particular pixel, to the normalized gray levels of the corresponding pixel of the reference image. Reference images are to be chosen by the user from the image database. An example of a pattern generated by the model is shown in figure 6.3.

6.2.2 Spatially inhomogeneous texture with controlled variances ('multiplicative noise')

In this version of the PWN model, generated are zero mean pseudo-random images with normal distribution and standard deviation proportional, for each pixel, to the normalized gray level of the corresponding pixel of a reference image. This type of pseudo-random image simulates signal dependent multiplicative noise. As seed images, pseudo-random numbers with normal distribution taken from the standard MATLAB® pseudo-random number generator are used. The amplitude transfer function of the 'nonlinearity' is a parabolic transfer function, which spans within the image dynamic range ([0–255]) with a slope proportional to its argument, the gray level. As in the previous exercise, reference images are to be chosen by the user. Figure 6.4 presents an example of an image generated in this way and its corresponding reference image.

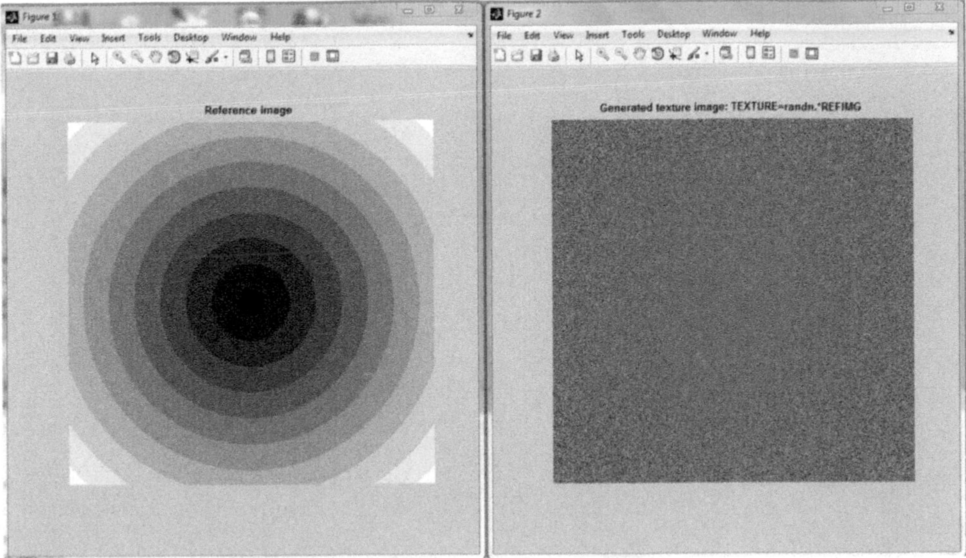

Figure 6.4. PWN model: a reference image (left panel) and an example of a pseudo-random image with pixel gray level standard deviations proportional to gray levels of corresponding pixels of the reference image (right panel).

6.2.3 Spatially inhomogeneous texture with controlled local histograms

This implementation of the model enables generation of pseudo-random images with local histograms within windows of a given size identical to local histograms of a reference image in corresponding positions of windows. As seed images, arrays of uniformly distributed pseudo-random numbers generated by the standard MATLAB® random number generator are used. The model nonlinearity is the one that converts uniform distribution of pseudo-random numbers into a given distribution. It is inverse to the *histogram equalization* transformation. The reference images as well as vertical and horizontal dimensions of the window for computing local histograms are to be chosen by the user. A result of the work of the model is illustrated in figure 6.5.

6.3 LF models

6.3.1 Introduction

While PWN models control image gray level distribution histograms, linear filter (LF) models generate images with pre-defined power spectra (or, correspondingly, autocorrelation functions). It is noteworthy that, by virtue of the central limit theorem of the probability theory, gray level distributions of images generated by LF models tend to a normal (Gaussian) distribution.

Exercises in this section demonstrate synthesized images for several types of image spectrum and a possibility of generating images that imitate certain types of natural texture. Linear filters in the models are implemented in spectral DFT or DCT domains: seed arrays of pseudo-random uncorrelated zero mean numbers with

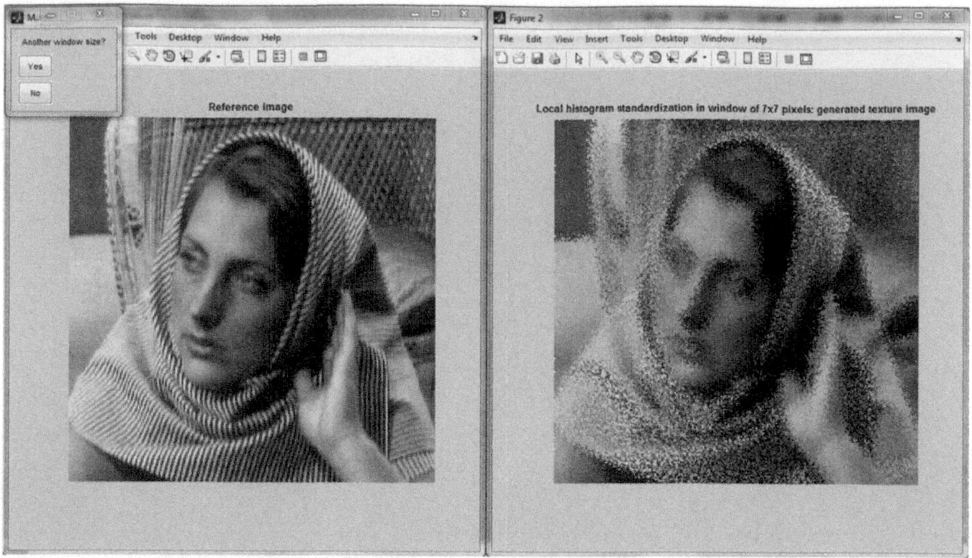

Figure 6.5. PWN model: a reference image (right) an example of a pseudo-random image with local histograms over a certain window identical to local histograms of the reference image in corresponding 7 × 7 pixel window positions.

uniform distribution in the range [−0.5, 0.5]) from the standard MATLAB® random number generator are multiplied by spectral masks of certain chosen by the user forms or controlled by a reference image, and the images are obtained by inverse DFT or DCT transform. Thus, power spectra of generated images are specified by the spectral masks, while spectra phase components are determined by the pseudo-random numbers. Types of texture images that can be generated are listed in the start menu in figure 6.6.

6.3.2 'Ring of stars', circular and ring-shaped spectra, 'fractal' textures

'Ring of stars' textures are generated in the DFT or in DCT domains using spectral masks in the form of a 'ring of stars' (several spectral components uniformly arranged over a circumference of a circle (for DFT) or of a pie-sector (for DCT) of certain radius centered at the DC component). For generating circular and ring-shaped spectra textures, spectral masks in the form of circles and rings, for DFT, or pie-sectors and quarters of rings, for DCT, are used. For generating 'fractal' textures, one uses spectral masks in the form of the DC component centered at the spectrum circularly symmetrical surfaces that decay inversely proportionally to the 0.5th; 1st; 1.5th; and 2nd powers of the distance from the DC component ('$1/f^{P}$'-type spectra).

For generating 'ring of stars' textures, the user is prompted to choose DFT or DCT transform domains for filtering, set the radius of a circle as a fraction of the image size, and the number of spectral components ('stars') uniformly arranged on the circumference of the circle or, correspondingly, pie-sector. For textures with

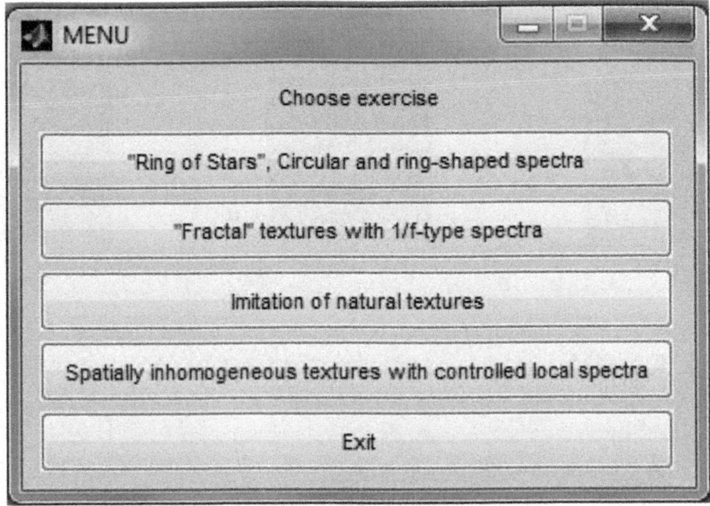

Figure 6.6. LF models: start menu.

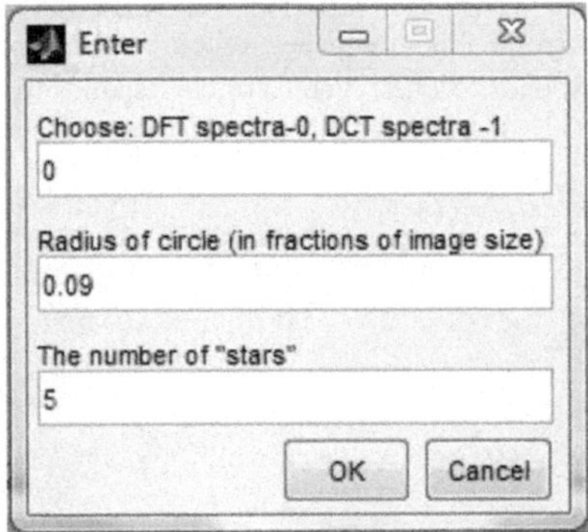

Figure 6.7. LF model, 'ring of stars', circular and ring-shaped spectra: menu of parameters.

circular or ring-shaped spectra, the user defined parameters are corresponding radii (figure 6.7).

The program can be run many times producing different realizations of this type of textures with the same parameters. Examples of the resulting images are presented in figure 6.8.

If the option 'fractal' textures with 1/f-type spectra is chosen, the program automatically generates all four special cases of fractal textures with $1/|f|^P$ spectra for $P = 0.5$, $P = 1$, $P = 1.5$ and $P = 2$ (figure 6.9).

6.3.3 Imitation of natural textures

A remarkable property of LF models is their capability of imitating many types of natural texture. This can be done by assigning to arrays of pseudo-random images the power spectrum of a template texture images to be imitated. To demonstrate this

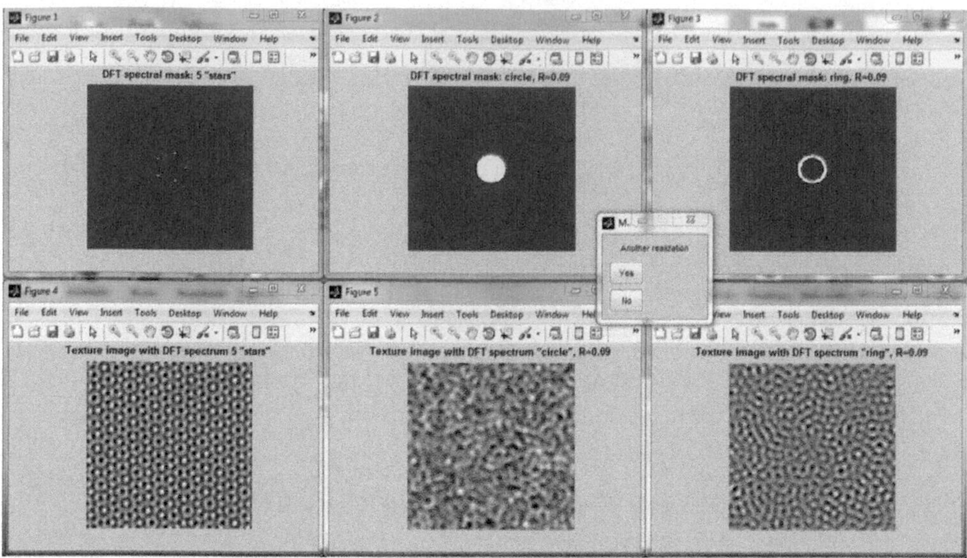

Figure 6.8. LF models, 'ring of stars', circular and ring-shaped spectra. Shown are examples of generated images (bottom row) along with corresponding frequency responses of linear filters of the models. (Yellow color in images of spectral masks corresponds to ones; blue color corresponds to zeros in the frequency responses).

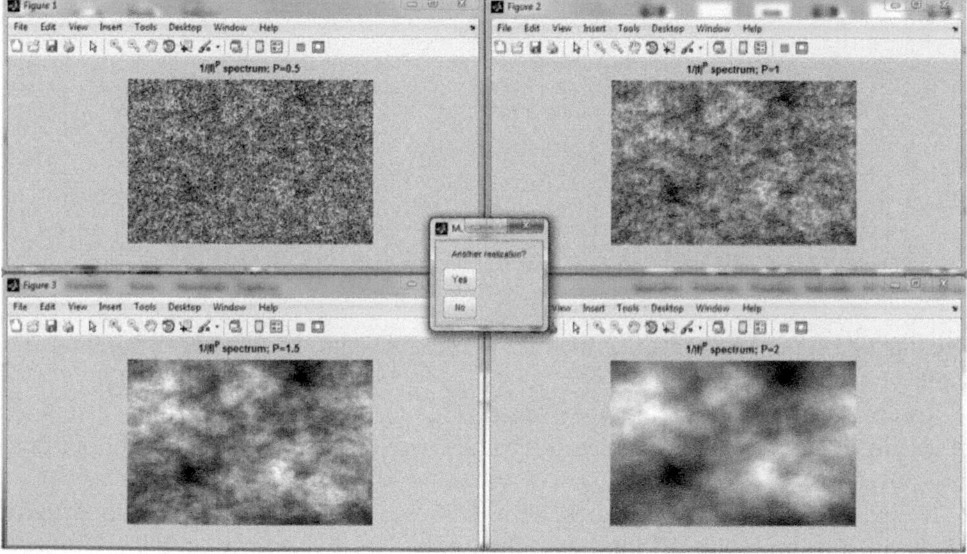

Figure 6.9. LF models, 'fractal' textures with circular symmetric power spectra that decay inversely proportionally to powers 0.5, 1, 1.5 and 2 of the spatial frequency.

capability, two options are offered in the exercise for choosing the template texture: (i) three types of natural textures, a 'wood' texture of wooden furniture, a 'mohair' texture of weaved woolen fabric and another texture, 'textile', of woven fabric, and (ii) arbitrary texture image from the image database. The latter option is intended

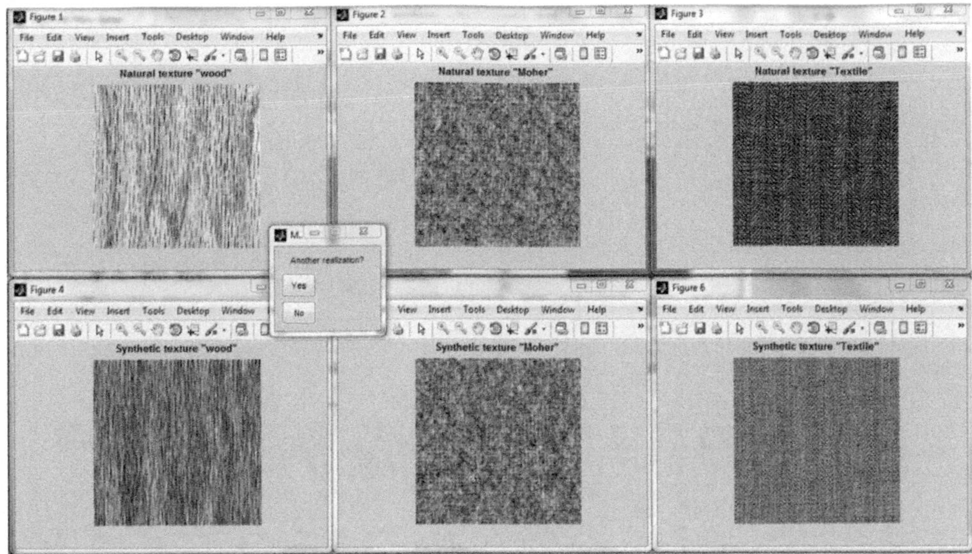

Figure 6.10. LF models: samples of natural textures (upper row) and their computer generated imitations (lower row).

for demonstration that not all natural texture can be imitated using the LF model. The program can be run many times to generate different realizations of texture images of the same type, which, in this case, is defined by the power spectrum of template images. Examples of generated texture images that imitate natural prototypes are shown in figure 6.10.

6.3.4 Spatially inhomogeneous textures with controlled local spectra

In the previous exercise, LF models are applied globally, i.e. to spectra of whole images. Resulting textures are, therefore, spatially homogeneous (in terms of their local spectra). Local application of LF models enables generating spatially inhomogeneous textures. This can be done, for instance, using as a control signal, an auxiliary image, whose local parameters determine parameters of local spectra of textures to be generated.

This idea is implemented in the exercise in the following way. Two types of spectral masks for the LF model are pre-defined: circular masks of different radii and elliptical masks of different orientations. For circular spectral masks, mask radius is the controlled parameter. For elliptical spectral masks, their angular orientation is the controlled parameter. In the process of generating texture images, those parameters are, pixel by pixel, determined by gray levels of pixels of the reference image chosen by the user. Figure 6.11 illustrates the work of the model.

6.4 PWN&LF and LF&PWN models

PWN&LF and LF&PWN models are examples of two-stage (cascade) models with point-wise nonlinearity and linear filter applied to input seed images one after another in different order.

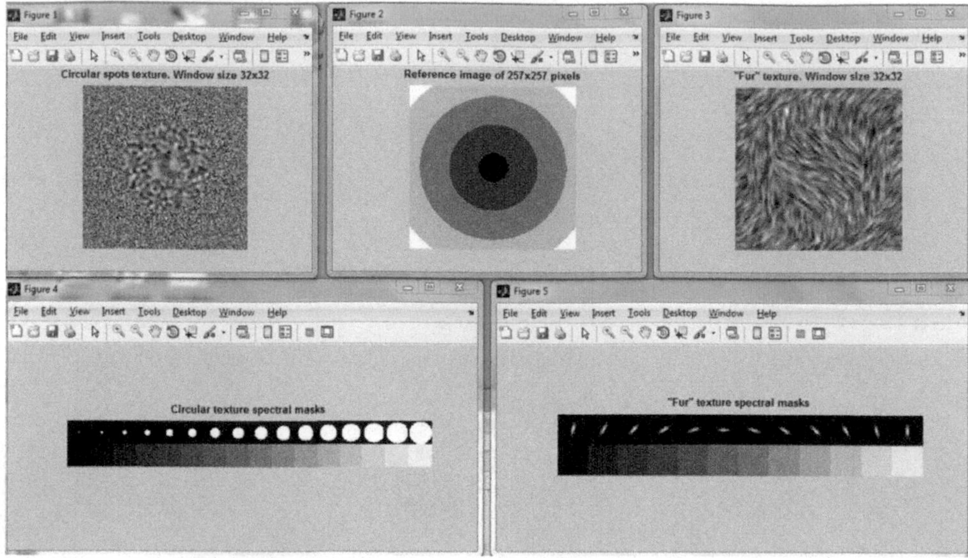

Figure 6.11. LF models: spatially inhomogeneous textures (upper left and right panels) with circular (bottom left) and elliptic (bottom right) local spectra controlled by the reference image (upper middle panel).

A version of the PWN&LF model implemented here imitates 'randomly' tossing an image of a one cent coin onto a plane. To this goal, the model generates in the first stage an array of pseudo-random binary numbers with a certain, set by the user, probability of 'ones'. Then this array is convolved with an image of a cent coin, which plays here the role of the impulse response of the linear filter. As a result, images of cent coins are placed in the positions of ones of the binary array at the linear filter input. The program runs this procedure several times and displays obtained realizations of images as video frames. The number of runs is a user-defined parameter as well. Figure 6.12 shows one frame of such a run.

In the LF&WPN-model, linear filters and point-wise nonlinearities act in the inverse order with respect to the previous case. First, arrays of correlated pseudo-random numbers are produced from a seed array of uncorrelated pseudo-random numbers by a linear filter with a preset frequency response, and then the result is subjected, pixel by pixel, to a certain user-defined nonlinear transformation. The types of filter masks used here are the same as in the above described exercise with the LF model. As for the nonlinearity, two options are offered: threshold non-linearity and sinusoidal one. The threshold nonlinearity replaces positive input signal values by 'ones', and negative values by 'zeroes'. The sinusoidal nonlinearity replaces input signal values by a cosine of two π times signal value normalized to the unity. Figures 6.13 and 6.14 illustrate output displays.

6.5 Evolutionary models

As was mentioned, evolutionary models are iterative models, i.e. models with feedback. They work with the initial 'seed' image in an iterative way, applying, at

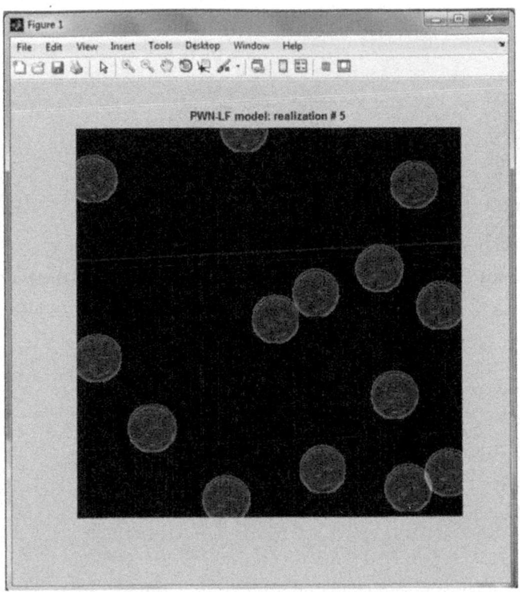

Figure 6.12. PWN&LF model: images of cent coins placed 'randomly' over an empty frame (shown using the MATLAB® color map 'copper').

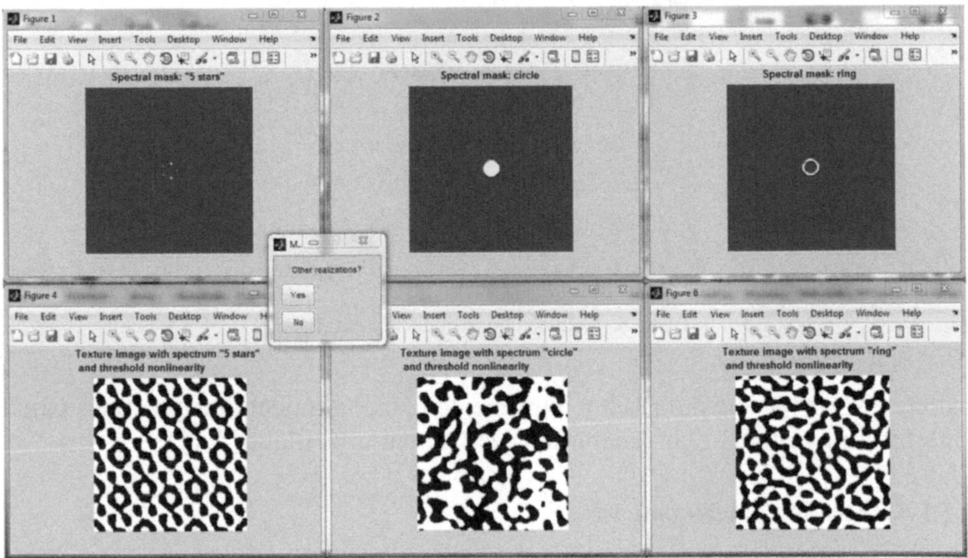

Figure 6.13. LF&PWN model, the threshold nonlinearity. Yellow color in images of spectral masks corresponds to ones and blue color corresponds to zeroes in the frequency responses.

each iteration step, a certain image transformation specific for the model to the result obtained at the previous step. A critically essential feature of evolutionary models is the presence of irreversible non-linearity in the feedback loop. This enables generating nontrivial patterns in the process of iteration, i.e. of evolution of the

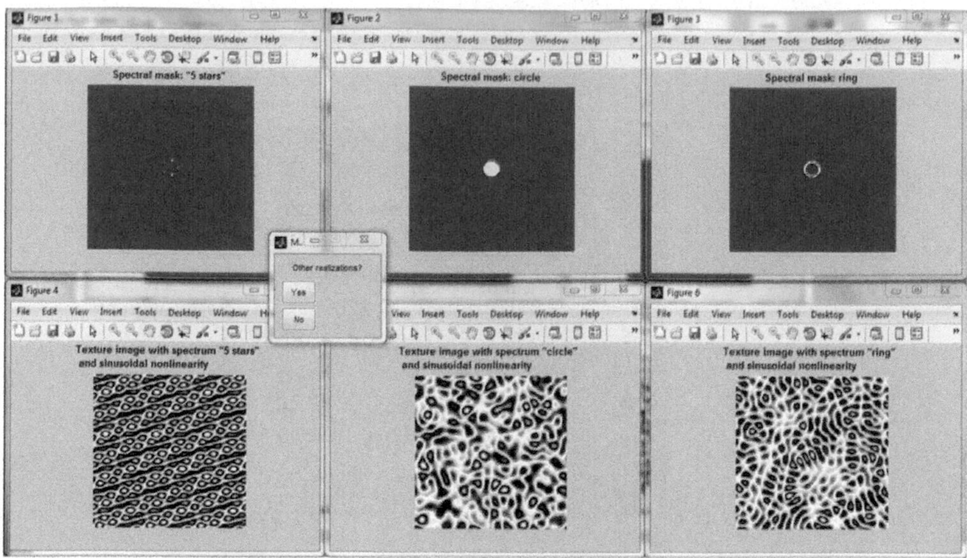

Figure 6.14. LF&PWN model, the sinusoidal nonlinearity. Yellow color in images of spectral masks corresponds to ones and blue color corresponds to zeroes in the filter frequency responses.

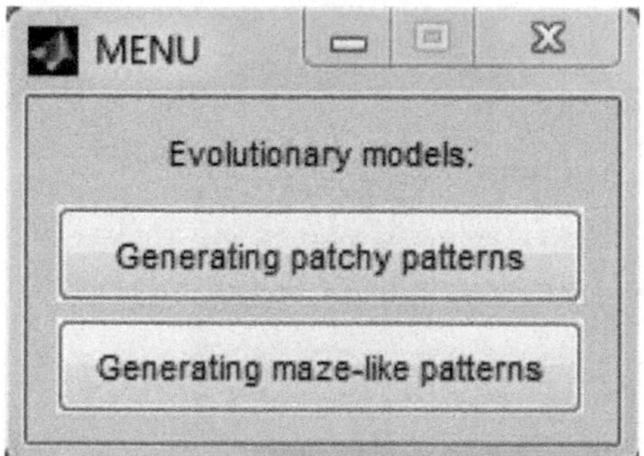

Figure 6.15. Evolutionary models: start menu.

patterns. Two specific models are implemented here: a model that generates patchy patterns and a model that generates maze-like patterns (figure 6.15).

6.5.1 Generating patchy patterns

In this model, images are iteratively subjected to filtering in a running (row-wise and column-wise) window that, at each position of the window, replaces the gray level of the window central pixel by the gray level of the mode of the histogram over the window, i.e. by the gray level, which is the most frequent in the window. This filter belongs to a family of rank filters that will be studied later in chapters 8 and 9. Being applied iteratively, it tends to produce piece-wise constant patchy patterns.

For experimentation with this model, the user is first prompted to choose, as a seed image, either an array of pseudo-random uncorrelated numbers or any natural

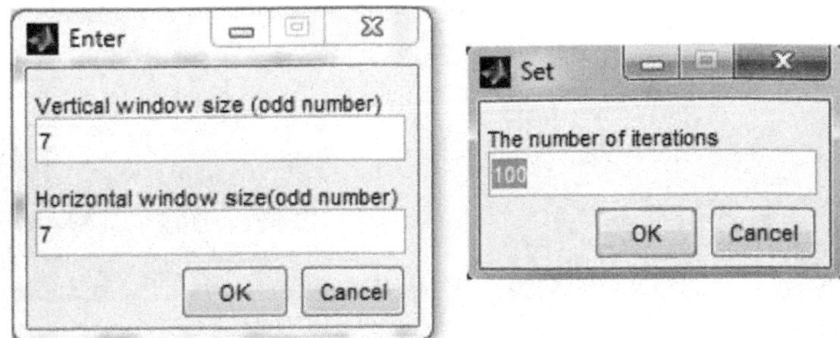

Figure 6.16. Evolutionary models: generation patchy patterns parameter menu.

image from the image database and after that to set the filter window horizontal and vertical dimensions and the number of iterations (figure 6.16).

The program displays the input seed image and, at each iteration, the output image and plots of the number of image pixels modified at this iteration and of the number of histogram bins in the output image versus the number of iteration. The first plot provides an indication of the convergence of the output image to a model 'fixed point', i.e. to a stable image, which, once it has appeared, is not modified anymore in the process of iterations. In this case the number of modified pixels becomes zero. The second plot shows the number of image histogram non-zero bins in the iteration process. Decrease of this number evidences the convergence of the seed image to a patchy piece-wise constant image.

After the chosen number of iterations is executed, the user has an option either to further continue iterations or to stop iterations and display the pattern of edges of the produced patchy pattern. The edges are detected by computing pixel wise differences between output image maxima and minima in a running window of 3 × 3 pixels. An example of the final display is shown in figure 6.17.

6.5.2 Generating maze-like patterns

The exercise in this section implements a stochastic modification of the mathematical game, the 'Game of life', invented by a British mathematician John Conway. In the standard model 'Game of life', a square array of 'cells', which may be in one of two states, one ('live') and zero ('empty') and forms a binary pattern with pixels representing the cells, evolves from a certain seed pattern according to the three simple rules:

1. If a 'live' cell has in its closest 3 × 3 pixel spatial neighborhood less than two or more than three 'live' cells, it will 'die' at the next evolution step, i.e. one will be replaced by zero in the corresponding pixel.
2. If an 'empty' cell has in its closest 3 × 3 pixel neighborhood exactly three 'live' neighbors, this cell will give 'birth' at the next evolution step, i.e. zero will be replaced by one in the corresponding pixel.
3. Otherwise nothing happens.

The 'births' and 'deaths' events in the standard model happen at each evolution step synchronously in all cells of the array, where they must happen according to the

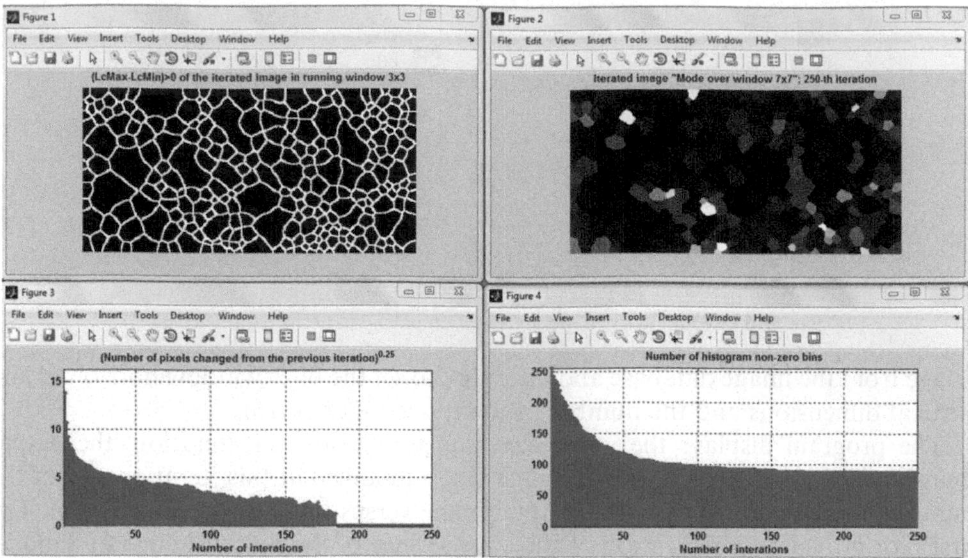

Figure 6.17. Evolutionary models: iterative local histogram modes over a running window. The graph of the number of pixels changed from the previous iteration shows that the model reached its fixed point at about the 170th iteration.

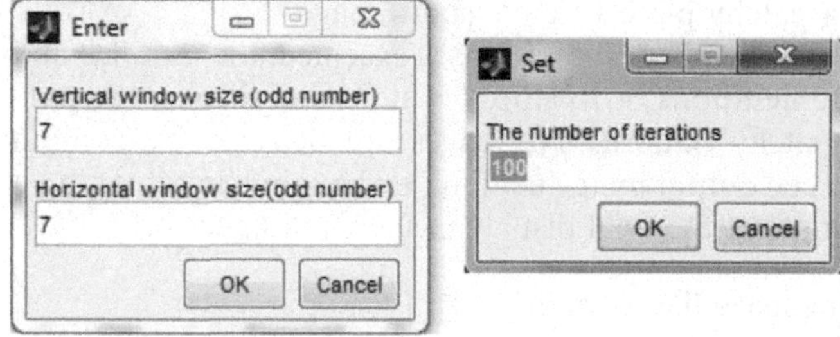

Figure 6.18. Evolutionary models, generating maze-like patterns: parameter menus.

above rules. In the stochastic modification of the model that is offered for experimentation here, the 'birth' events occur in all cells of the array, where they must occur according to the above rule, whereas 'deaths' occur only in a subset of the relevant cells. Pixels of this subset are selected, using a pseudo-random number generator, with a certain probability, which we call the 'probability of death' P_{death}. This is a model parameter that the user has to set along with the initial probability of 'live' cells in the binary pseudo-random seed pattern that the program will generate at its start (figure 6.18).

For the standard, non-stochastic, model $P_{\text{death}} = 1$. The standard 'Game of life' model produces, in the course of evolution from an arbitrary seed pattern, three types of patterns: (i) stable formations that, once appeared, remain unchanged unless they collide with neighbor formations, which might happen in the course of evolution; (ii) periodical formations ('oscillators'), which repeat themselves after a certain number of evolution steps; obviously, the above-mentioned stable patterns

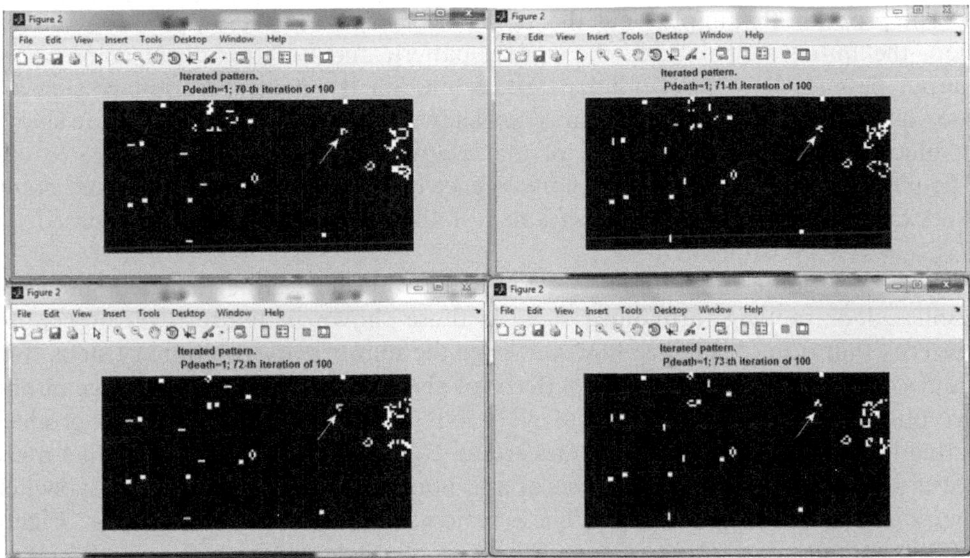

Figure 6.19. Game of Life standard model: four consecutive frames of the evolutional pattern, in which stable, periodical and moving patterns are present. The latter are marked by the arrow.

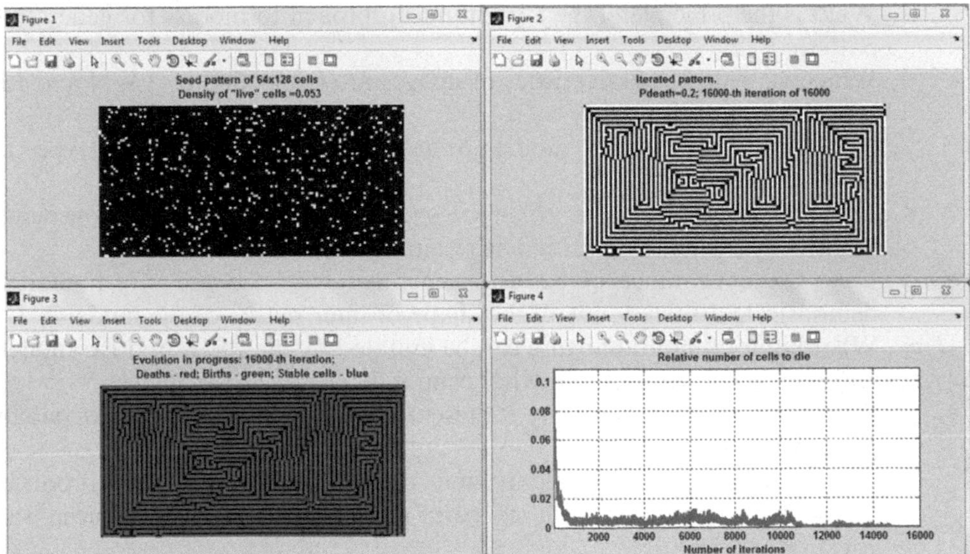

Figure 6.20. Evolutionary models: stochastic modification of the 'Game of Life'. The bottom image, in which stable cells are shown in blue, and plot evidence that the model reached a fixed point after about 15 000 iterations.

can be regarded as a special case of periodical formations with a period of one step; (iii) self-replicating 'moving' formations, or 'gilders', which move across the lattice and replicate themselves in a shifted position after a certain number of steps; this can be regarded as a general 'space–time' periodicity.

The program that implements the model displays, at each iteration, i.e. evolution step, the initial seed pattern, the output pattern and additionally a color coded output pattern, in which cells that are to 'die' on the next evolutionary step are shown in red, cells that will give 'birth' are shown in green, and stable cells are shown in blue. Displayed is also a plot of the relative number of cells that are to die. The plot serves as an indicator of convergence of the pattern to a stable fixed point. An example of four consecutive frames of the evolutional pattern observed for $P_{\text{death}} = 1$ is shown figure 6.19.

For P_{death} larger than about 0.3, the model produces either isolated stable, or oscillated or moving formations such as those shown in figure 6.19, or chaotic patterns that do not stabilize however large the number of evolutionary steps. For values of P_{death} lower than ~0.3, patterns of chaotic formations that emerge at first evolution steps tend, in the course of evolution, to stabilize and to gradually produce stable homogeneous patterns with a certain degree of order, which look like maze patterns of alternative straight vertical and horizontal lines that chaotically switch their direction and/or positioning. These patterns are the model 'fixed points'. Figure 6.20 illustrates an outcome of one of the runs of the model with $P_{\text{death}} = 0.2$.

Questions for self-testing

1. What is the principle of the algorithmic approach to models for generating patterns?
2. Which statistical characteristics of images are controlled by PWN and LF models?
3. How can PWN and LF models be used for imitating different types of image noises?
4. Do 'fractal' textures with $1/f^P$-type spectra and spatially inhomogeneous textures generated by LF models resemble any natural textures?
5. Does the appearance of textures generated with the use of LF models demonstrate association with the shape of filter masks of the models?
6. What kinds of natural texture can be imitated by the PWN and LF models and their combinations and what cannot?
7. What irreversible nonlinearity is present in the model that generates patchy patterns?
8. Define, in terms of the algorithmic approach, a model that produces 'random net' patterns such as patterns of edges of patchy piece-wise constant images.
9. Do maze-like patterns generated by the evolutionary 'Game of life'-based model resemble some natural patterns?
10. What irreversible nonlinearity is involved in the model that produces maze-like patterns?
11. Suggest some other multi-level and multi-branch algorithmic models as an extension of those implemented in the exercises.

IOP Publishing

Advanced Digital Imaging Laboratory Using MATLAB®

Leonid P Yaroslavsky

Chapter 7

Image correlators for detection and localization of objects

7.1 Introduction

Object detection and localization is one of the basic tasks in image processing. This task assumes availability of a template image of the sought target object and solving this task requires one method or another of numerical evaluation of similarity between the template image and fragments of observed images in which the presence of the target object is expected. If the image contains, in some place, a precise copy of the target template, any reasonable similarity measure can be used for target detection equally successfully. This, however, never happens: images of target objects are never precise copies of their templates. The fundamental reason for that is the presence of sensor random noise in observed images. Other image distortions are also possible. In the presence of noise, no method is capable of unerring detection and localization of objects. Therefore, one should find optimal methods that secure the most reliable detection and accurate localization of targets in the presence of image distortions and noise.

For the case when an image containing a target object has an empty background and the only obstacle for target localization is contamination of the image by additive signal independent uncorrelated Gaussian noise, the optimal method for target detection and localization is known. It consists in computing image correlations with the target object template and locating coordinates of the correlation maximum. These coordinates are statistically the best possible estimate of the target object position in the image. This process is also called 'matched filtering', and the image correlator that implements it is called '*matched filter correlator*'.

There are a number of real applications, in which such a model of target localization in images with empty background and with signal independent uncorrelated Gaussian noise is sufficiently adequate. A typical example is navigation in space by stars. The importance of this model is also associated with the fact that it is a

doi:10.1088/978-0-7503-1233-2ch7

special case of the more fundamental and general problem of parameter estimation in images, for which it gives an example of the existence of an ultimate solution.

However, in a much larger number of applications such a model is too simplistic. First of all, the assumption of empty background does not hold often. Background parts of images either contain a number of non-overlapping non-target objects, as, for instance, in the case of character recognition in text, or, even worse, contain clutters of overlapping non-target objects, which can be confused with the target under search.

The exercises in this chapter are targeted at studying the performance of the standard matched filter image correlators in different circumstances and its adaptive modifications optimized for reliable target detection in cluttered images. The exercises are listed in the start menu of this chapter, shown in figure 7.1.

7.2 Localization of a target on images contaminated with additive uncorrelated Gaussian noise. Normal and anomalous localization errors

This section contains exercises that simulate the matched filter correlator for localization of target objects in images contaminated by additive signal independent uncorrelated Gaussian noise and demonstrate its performance in terms of the *localization accuracy and reliability*. It includes three exercises listed in the start menu shown in figure 7.2.

7.2.1 Localization of a target on uniform background

For this exercise, two test target objects are prepared, 'Constellation' and 'character "o"', which have different signal energy (sum of squared pixel gray values) (figure 7.3).

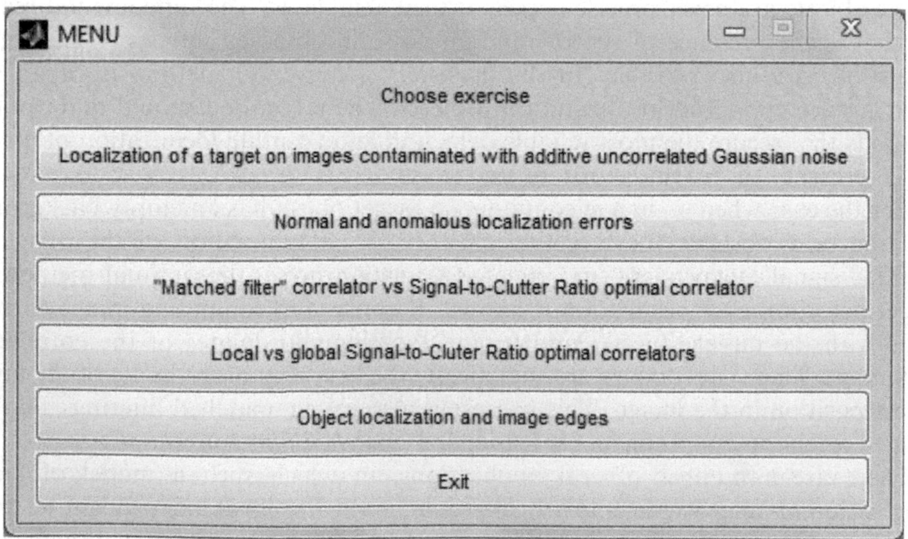

Figure 7.1. Image correlators for localization of objects: start menu.

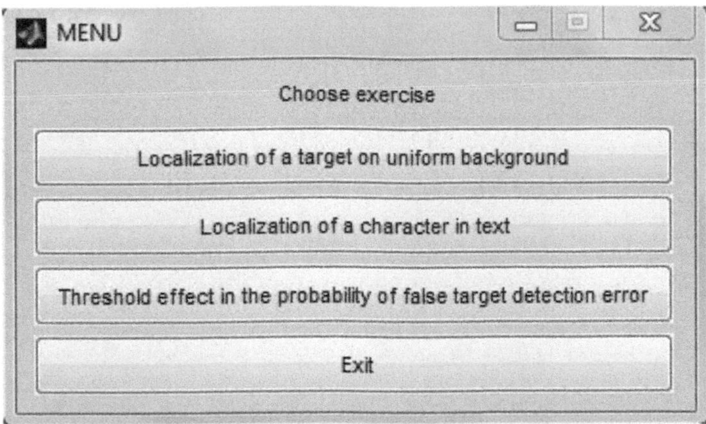

Figure 7.2. Localization of a target on images contaminated with additive uncorrelated Gaussian noise.

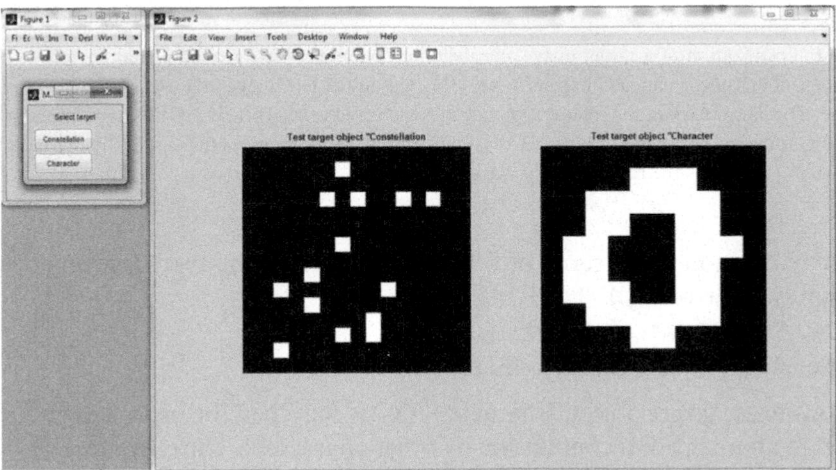

Figure 7.3. Localization of a target on uniform background: two template images.

The exercise visualizes results of 25 runs of localization of the chosen target using matched filter correlator on images with different realizations of additive uncorrelated Gaussian noise to show that, when noise level is sufficiently low, the matched filter correlator successfully detects the target in a close vicinity of its actual position, whereas, when noise level is sufficiently high, it frequently happens that the matched filter correlator confuses the target with some fragment of pure noise and erroneously the target far away from its actual position. The noise intensity and the number of realization are parameter set by user. The two prepared target objects have different energies. This enables comparison of the probability of errors for them for same intensity of noise. Displayed are a noisy test image with target randomly placed randomly in different positions, output of the matched filter correlator (figure 7.4) and, in the title, numerical parameters of the experiment: signal-to-noise ratio, index

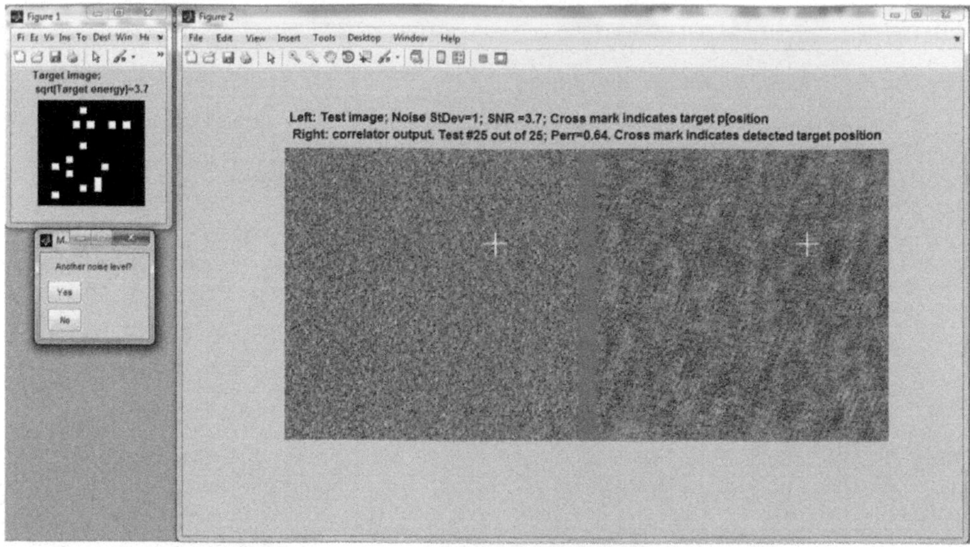

Figure 7.4. Localization of a target image 'constellation' on empty background contaminated with additive signal independent uncorrelated Gaussian noise. The cross in the left image indicates position of the target in the image. The cross mark in the right image indicates the result of localization of the target in the position of the highest, for each particular realization of additive noise, maximum at the output of the matched filter correlator. P_{err} indicates the rate of wrong detections.

of noise realization in the series of runs and the relative number of wrong detections (probability of error P_{err}).

7.2.2 Localization of a character in text

In this exercise, target object 'Character "O"' is searched for in an image of printed text, i.e. in an image that contains many other characters. The exercise demonstrates that if the image contains non-target objects, with which the target object might be confused, the probability of false localization of a target object substantially rises, compared to the case of target localization on empty background for the same noise level. The experiment runs, for each of value of noise standard deviations chosen by the user, 25 times with 25 different realizations of noise, and the user can see how frequently false detections happen and what characters are most frequently confused with the test character. Figure 7.5 shows an example of one of the experiment's runs. Displayed are the results of localization, indicated by a cross mark in the noisy image, and, as a reference, the position on a noise-free image of the target detected on the noisy image. Standard deviation of noise, signal-to-noise ratio and the number of noise realizations are given in the titles of the images.

7.2.3 Threshold effect in the probability of false target detection error

A fundamental phenomenon in target detection in additive Gaussian noise is the threshold effect in the probability of false detection error: if signal-to-noise ratio

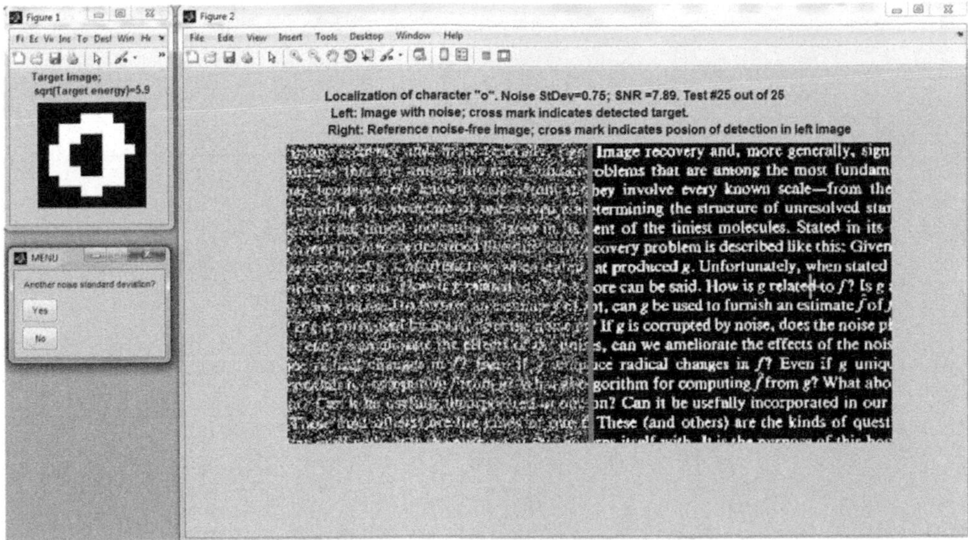

Figure 7.5. Localization of a character in text.

(SNR) falls below a certain threshold level, the probability P_{err} of false localization of target far from its actual position rises very rapidly to one with lowering of SNR. The speed of growth tends to infinity with the number Q of possible positions of the target object within the image (it is roughly equal to the ratio of the area of search to the area occupied by the target object). Theoretical value of the threshold is defined by the inequality $\text{SNR} = E_{\text{tgt}}/\sigma_{\text{n}}^2 > 2 \ln Q$, where σ_{n}^2 is variance of the additive noise, E_{tgt} is target image energy (the sum of squared pixel gray values).

The exercise demonstrates this phenomenon experimentally. The program simulates detection of a test object, a uniform square of 8 × 8 pixels, on an image of six sizes (64 × 64, 128 × 128, 256 × 256, 512 × 512, 1024 × 1024 and 2048 × 2048 pixels) with empty background in the presence of additive Gaussian noise. The detection is carried out in a number of runs chosen by the user for different realizations of additive noise for nine preset levels of noise and for five values of the ratio of the area of search to the target area Q = 64, 256, 1024, 4096 and 16396. Upon completion of all runs for each noise level, the rate of false detections is evaluated and taken as an estimate of the probability of detection error. Detection results are qualified as false if the target is localized outside the target object area centered at true target position. The results are plotted in graphs of probability of false detection versus the ratio $\sqrt{2\sigma_{\text{n}}^2 \ln Q/E_{\text{tgt}}}$ for five values of the ratio Q of the area of search to the target area (figure 7.6). The dashed line indicates in the plot the theoretical threshold value $\sqrt{2\sigma_{\text{n}}^2 \ln Q/E_{\text{tgt}}} = 1$ of noise-to signal ratio.

7.3 Normal and anomalous localization errors

Full statistical characterization of target localization errors is provided by distribution density of localization errors. Although exact theoretical distribution density of

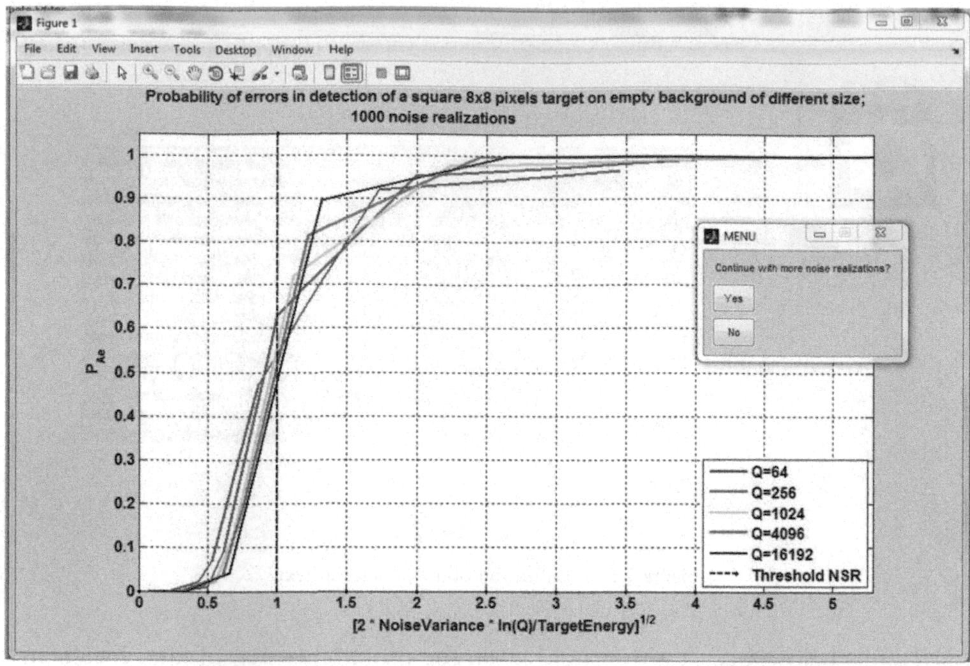

Figure 7.6. Threshold effect in the probability of false target detection error.

localization errors is not known, it is known that for small errors, which are substantially less than the linear size of the target, it can be approximated by normal distribution density and that for errors larger than the linear size of the target, this function has uniform tales. The area of these tales is the probability of target detection error studied in the previous exercise. Small localization errors are called 'normal' errors; large localization errors are called anomalous errors. The exercise 'Normal and anomalous localization errors' enables experimental observation of these two components of the localization error distribution density. The program simulates matched filter correlator for localization of an impulse of Gaussian shape observed in additive signal independent uncorrelated Gaussian noise and measures the distribution density of localization errors (differences between actual positions of the impulse and their estimates made by the matched filter correlator) for different variances of noise. In order to obtain sufficiently good statistical estimation of probabilities of errors, the program runs, for each specific level of noise, a user defined number of times with different realizations of noise.

At the start of the experiment, the user is prompted to set the width of the test impulse of Gaussian shape (in number of samples), the start value of standard deviation of noise, the number N_{nsr} of noise levels to be tested and increments of this value ($\text{DELTA}_{\text{nsr}}$) as well as the number N_{iter} of noise realizations to be tested for each noise level (figure 7.7).

For each value of noise variance, the program runs the chosen number of runs with different realizations of noise. Upon completion of all runs, distribution

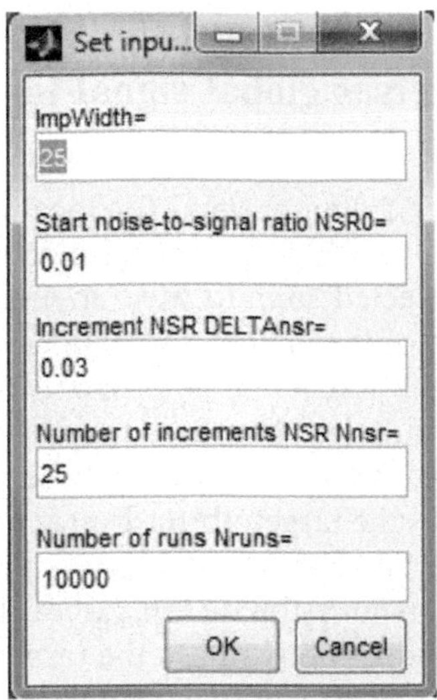

Figure 7.7. Normal and anomalous localization errors: parameter panel.

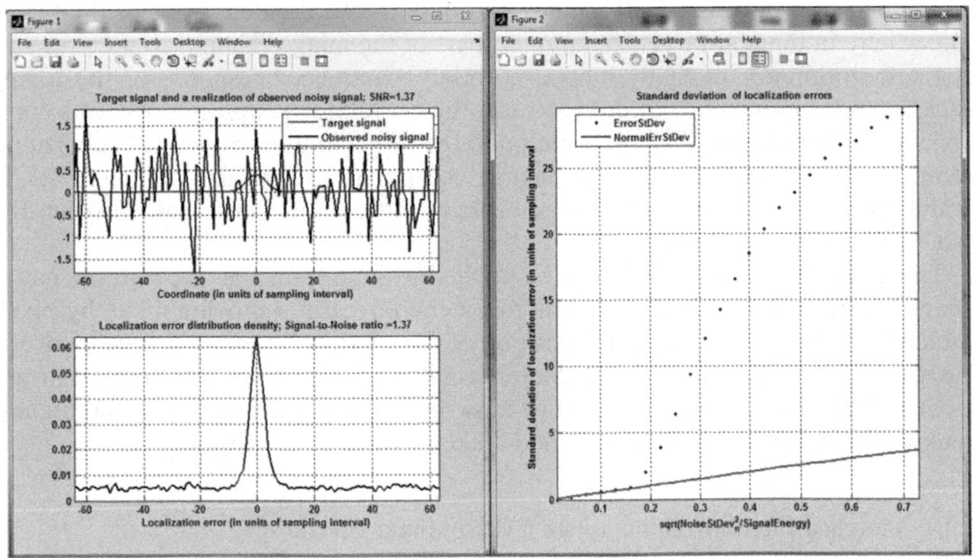

Figure 7.8. Normal and anomalous localization errors: an example of final display.

histogram of localization errors and error variance are evaluated. For each value of noise variance, the program plots the test impulse and its mixture with noise, the probability distribution functions of localization errors, and, additionally, estimates of the localization error variance. The latter is plotted along with plot of theoretical estimates of normal error standard deviation, which extrapolate to large noise levels values obtained for small noise levels. All this is repeated for all chosen numbers of signal-to-noise ratios. An example of the final display is presented in figure 7.8.

7.4 Matched filter correlator versus signal-to-clutter ratio-optimal correlator. Local versus global signal-to-clutter ratio-optimal correlators

The matched filter correlator, being optimal for localization of targets in uncorrelated additive noise, shows a very high rate of false detections in most applications, when targets should be detected and located in images that contain cluttered background. A modification of the matched filter correlator called *optimal adaptive correlator*, or *signal-to-clutter (SCR) optimal correlator*, exhibits a substantially better capability of discrimination between targets and non-target objects. In distinction from the matched filter correlator, whose frequency response is just a complex conjugate $(Sp_{tgt})^*$ to the target object Fourier spectrum Sp_{tgt}, in frequency response of the SCR optimal correlator, complex conjugate $(Sp_{tgt})^*$ to target object Fourier spectrum is divided by an estimate $|Sp_{img}|^2$ of the power spectrum of image background component that does not contain the target. This frequency response is obtained by maximization, over all possible frequency responses of linear filters, of the ratio of the signal value in the target position to the signal standard deviation over the non-target background part of the image (signal-to-clutter ratio, SCR). It is assumed that maximal SCR secures a minimum of false detections of the target somewhere in the non-target background part of the image. Thanks to the presence in the denominator of SCR optimal correlator frequency response of the image background component power spectrum, the correlator suppresses spectral components of input image that are common to the target and to the image background component and enhances their distinctive components. This also makes the SCR optimal correlator adaptive to image background components, against which the target should be discriminated.

The SCR optimal correlator can be applied to search for the target in the entire image, i.e. globally, or locally, to search for the target in a moving, pixel by pixel, window. In the latter case, at each position of the window, the correlator response at the window central pixel is recorded into its corresponding pixel of the output array. Upon finishing image scanning and window processing, the position of the highest peak in the output array is found and is taken as the target position.

7.4.1 Matched filter correlator versus SCR optimal correlator

The first exercise in this group implements localization of a fragment of one of two stereo images in the second image. At the start, the user is prompted to choose, using a cross mark, a position on the displayed image of its fragment to be detected (figure 7.9). Then a panel (also shown in figure 7.9) is opened for setting the size, in pixels, of the fragment that contains the chosen target. The larger the size, the better the reliability of target detection. Once the target size is chosen, the program displays (i) both stereo images side by side with the chosen target highlighted in the left image, (ii) results of localization of the chosen fragment by the matched filter correlator and by the SCR optimal correlator with detected target positions indicated by crosses in corresponding images, (iii) images of outputs of both

Figure 7.9. Matched filter correlator versus SCR optimal correlator: choosing target position.

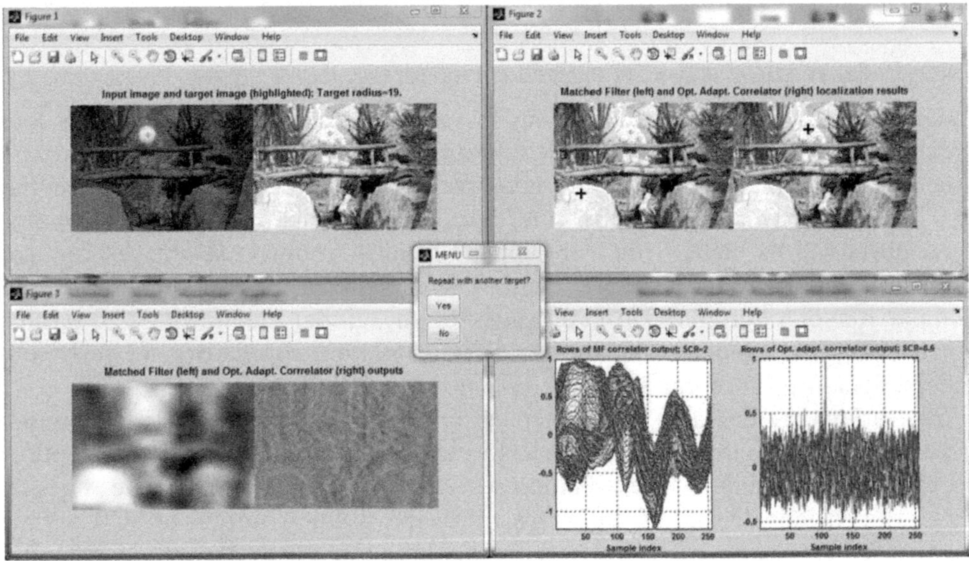

Figure 7.10. Matched filter correlator versus SCR optimal correlator. The localization results are marked by crosses. The sharp peak in plots of rows of output of the SCR optimal correlator indicates position of the target.

correlators and (iv) plots of all rows of the corresponding correlator outputs, in which one can see the highest peak that corresponds to the found position of the target. In titles to the plots, SCRs of corresponding signal maxima at the target location to standard deviations of the corresponding correlator outputs are given. Figure 7.10 presents an example of the program output. The experiment can be repeated with another image fragment as a target.

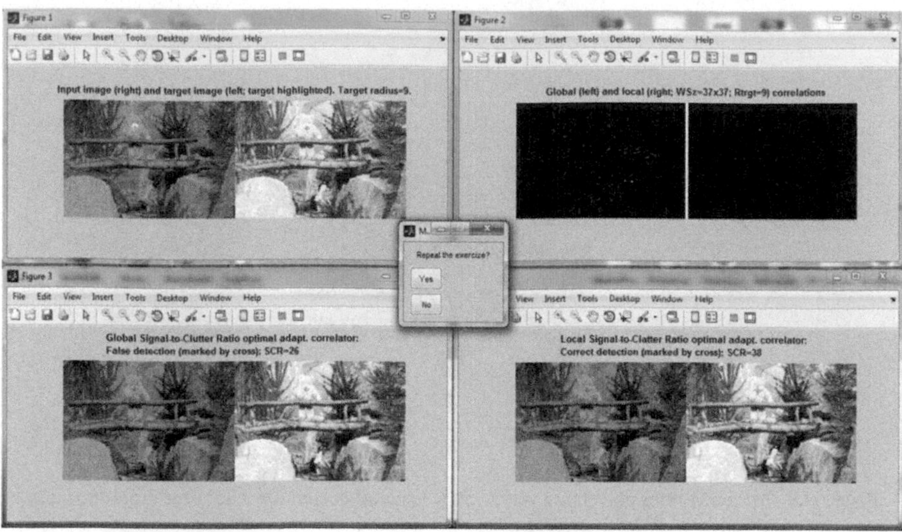

Figure 7.11. Local versus global SCR optimal correlators: final display.

7.4.2 Local versus global SCR optimal correlators

Images are, as a rule, inhomogeneous in terms of 'local' spectra, i.e. their local spectra have high variability and may substantially differ from image global spectra. Since SCR optimal correlators are adaptive to spectra of images, to which they are applied, one can expect that the discrimination capability of SCR optimal correlators will be better if they are applied locally to individual image fragments rather than globally to the entire image. The exercise in this section is targeted at comparison of discrimination capabilities of the global and local SCR optimal correlators and demonstrating that local SCR optimal correlators are capable of reliable localization of much smaller targets than global ones.

As test images, the same pair of stereoscopic images as in the previous exercise is used, and the exercise is performed in the same way. For the local SCR optimal correlator, dimensions of the scanning search window are taken as five times the target dimensions. Displayed are both stereoscopic images, outputs of SCR optimal correlator in real time of window processing, and, upon completion of scanning of the entire image, results of target detection by SCR optimal correlators in both global and local implementations. As a numerical measure of discrimination capability of the correlators, SCR ratios are given in the titles of the output images. Figure 7.11 illustrates how the results are displayed.

7.5 Object localization and image edges

The exercises of this group are intended to provide a deeper insight into the work of SCR optimal correlators. As was mentioned, frequency responses of SCR optimal correlators are the ratio $(Sp_{tgt})^*/|Sp_{img}|^2$ of complex conjugate to the target image spectrum $(Sp_{tgt})^*$ to the image power spectrum $|Sp_{img}|^2$. The ratio $(Sp_{tgt})^*/|Sp_{img}|^2$

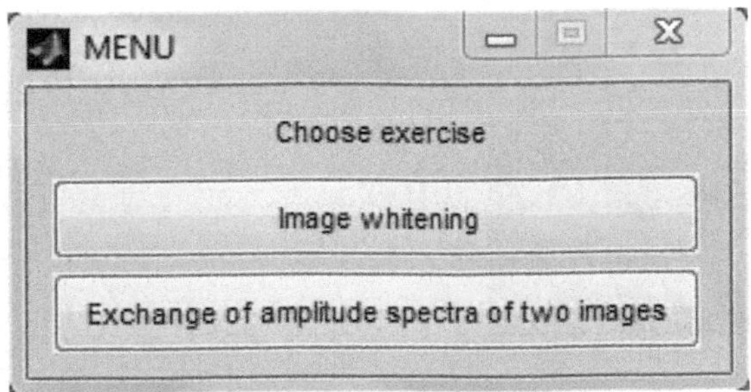

Figure 7.12. Object localization and image edges: start menu.

can be represented as a product of two terms: $1/|Sp_{img}|$ and $(Sp_{tgt})^*/|Sp_{img}|$. Therefore, the work of SCR optimal correlators can be treated as a two-step image filtering: first by the filter with frequency response $1/|Sp_{img}|$ and then by the filter with frequency response $(Sp_{tgt})^*/|Sp_{img}|$. The first filter makes amplitude of the spectrum of the input image uniform (similarly to the uniform spectrum of white light). Thus it is called *'whitening' filter*. The second filter is, obviously, the filter matched to the 'whitened' target object modified by the first filter. This means that SCR optimal correlators can be treated as the matched filter correlators for 'whitened' input and target images.

Thanks to the energy compaction capability in the Fourier transform, intensities of Fourier spectral components of images more or less rapidly decay with frequency as a rule. Therefore, whitening filters, whose frequency response is inverse to the module of the image Fourier spectrum, correspondingly amplify high-frequency image components. In images that contain sets of objects separated by their borders, image whitening results in what can be called *edge enhancement*.

Two exercises offered in this section are listed in the start menu shown in figure 7.12.

7.5.1 'Image whitening'

This exercise demonstrates image edge enhancement on test images chosen by the user. Along with whitening, test images are also subjected, for comparison, to the filtering using 2D *'Laplacian' operator,* a quite popular method of edge detection. Implemented is a version of Laplacian with 2D point spread function, in MATLAB® denotations, [−0.1 −0.15 −0.1; −0.15 1 −0.15; −0.1 −0.15 −0.1]. In addition, local means in the window of 9×9 pixels over the squared modulus of the whitened image are computed. Theoretically, they represent, for all pixels, potential SCRs at the output of the SCR optimal correlator for 9×9 pixels image fragments centered at these pixels, if they were used as target objects. These ratios characterize the potential 'goodness' of these fragments for their reliable localization in the given image. They are displayed in a separate panel and, in addition, are shown overlaid on the test image in order to ease their association with objects present in images. The results are displayed as illustrated in figure 7.13.

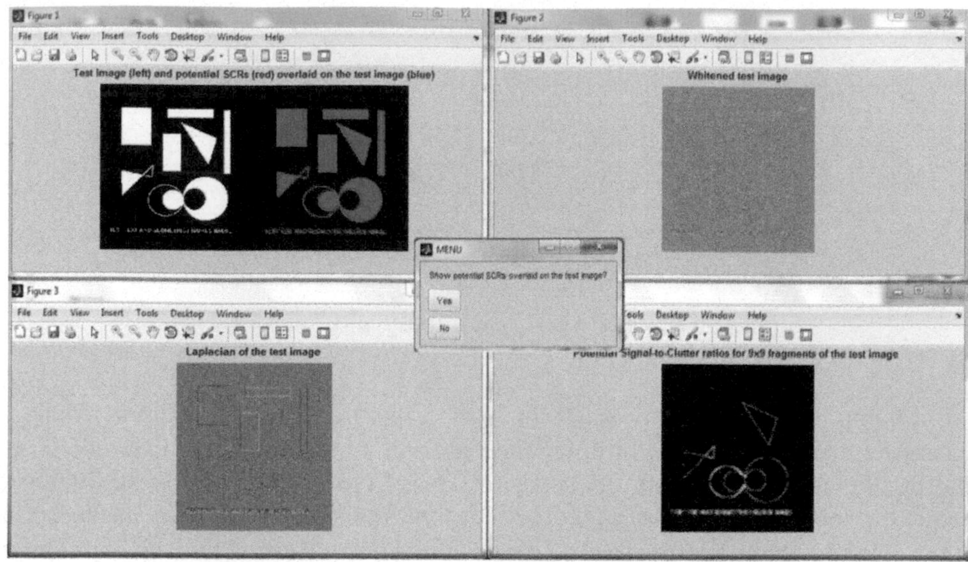

Figure 7.13. Object localization and image edges: image whitening and Laplacian.

Figure 7.14. Exchange spectra magnitude components between two images: a result for 'Mona Lisa' and 'Barbara' test images.

7.5.2 Exchange of amplitude spectra of two images

Comparison of the matched filter correlator and SCR optimal correlators evidences that image whitening that makes the image amplitude spectrum uniform, is a key reason for the improved discrimination capability of SCR optimal correlators. In whitened images, only the spectrum phase component of the initial image spectrum is kept. This tells us that it is the phase component of image spectra that contains all the information needed for the detection of objects and discriminating between objects.

The exercise 'Exchange of amplitude spectra of two images' provides a vivid illustration of the importance of image spectra phase components. As a test pair of images, either prepared test images 'Mona Lisa' and 'Barbara' or any other pair of images from the image database can be used. The program computes Fourier spectra of images, exchanges their amplitude components, restores images with modified amplitude component and displays the restored images under the corresponding original images (figure 7.14).

It is recommended to conduct exercises with different pairs of test images, those that contain individual objects and images that do not contain individual objects such as textures used in exercises with LF models in chapter 6.

Questions for self-testing

1. In the experiment on target localization, does the matched filer correlator perform similarly for both test targets for the same noise level?
2. In experiments on the detection of a character in text, what other characters are most frequently confused with the test character 'o' and why?
3. How would you explain, in intuitive terms, the threshold effect in the probability of false detection of objects?
4. Can you distinguish in the localization error distribution density areas that correspond to normal (small) and anomalous (large) localization errors?
5. Why are the tails of the distribution density of localization error for large noise levels uniform?
6. How can one explain the substantial increase of the localization error variances compared to their theoretical estimates for a sufficiently large level of noise obtained by extrapolation from low noise level data?
7. Using the results of performance of SCR optimal correlators (section 7.4.1), how can one explain their variability for different image fragments chosen as target objects?
8. Do local SCR optimal correlators perform better than global ones in terms of reliability of localization of small targets and, if yes, how much?
9. In the experiment on image whitening with test image 'Geometrical figures' illustrated in figure 7.13, some characters promise, according to the maps of potential SCRs, substantially larger SCRs than others. How can one explain that?
10. Why are the vertical and horizontal edges of rectangles in the test image 'Geometrical figures' shown in figure 7.13 not enhanced in the whitened image as much as the edges of other figures? Which features of test figures are most enhanced and why?
11. Why is image Laplacian a good candidate for edge detection? Does this hold for images composed of patches of different textures?
12. What is the rational explanation for a common belief that edge enhancement and extraction is useful for recognizing images?

13. Is it true for all types of images that the phase rather than the amplitude components of image spectra carry information needed for image recognition and identification?
14. What would you expect to obtain from exchanging phase and amplitude components between images that contain some objects separated one from another by their borders and homogeneous texture images, such as images of grass, textile or similar?

Chapter 8

Methods of image perfecting

8.1 Introduction

Image perfecting is a primary task of image processing. It is aimed at producing, from raw images generated by real imperfect imaging systems, images without, as much as is possible, degradations due to imperfections of imaging systems. Typical image degradations in imaging systems are

- degradations due to nonlinearity of system *gray scale transfer functions*, which ideally must be linear within the image dynamic range
- image blur due to imperfection of the imaging system *frequency transfer functions*, which ideally must be uniform in the image base band
- degradations due to various random noises.

The exercises in this chapter listed in the start menu shown in figure 8.1 are designed for practicing with methods of correcting these typical image degradations.

8.2 Correcting imaging system transfer functions

This section contains exercises on correction of the imaging system gray Scale transfer function, both known and unknown, and correction of the imaging system frequency transfer function (figure 8.2).

They implement a straightforward approach of '*inverse filtering*', i.e. image distortions are corrected by means of applying to distorted images a transformation inverse to that which caused the distortions. This approach works if the noise level in the image signals is sufficiently low.

8.2.1 Correction of imaging system gray scale transfer function

Two exercises in the correction of imaging system gray scale transfer function are offered (figure 8.3):

doi:10.1088/978-0-7503-1233-2ch8

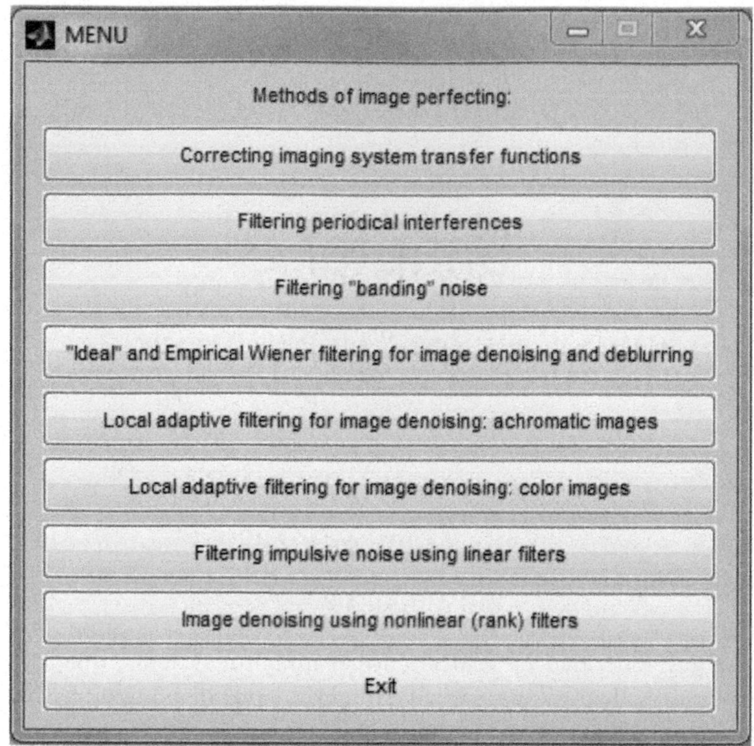

Figure 8.1. Methods of image perfecting: start menu.

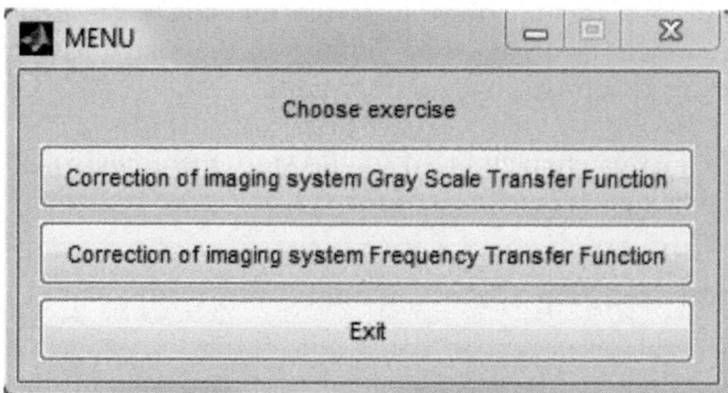

Figure 8.2. Correcting imaging system transfer functions: start menu.

Known system gray scale transfer function

In the exercise 'Known system gray scale transfer function', a test image chosen by the user is subjected to a point-wise non-linear *P*th law transformation according to the equation:

$$\mathrm{INPIMG\_NL} = \mathrm{round}(128*(1 + \mathrm{sign}(\mathrm{INPIMG}-128).*\mathrm{abs}(\mathrm{INPIMG}/128-1).\hat{}P))$$

where INPIMG and INPIMG_NL are non-distorted test image and distorted image, both with quantized gray scale values in the range [0–255]. Parameter *P* of

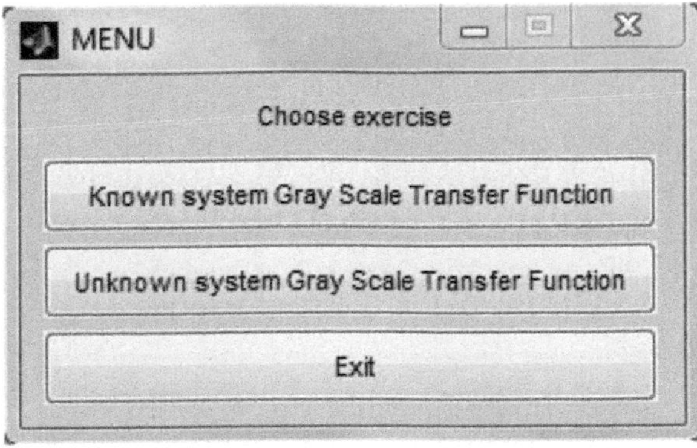

Figure 8.3. Correction of imaging system gray scale transfer function: menu.

the transformation is to be set by the user along with peak signal-to-noise ratio (PSNR), which determines intensity of normal noise to be added to the *P*th low transformed image. Adding the noise simulates noise that might be present in the raw image signal generated by the image sensor. The image distorted in this way is then subjected to the correcting inverse 1/*P*th law transformation

$$\text{OUTIMG} = \text{round}(128{*}(1 + \text{sign}(\text{INPIMG\_NL}-128).\\ {*}\text{abs}(\text{INPIMG\_NL}/128-1).\hat{\ }1/P))$$

The result is displayed as exemplified by figure 8.4. Displayed are the initial test image, distorted test image, corrected image, plots of initial and corrected image histograms and plots of distortion and correction gray scale transfer functions.

As an option, the program offers to display, in place of plots of distortion and correcting functions, the difference between initial test and corrected images (correction error) in order to enable visual and quantitative (in terms of the restoration error standard deviation) evaluation of the correction quality. The exercise can be repeated with the same test image and other distortion parameters as well as with another test image.

The goal of this exercise is to show that correcting the inverse transformation non-linear transformation by an 'inverse' transformation is feasible only if PSNR is sufficiently large.

Unknown system gray scale transfer function

Point-wise nonlinear distortions of images affect their histograms. Therefore, if an undistorted histogram of a distorted image is available, conversion of this image into the image with this undistorted histogram corrects the distortion. As a source of undistorted, or the 'etalon', histogram, images can be used that belong to the same family of images as the given distorted image, and are known or regarded as undistorted etalon images. For instance, for images of optical interferograms, which are very frequently recorded with distorted gray levels, simulated computer generated phase modulated sinusoidal patterns can be used as a source of the etalon

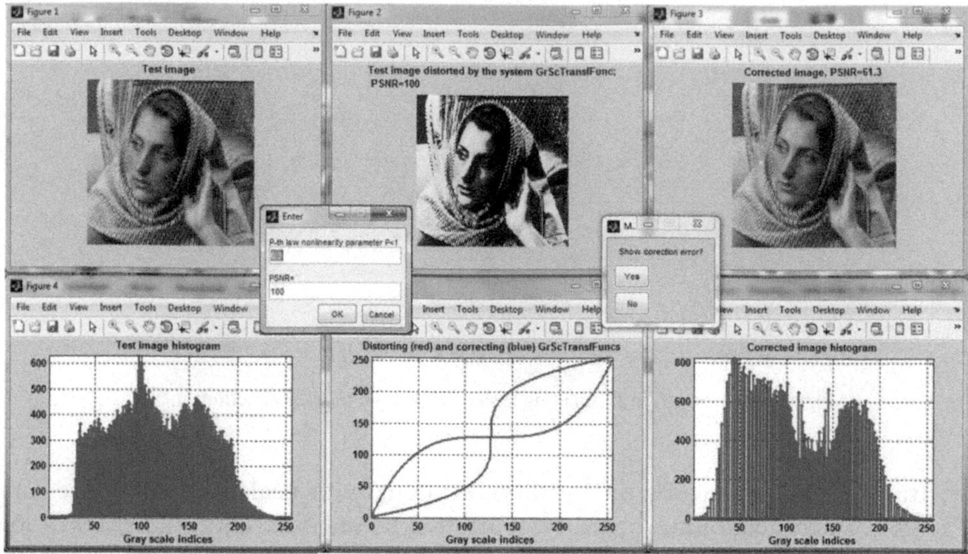

Figure 8.4. Correction of a known system gray scale transfer function: final display. Panel for setting image distortion parameters appears before executing correction once a test image is chosen.

histogram. Conversion of an image into the image with a given histogram is called *histogram standardization*.

For experimentation two options for test images are offered: (i) a distorted interferogram, for which simulated undistorted interferogram serves as a reference 'etalon' image, (ii) and an option of using arbitrary pairs of images from the image database, the first of which is regarded as the distorted image and the second as its etalon. Similarly to the previous experiment, the user is also prompted to set PSNR for noise that will be added to the image to be corrected before it will be subjected to correction by means of histogram standardization.

Once test images and SCR are chosen, the program performs histogram standardization and displays for visual evaluation (i) the chosen distorted image to be corrected, (ii) the reference image, (iii) the corrected image, (iv) plots of histograms of the distorted and reference images and (v) plots of middle rows of both images (figure 8.5). The exercise can be repeated with another PSNR and with another pair of images.

8.2.2 Correction of imaging system frequency transfer function

This exercise is intended to demonstrate correction of degradations of image sharpness due to finite sizes of apertures of image sensors, such as scanners or photographic cameras, and of image display devices, using the 'inverse filtering' approach. Frequency transfer functions of image sensors and display devices are Fourier transforms of their aperture, or point spread functions. *Overall frequency responses* of imaging systems that consist of image sensors and display devices are products of those frequency responses.

The exercise is designed in the assumption that sensor and display apertures have a square shape of the size defined by so called fill-factors, determined by the

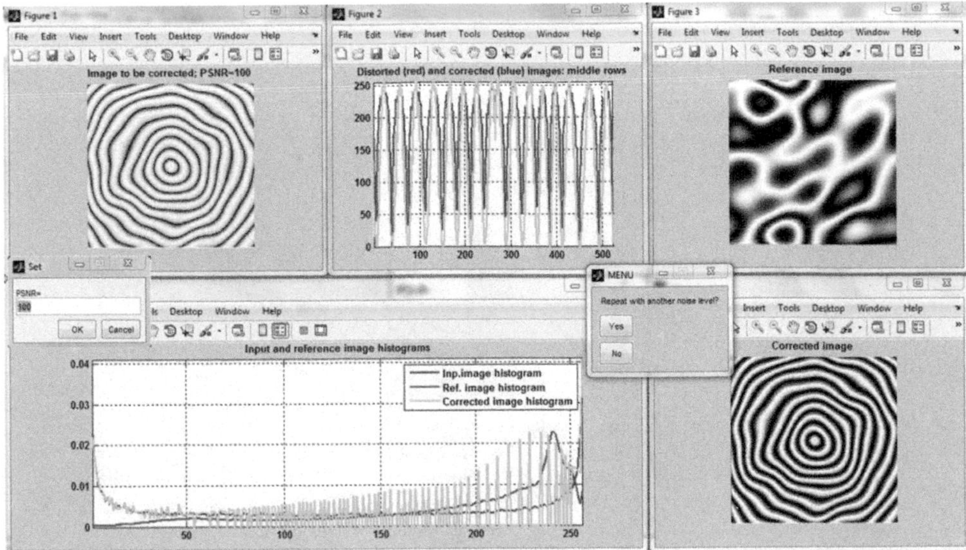

Figure 8.5. Correcting unknown gray scale transfer function: final display. Panel for setting SCR appears before the final display just after choosing test images.

fractions of the sampling interval occupied by apertures of the sensor and, correspondingly, the display device. The larger the fill factors the more severe are image sharpness degradations due to weakening of the image high-frequency spectral components in image sensor and display devices. Frequency response of the *inverse filter* that corrects these distortions is inversely proportional to the overall frequency response of the imaging system. For frequencies where sensor or/and display device frequency responses are equal to zero (or, generally, are smaller than a certain threshold), the correcting frequency response is set to zero in order to prevent over-amplification of noise, which is always present in the image and otherwise is negligible.

As a test image, a prepared 'Barbara' image is suggested, though the user can choose any other test image from the image database as well. The user is also prompted to set camera and display fill factors and PSNR of noise to be added to the chosen test image in order to imitate sensor noise. Once this is done, the program displays input and corrected images (figure 8.6) and an additional option is offered of displaying imaging system frequency response and a difference between initial and corrected images (figure 8.7). The latter represents an image component added to the initial image for its correction.

8.3 Filtering periodical interferences. Filtering 'banding' noise

8.3.1 Introduction

Noise in imaging systems is a fundamental factor that limits image suitability for visual perception and for analysis as well as possibilities of correcting other image distortions. In cases when noise cannot be tolerated, image denoising is required.

Figure 8.6. Correction of imaging system frequency transfer function: initial test image, corrected images and prompt panels (appear before and, correspondingly, after displaying results).

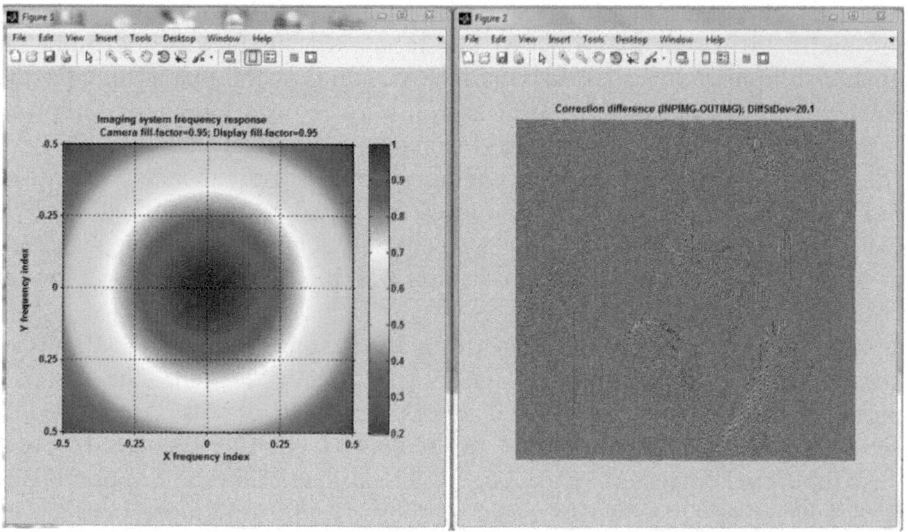

Figure 8.7. Correction of imaging system frequency transfer function: imaging system frequency response (shown in pseudo-colors coded accordingly to the color bar) and correcting image component added to the initial image to correct degradations of its sharpness.

There are many methods of image denoising, linear and non-linear filtering ones, aimed at image cleaning from different types of noise. Exercises in this section demonstrate denoising images distorted by *narrow band noise*. Specifically, linear filtering methods for image cleaning from periodical interferences and *banding noise* are dealt with. In chapter 6, methods for diagnostics of parameters on these types of

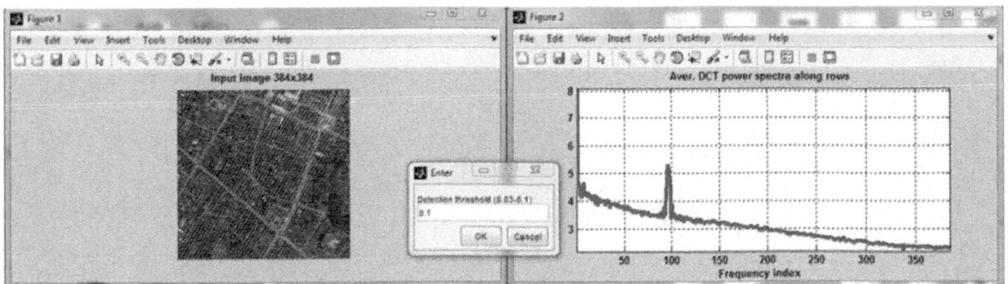

Figure 8.8. Filtering periodic interferences: test image, its average row-wise spectrum and prompt for setting threshold for detecting noise spectral components.

noise were demonstrated. These methods are used in the denoising at the stage of design of noise cleaning filters.

Theoretically, using linear filtering for image denoising is based on the ideas of *empirical Wiener filtering*. Although, in general, the capability of Wiener filtering for image cleaning from additive noise has certain limitations, as will be demonstrated later in the exercises of this chapter, in its application to cleaning narrow-band noise empirical Wiener filtering proved to be very efficient.

8.3.2 Filtering periodical interferences

As was already mentioned in chapter 5, one of the typical types of narrow-band noise is *periodical noise* (*moiré noise*), which contains only a few isolated components in its DFT or DCT spectra. This exercise demonstrates *rejecting filtering* for image cleaning from this type of noise. Rejecting filtering is a special case of *empirical Wiener filtering*. Empirical Wiener filtering requires detection of noise spectral components and evaluation of their intensity. For this, methods of noise diagnostics demonstrated in chapter 6 can be used. Rejecting filtering requires only detection of moiré noise spectral components because in rejecting filtering the detected noise components are simply eliminated. Two implementations of the rejecting moiré noise filtering are offered: filtering in DFT and filtering in DCT domains. As a test image, one of two prepared images with real (not simulated) noise are suggested in the exercise; the use of another image from the image database is possible as well. As soon as a test image is chosen, the program displays this image and plots row-wise averaged DFT or, correspondingly, DCT power spectrum of image rows and the user is prompted to set a threshold for detecting noise peaks (figure 8.8).

Once the detection threshold is set (values in the range 0.03–0.1 are recommended for the particular program that performs detection of noise spectral component), the program displays the result of the filtering, the difference between initial and filtered images, i.e. filtered noise component, and averaged power spectrum of filtered image rows overlaid on that of the initial image (figure 8.9).

8.4 Filtering 'banding' noise

As was mentioned in chapter 5, 'banding' noise causes chaotic distortions of image signal mean values along a certain direction, usually along image columns or rows.

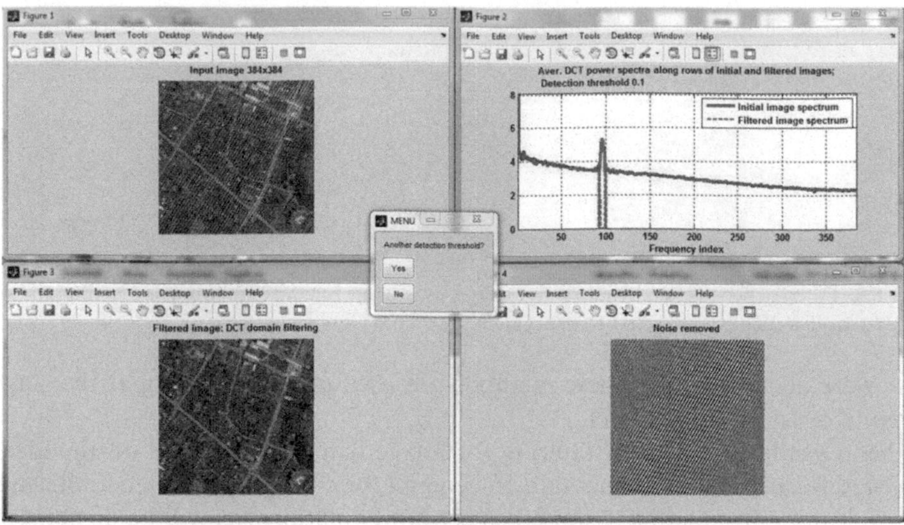

Figure 8.9. Filtering periodical interferences in DCT domain: an example of the final display.

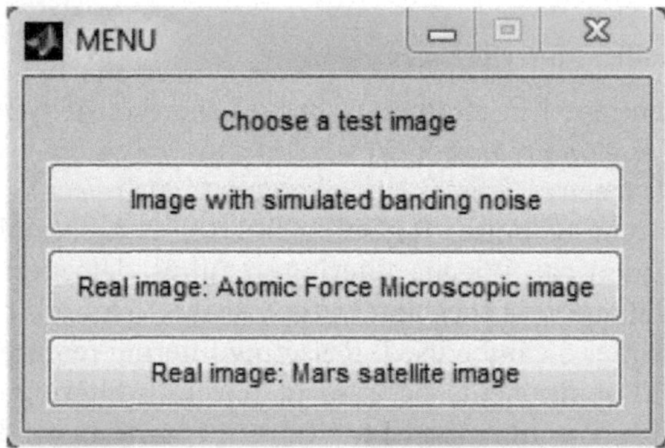

Figure 8.10. Filtering banding noise: start menu.

The latter case is assumed by default in the exercise. Banding noise can be treated as a narrow band noise concentrated in the corresponding projection of image radon transform. To remove this noise, the principle of empirical Wiener filtering can be used. Using noise diagnostic methods demonstrated in section 5.7, the sequence of averaged image mean values along the direction is smoothed, similarly to smoothing averaged image DFT/DCT row-wise spectra in the previous exercise on filtering 'moiré' noise, and then the difference between the initial sequence of image row-wise means and its smoothed copy is subtracted from all pixels of the corresponding image rows.

As test images, three options are offered: simulated banding noise and two images with real not simulated banding interferences (figure 8.10).

If the option 'Image with simulated banding noise' is chosen, the user is prompted to load a test image from the image database and then to set banding noise dynamic

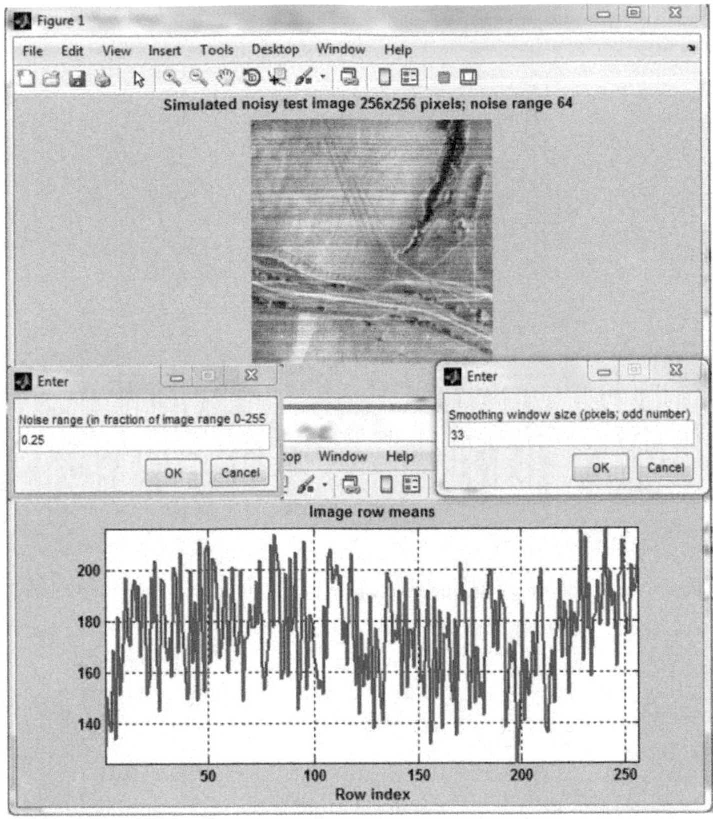

Figure 8.11. Filtering banding noise, case of simulated noise: simulated distorted image, a plot of image row-wise means and prompt panels for setting banding noise dynamic range and window size for smoothing image row-wise means.

range (in fractions of the image range [0–255]). Then the program displays the noisy image and a plot of its row means, after which it prompts the user to set the size of the smoothing window that will be used for smoothing the sequence of local means, using 1D local medians (see chapter 5), in subsequent detection of noise outbursts (figure 8.11).

Once the window size is specified, the program performs the above described estimating banding noise for image rows and removing it and displays the result, as shown in figure 8.12.

When one of two images with real banding noise is chosen for testing, the user has to only set the size of the row-wise means smoothing window. Note, that the test image 'Mars satellite image' is distorted by both row-wise and column-wise banding noise. Therefore, noise cleaning of this image is performed in two passes: row-wise cleaning and then column-wise cleaning. At each pass, smoothing window size is requested and filtering can be repeated with another window size. The resulting display is shown in figure 8.13.

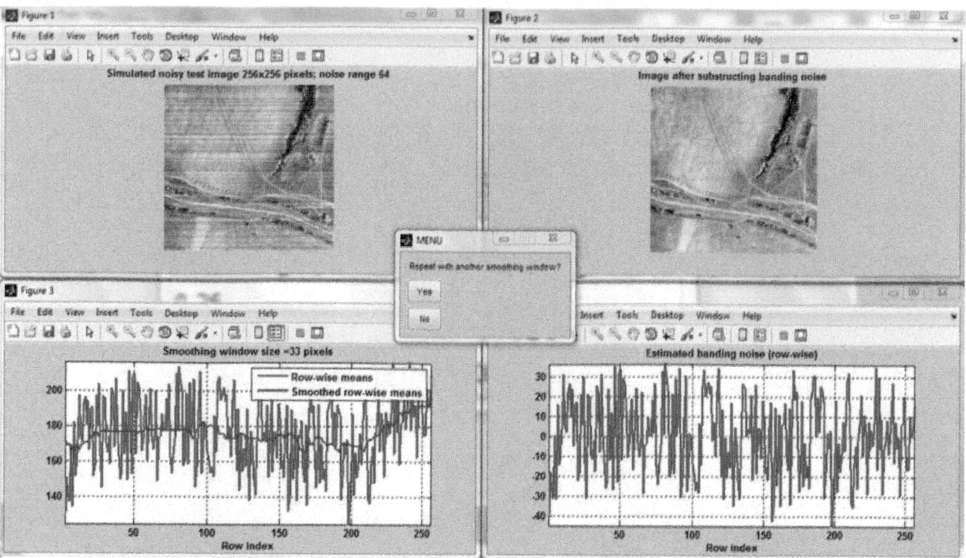

Figure 8.12. Filtering banding noise, case of a simulated noise: final display.

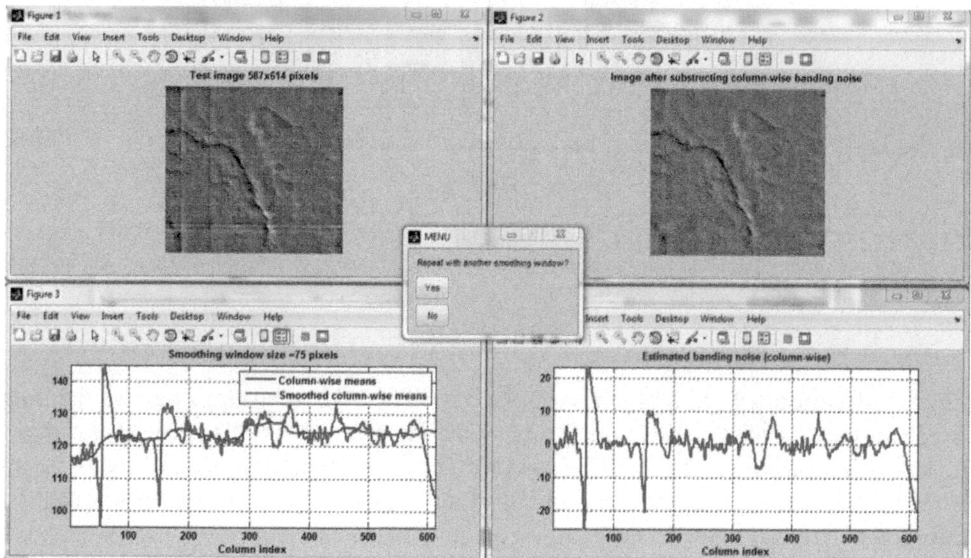

Figure 8.13. Filtering banding noise: real image. Shown is the result of the second pass (column-wise) of the filtering.

8.5 'Ideal' and empirical Wiener filtering for image denoising and deblurring

8.5.1 Introduction

Theoretically, Wiener filtering can be used for both noise cleaning and for correcting image blur caused by weakening image high-frequency components in imaging

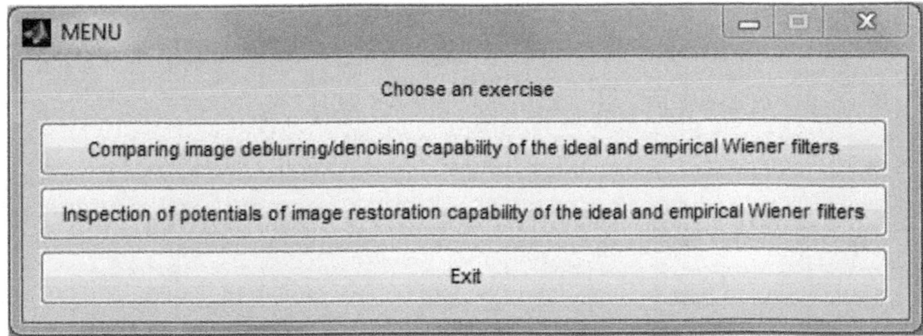

Figure 8.14. Ideal and empirical Wiener filtering: start menu of exercises.

systems. As was mentioned, Wiener filtering is quite efficient for image cleaning from narrow band additive noise, but it has a limited capability of cleaning images from additive broad band noise. Image deblurring capability of Wiener filtering is also limited by the presence of noise.

For designing the ideal Wiener filters, one needs to precisely know power spectra of noise and of the noiseless image. In reality, power spectrum of the noiseless image is not known and the ideal Wiener filter can only be implemented in computer simulation with a known image. For real images, empirical Wiener filters are used. They are designed by means of empirically estimating power spectra of noise and of the noiseless images from spectra of the observed noisy images. Methods for empirical estimation of power spectra of wide band and narrow band noises in images are demonstrated in exercises in chapter 5. Exercises described in section 8.2.2 demonstrate how these estimates can be used for designing empirical Wiener filters for cleaning images from narrow band noise. In exercises in this section listed in the start menu (figure 8.14) ideal and empirical Wiener filter are compared in terms of their capability of denoising images distorted designed by white, i.e. wide band, additive noise.

8.5.2 Comparing image deblurring/denoising capabilities of the ideal and empirical Wiener filters

In this exercise, the ideal and empirical Wiener filter filters are compared in terms of usability for visual analysis of a test image restored (denoised and deblurred) by the filters from its noisy and blurred original for different levels of additive uncorrelated (white) noise and for different degrees of blur by a 'Gaussian' blur function. Both noise and image blur are simulated. Variance of noise is assumed to be known in the simulation. Power spectrum of the noiseless image is estimated as the difference between power spectrum of the distorted image and a known variance of noise times certain noise variance estimation factor of the range (1–2). The latter is needed because power spectra of particular realizations of noise are not uniform and their variances are not exactly equal to the known statistical variance.

For experiments, using as test image of a prepared image 'text' is suggested, although any other image from the user's image data set can be used as well. Before

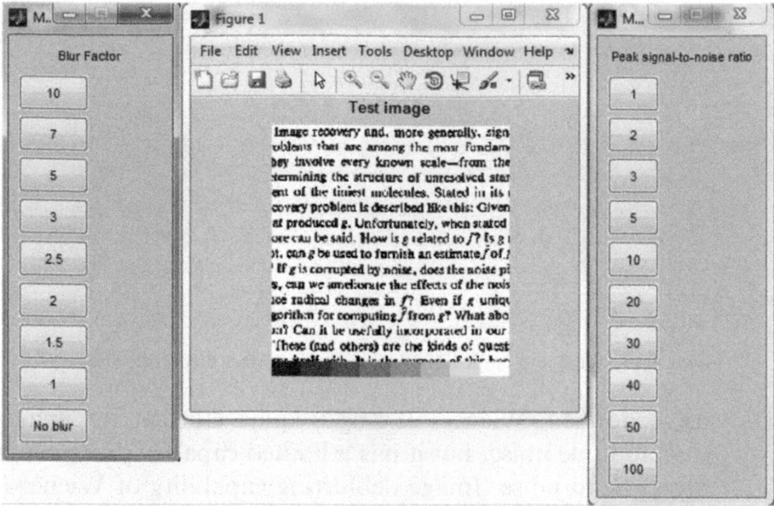

Figure 8.15. Comparing image deblurring/denoising capabilities of the ideal and empirical Wiener filters: parameter menus.

running the program, the user is prompted to choose, from the displayed menus, a blur factor and peak SCR (figure 8.15).

Blur-factor is a value that, roughly, is inversely proportional to the width of Gaussian frequency response of the image blurring filter that will be applied to the test image in order to simulate its blur. There is a 'no blur' option in the menu as well. PSNR is the ratio of image range maximum to the standard deviation of uncorrelated noise added to the blurred image. Once these settings are done, ideal Wiener filtering is performed and the difference between initial non-distorted and distorted images and between the initial image (image distortion) and the image restored by the 'ideal Wiener' filter (restoration error) are displayed for visual evaluation (figure 8.16).

Then the user is prompted to set the noise variance estimation factor needed for implementing the empirical Wiener filter for image denoising and deblurring. Once the setting is done, the filtering is performed and the image restored by the empirical Wiener filter is displayed along with the empirical Wiener filter restoration error. If the empirical Wiener filtering restoration result is not satisfactory, another, usually larger, noise variance estimation factor should be set. An illustrative example of final display is presented in figure 8.17.

8.5.3 Inspection of potentials of image restoration capability of the ideal and empirical Wiener filters

This exercise is aimed at quantitative evaluation of image restoration capability limits of the 'ideal' and empirical Wiener filters, i.e. at determination of the border line in coordinates 'the degree of image blur' and PSNR, above which restoration is possible and beneath which it is not. To this goal, for each particular PSNR from the

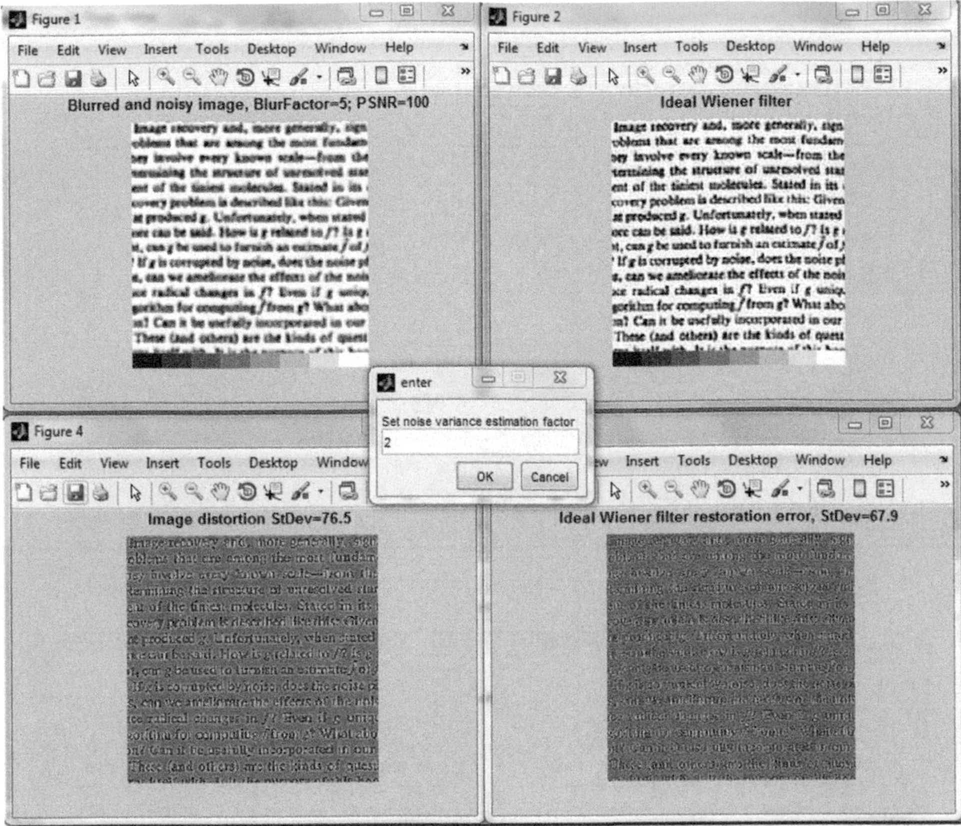

Figure 8.16. Comparing image deblurring/denoising capabilities of the ideal and empirical Wiener filters: an intermediate display and a prompt panel for setting noise variance estimation factor.

set of values (1, 2, 3, 5, 10, 20, 30, 40, 50, 100), the image is subjected to blur with different blur factors, one by one, and then the image distorted in this way is restored by the ideal and by the empirical Wiener filters. Results are displayed one after another, and the user has to decide whether the restored image is readable. One of the intermediate displays is shown in figure 8.18.

Once an acceptable readability is confirmed by the user, the corresponding pair of blur factor and PSNR are stored and the experiment is repeated for the next level of PSNR. As soon as all values of PSNR have been tested for all blur factors, the program plots the stored 'threshold effective bandwidth', corresponding to used blur factors versus respective PSNRs for both 'ideal' and empirical Wiener filters. The meaning of these plots is simple: for pairs 'effective bandwidth' and 'PSNR', which correspond to points above the corresponding curves, filters restore the degraded image satisfactorily, for pairs 'effective bandwidth' and 'PSNR', which correspond to points beneath the curves, filters are not able to satisfactorily restore images. An example of such 'threshold' plots is shown in figure 8.19.

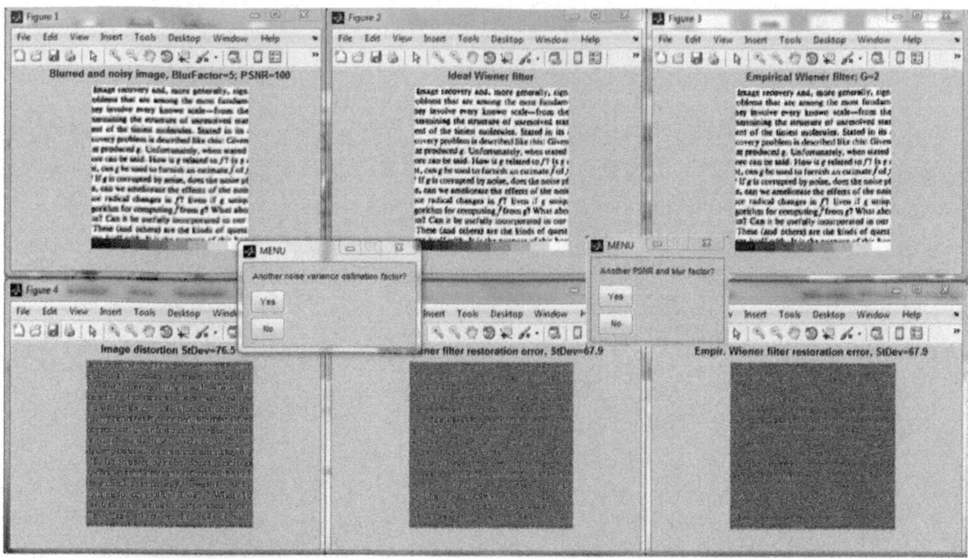

Figure 8.17. Image denoising and deblurring by the 'ideal' and empirical Wiener filters.

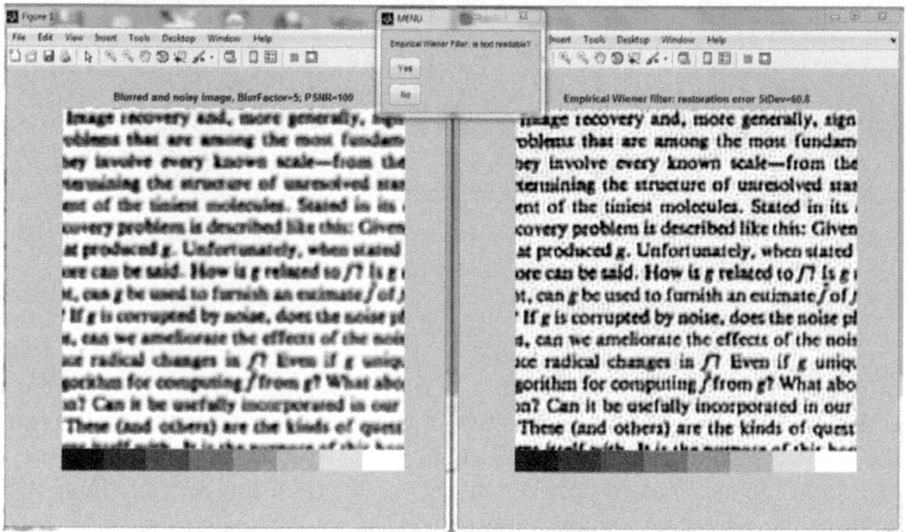

Figure 8.18. Inspection of potentials of image restoration capability of the ideal and empirical Wiener filters: one of the intermediate displays.

8.6 Local adaptive filtering for image denoising: achromatic images

8.6.1 Introduction

Noise suppressing capability of Wiener filters is rooted in the energy compaction property of the transforms studied in the exercises of chapter 2. In the previous

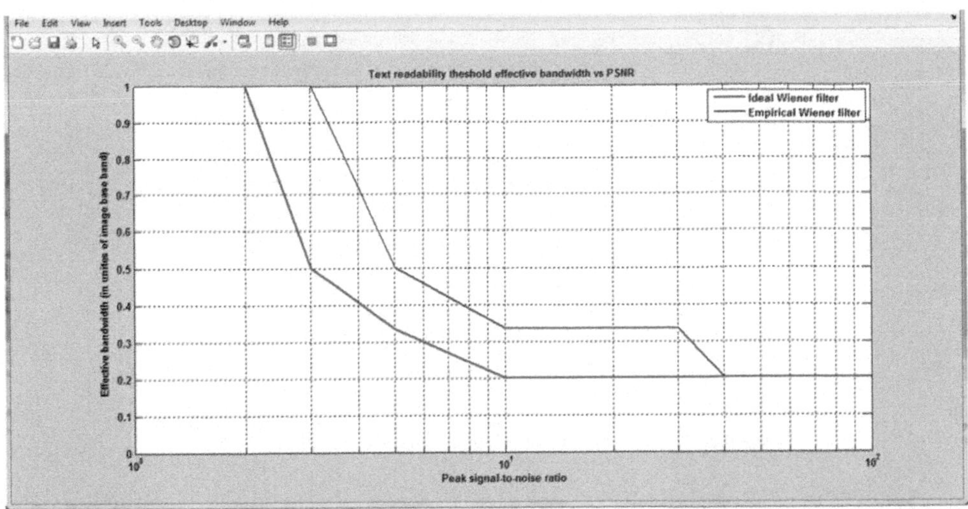

Figure 8.19. Inspection of potentials of image restoration capability of the ideal and empirical Wiener filters: final plots of restoration capability thresholds.

exercises in this chapter, Wiener filtering was applied 'globally', i.e. to entire image frames. However, images that contain sets of isolated objects separated by object borders are very inhomogeneous in terms of their local spectra: local spectra of sufficiently small image fragments, which, at the same time, are large enough to contain at least one object, vary very substantially from one fragment to another. The exercise 'Image power spectra' in chapter 5 demonstrates this phenomenon. Therefore, to make full use of the transform energy compaction property, one should apply Wiener filtering locally to image individual fragments rather than globally. Such filtering will obviously be local adaptive as filter frequency responses will be built on the base of estimation of image local spectra in each window position.

Exercises in this section (figure 8.20) implement this idea of local adaptive empirical Wiener filtering in a running window.

8.6.2 1D denoising filtering

In the exercises in local adaptive filtering for denoising 1D signals, two options are offered for choosing test signals: realizations of computer generated pseudo-random piece-wise constant signals and a sample electrocardiogram. Filtering in two transform domains, Haar and discrete cosine transform, can be tested. Implemented is the *'rejective' filter* that sets transform coefficients, which are below a certain filtering threshold, to zero and does not modify all other coefficients. At the beginning, the user is prompted first to choose a test signal, then to choose a transform, in which domain filtering will be performed and finally to specify level of noise (in the units of the signal range) that will be added to test signal, filter window size (in the case of working in Haar transform domain window size must be an integer power of two) and the filtering threshold. The latter is determined by noise standard deviation and,

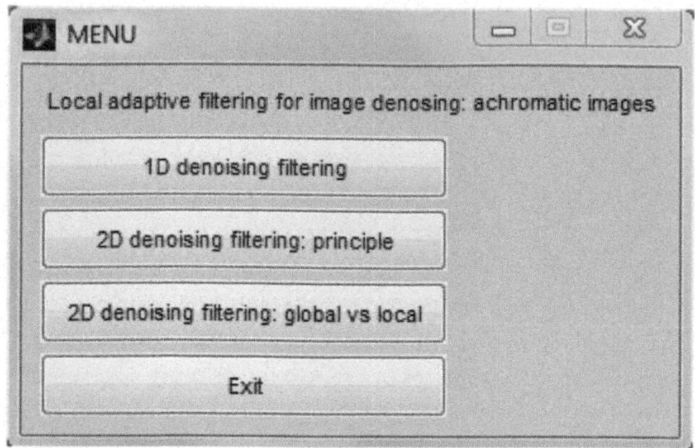

Figure 8.20. Local adaptive filtering for image denoising: start menu.

Figure 8.21. 1D denoising filtering: three successive pop-up menus.

therefore, has to be of the same order of magnitude. The three starting successive pop-up menus are shown in figure 8.21.

Once filtering parameters are set, the program performs filtering and displays results in four subplots, as illustrated in figure 8.22.

The first, from top to bottom, subplot is the chosen test signal with added noise. The second subplot is an image whose columns present for each position of the sliding window central sample, local transform spectra with intensities of spectral coefficients represented by gray levels of the corresponding pixels. The third subplot is the same spectral image after thresholding. These two subplots are what is called *'time-frequency' signal representation.* The fourth subplot shows output filtered signal. The user has a possibility to visually evaluate the filtering quality and to try to optimize filter parameters (window size and filtering threshold) to achieve the best possible result.

8.6.3 2D denoising filtering: principle

2D *local adaptive linear filtering* is performed by means of scanning the input image row-wise/column-wise with a moving window. At each window position, an estimate of the central pixel of the window is produced, using either empirical Wiener or

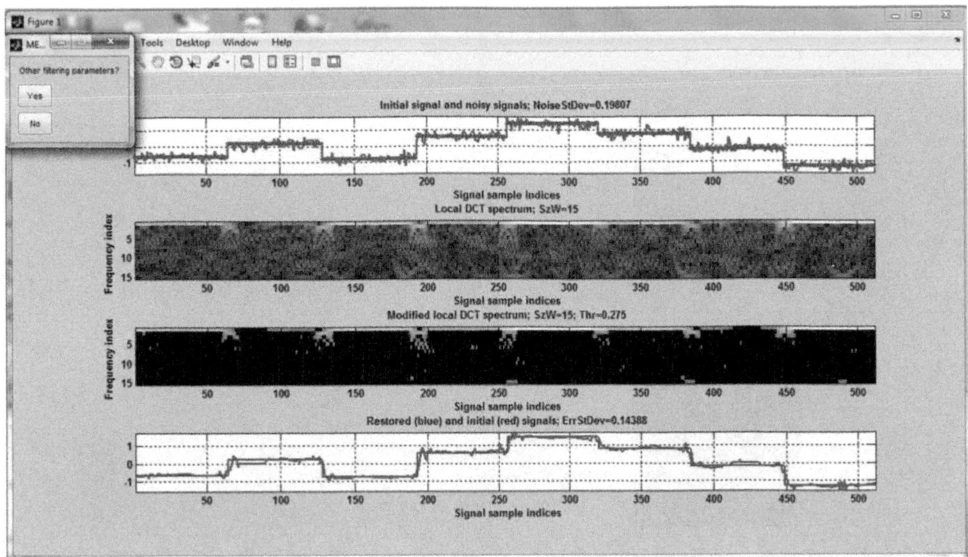

Figure 8.22. 1D denoising filtering: a pseudo-random piece wise constant test signal.

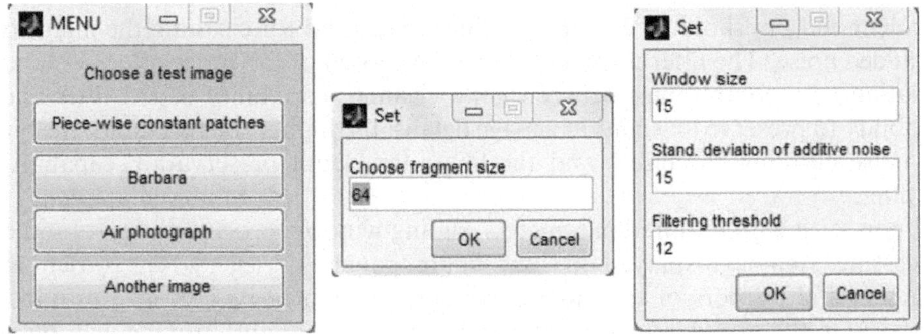

Figure 8.23. 2D denoising filtering: principle. Parameter pop up menus.

rejective filter designed in DCT domain for the image fragment within the window. In such a way, the output image is generated pixel by pixel. The exercisc in this section provides a vivid illustration of this filtering principle.

At the start, the program prompts the user to choose one of two prepared test images or any other image from the image database (figure 8.23, left panel). Then the chosen image is displayed and the user is prompted to set the size of a fragment of the chosen image to work with (figure 8.23, middle panel) and to choose the position of the fragment in the chosen test image. It is recommended to work with sufficiently small fragments, otherwise completion of the exercise may take considerable time, because displaying each step of sliding window processing is a very time consuming operation.

The third step at the start of the program is setting filtering parameters: window size, standard deviation of normal noise to be added to the chosen test image

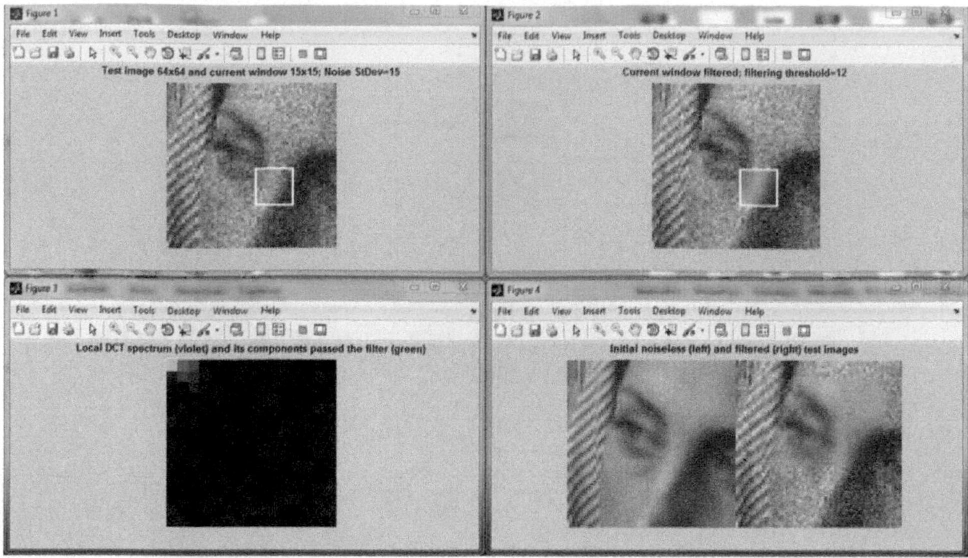

Figure 8.24. 2D denoising filtering: principle, a work in progress display.

fragment and threshold of the rejective filter to be used for cleaning the image from the added noise. The filter threshold should be chosen of the order of noise standard deviation as a compromise between noise cleaning capability of the filter and its capability to preserve low contrast image details: the higher the threshold, the higher the noise cleaning capability and the lower the detail preservation capability of the filter.

Upon setting all required parameters, sliding window processing starts and each processing step is displayed in four figure panels (figure 8.24): chosen noisy fragment and borders of the moving window in each of its current positions are displayed in the upper left panel; chosen noisy fragment and moving window with filtered window image are displayed in the upper right panel; current local DCT spectrum of the window is displayed in violet and its components that have passed the rejecting filter are displayed green in the bottom left panel; filtered chosen noisy fragment at the current filter window position is displayed in the bottom right panel. Note that only the inner part of the fragment is filtered, within a square bounded half window size from fragment borders. The experiment can be repeated with other filter parameters in order to explore their influence on output image quality.

8.6.4 2D denoising filtering: global versus local

This exercise allows one to evaluate noise suppression and edge preservation capability of local adaptive DCT domain empirical Wiener filtering and compare them with those of global filtering. For exercises, a prepared piece-wise constant image or any other image from the image database can be used as a test image.

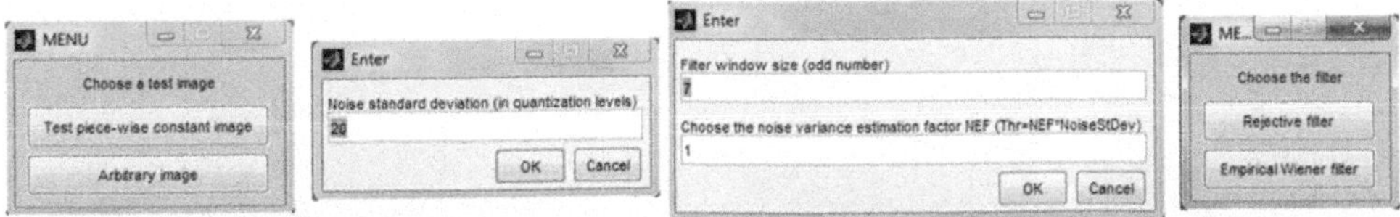

Figure 8.25. 2D denoising filtering: global vs local, parameter pop-up menus.

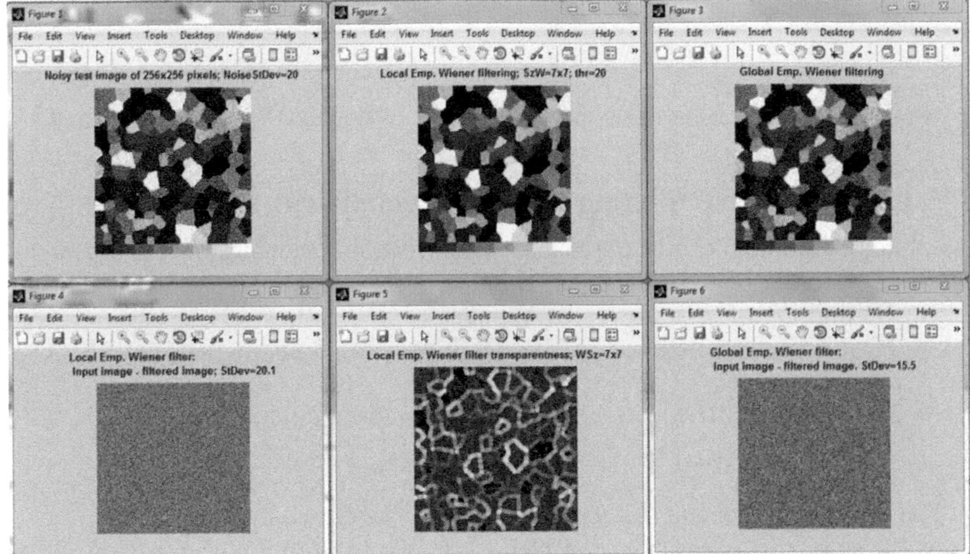

Figure 8.26. An example of 2D local adaptive image denoising filtering: piece-wise constant test image.

At the program start, it prompts the user to set standard deviation of noise (in units of image gray levels) to be added to the chosen test image, displays the noised image and then prompts one to set filter window size and the noise variance estimation factor, similarly to how it is done in the first exercise (global filtering), and finally to choose the filter type ('rejective' or 'empirical Wiener' filter). All these successive start menus are shown in figure 8.25.

Once filter parameters are set, the program displays the result of application of the chosen filter to the entire test image and the difference between input noiseless image and filtered noisy image and then starts local filtering. Results of local filtering are displayed after processing each of 16 rows. Displayed are input noisy image, output filtered images obtained by local and global filtering, corresponding differences between the initial noisy image and filtered images image and a map isomorphic to the image of the number of filter frequency response non-zero coefficients in the window (in fractions of the window size) for each window position in the scan process. This fraction, called the '*filter transparentness*', is a value between zero and one and is encoded, for display purposes, as image gray levels. Figure 8.26 illustrates the final display. The experiment can be repeated with other filter parameters in order to explore how filter parameters affect output image quality.

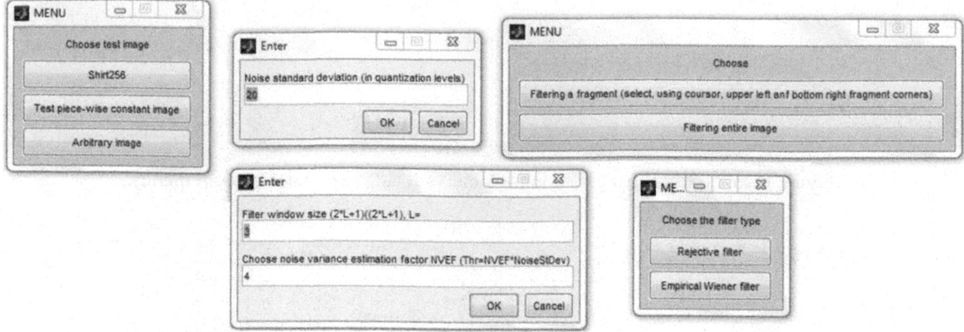

Figure 8.27. Local adaptive filtering for image denoising: color images, parameter pop-up menus.

8.7 Local adaptive filtering for image denoising: color images

Local adaptive filters can be applied for denoising color images in four ways:

- 2D filtering of separate R, G, B image components
- 2D filtering of separate Y, U, V image components
- 3D filtering carried out in 3D DCT spectral domain of image R, G, B components
- 3D filtering carried out in 3D DCT spectral domain of image Y, U, V components

The exercise implements all four of these options for comparison.

At the start, the user is first prompted to choose as a test image either one of two prepared images or any other color image from the image data set, then to specify standard deviation of noise to be added to the chosen test image for subsequent cleaning and to choose either to process an image fragment or the entire image. In the former case the user has to indicate on the displayed test image, using a cross cursor, upper left and bottom right corners of the chosen image rectangular fragment. The next two steps are setting filter window dimensions, noise variance estimation factor and choosing one of two modifications of the filter, rejective filter or empirical Wiener filter. Figure 8.27 shows these parameter prompt menus.

Once all required filter parameters are set, the program displays the initial noiseless test image, the test image with noise added and results of the above-mentioned four types of filtering. In the titles of corresponding figures, standard deviation of filtering errors, i.e. of differences between original noiseless image and results of filtering, are indicated.

8.8 Filtering impulsive noise using linear filters

Impulsive noise is a type of noise specifically characteristic for digital imaging systems. As indicated in chapter 5, impulsive noise results in the replacement of values of randomly, with a certain probability of error, selected pixels by random gray levels in the image dynamic range or with binary equiprobable gray levels of the minimum and maximum of the image dynamic range. In the latter case, noise is

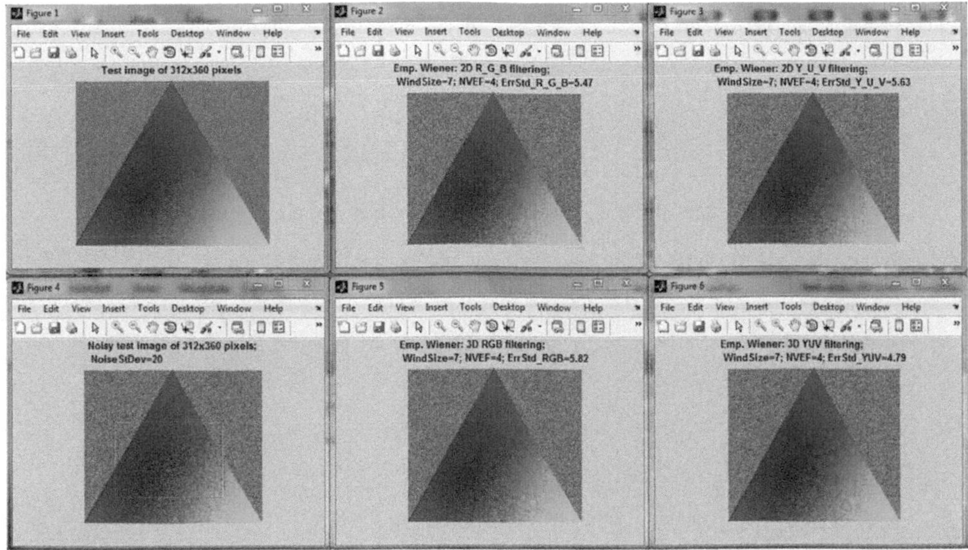

Figure 8.28. Local adaptive filtering for image denoising: color images. An example of a display with processing results. Borders of processed image fragment are shown in red in left bottom image.

called *pepper and salt noise*, as it appears as isolated contrast white and black dots in images.

The main problem in filtering impulsive noise is detection of distorted pixels. When distorted pixels are detected, their gray levels can be replaced by values obtained by means of one or another averaging of gray values of non-distorted pixels in their neighborhood. This is justified by the fact that normally gray levels of adjacent pixels do not differ much one from another.

For detecting distorted pixels, linear filters of SCR ratio optimal correlators for target detection addressed in chapter 7 can be used. Since in this particular case targets are individual pixels, image spectrum whitening using the 2D 'Laplacian' operator (section 7.5.1) proved to be a sufficiently good practical solution for image pre-filtering before comparing it with a detection threshold. One should note that unless the probability of distorting pixels is sufficiently low, there might be many places where two or more adjacent pixels are distorted. This may substantially hamper detection of distorted pixels.

In the exercise, two methods that use linear filters for detection and for filtering general impulsive and pepper and salt noise are demonstrated:

1. Iterative filtering, in which, at each iteration step, detection of distorted pixels is first performed by comparing the result of applying to the iterated image of the 2D Laplacian with a detection threshold. Then pixels detected as distorted are replaced by the average over those pixels in their 3×3 neighborhood, which were not marked as distorted at the detection stage. The detection threshold is proportional to the standard deviation of the difference signal; the proportionality factor is a user-defined parameter. The number of iterations is also to be set by the user.

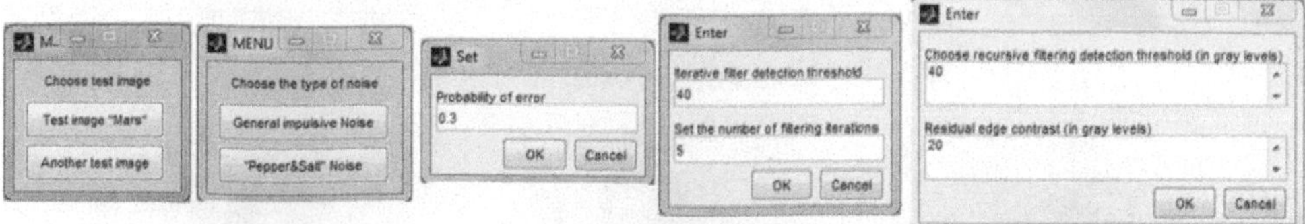

Figure 8.29. Filtering impulsive noise: parameter pop-up menus.

Figure 8.30. Filtering impulsive noise: filtering results.

2. Recursive filtering is performed in the process of image scanning row-wise/column-wise. In this process, for each current pixel, a difference between its gray level and the average AV over its four neighboring already processed pixels (three on the preceding row and one preceding pixel in the current row) is compared with a detection threshold. If this difference exceeds the threshold, the current pixel gray level is replaced by the above average plus or minus (depending on the sign of the difference), an edge preservation threshold ('residual edge contrast'). Both the detection threshold and the edge preservation threshold are user-defined parameters of the algorithm.

At the start of the exercise, the user is prompted to choose, as test image, either a prepared image, or any other image from the image database. Then the user has an option to choose perform the exercise with one of two types of noise: 'general impulsive noise' or 'pepper and salt noise'. For both types of noise, the user is then prompted to set the probability of error for simulation of noise as well as the detection threshold and the number of iterations for the iterative filter and the detection threshold and the 'residual edge contrast' for the recursive filter. These successive parameter menus are presented in figure 8.29.

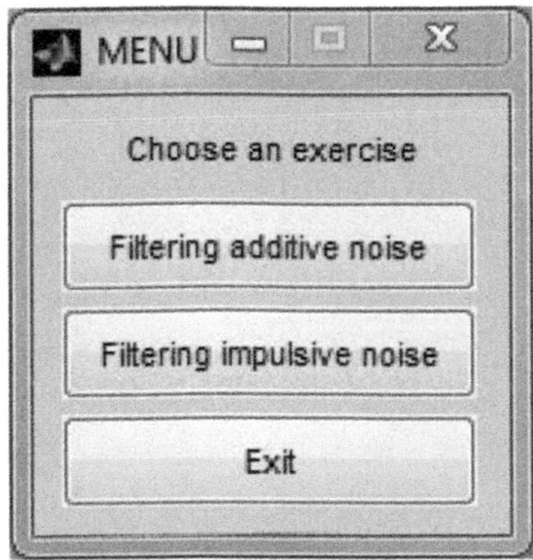

Figure 8.31. Image denoising using nonlinear (rank) filters: start menu.

The process of filtering is displayed in real time. Titles of the corresponding figures contain filtering parameters and standard deviation of filtering error (in units of gray levels). An example of the final display is presented in figure 8.30.

8.9 Image denoising using nonlinear (rank) filters

The main acting engine of the above filtering methods is linear filtering, i.e. weighted summation, for each pixel, of pixels in its spatial neighborhood for generating filtered image pixels or other relevant measures for deciding, when it is required, whether pixels are distorted. Theoretically, non-linear filters, being a general case, may have higher image denoising potentials.

An important subset of non-linear filters is that of '*rank filters*', which generate image pixel estimates on the base of image local order statistics or histograms. Exercises of this section demonstrate image denoising capability of two particular rank filters, one for cleaning additive noise and another for cleaning impulsive noise (figure 8.31).

8.9.1 Filtering additive noise

The first exercise demonstrates applying two kindred rank filters, *mean-EV filter* and *median-EV-filter*, for image cleaning from additive noise. The filters work in a moving window of a certain dimension as the above local adaptive linear filters do and generate estimates of pixel gray levels as a mean value, or, correspondingly, median over pixels' *EV-neighborhood* (see exercises in section 5.4.2). Window dimensions and lower and upper borders of EV-neighborhood are user-defined parameters. For better efficiency, the filtering is carried out iteratively, using, at each iteration, the image obtained in the previous iteration as the input to the filter. The number of iterations is also a user-defined parameter.

These filters are most efficient in cleaning noise with values in a limited range [−Min, +Max]. If the range is known, its borders can be taken as borders of EV-neighborhoods. In the program designed for this exercise, the noise dynamic

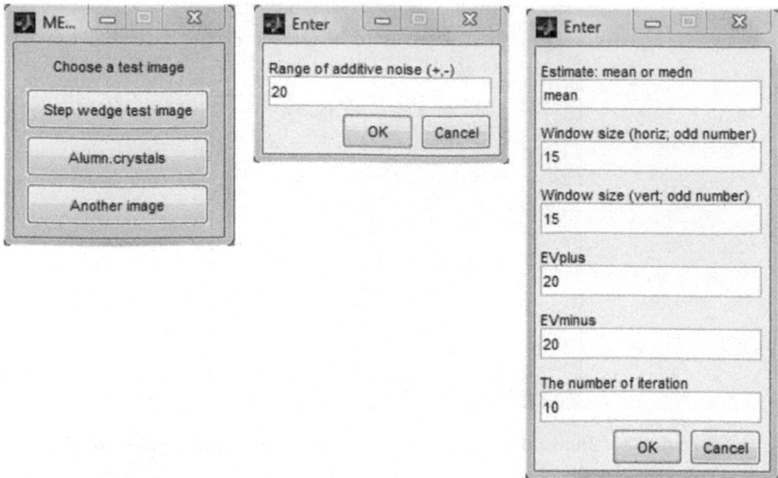

Figure 8.32. Filtering additive noise: filter parameter prompt panels.

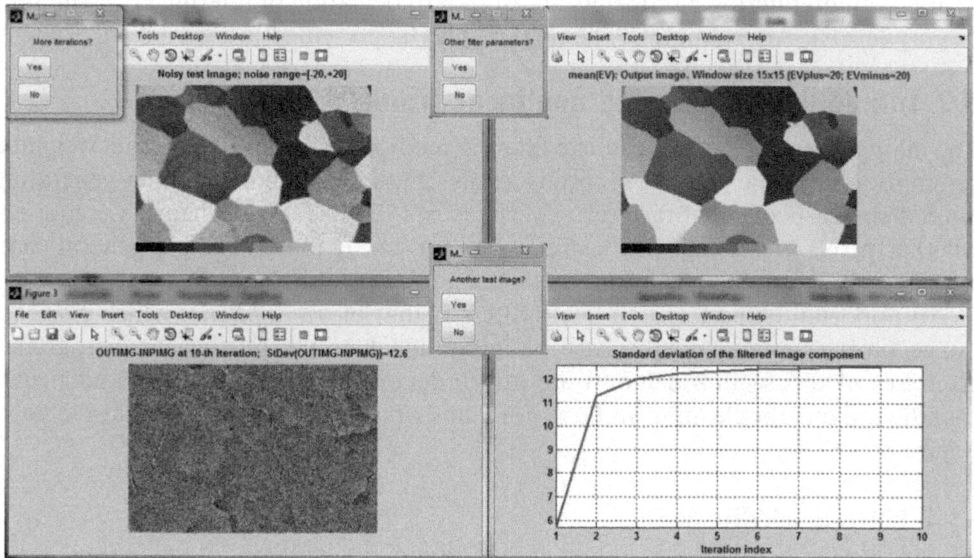

Figure 8.33. Mean-EV filtering additive noise of a limited range (Rng).

range is symmetrical with respect to zero (−Min = Max). This range is also a user-defined parameter. As test images, two prepared images as well as the option of loading another test image from the image data set are suggested. Figure 8.32 shows parameter pop-up menus for these filters.

Once the test image is chosen and filter parameters are set, the program starts filtering iterations. At each iteration, the program displays in real time of processing noisy input image, filtered output image, their difference, i.e. the filtered out component of the noisy image, and a graph of standard deviation of the difference as a function of the iteration number. A sample of the final display is presented in figure 8.33.

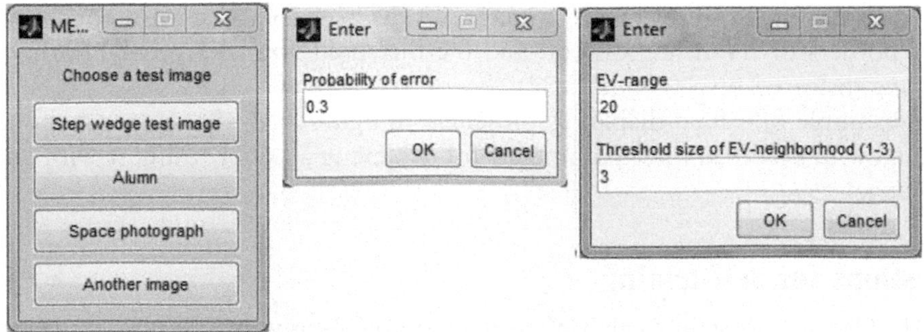

Figure 8.34. Filtering impulsive noise: parameter pop-up menus.

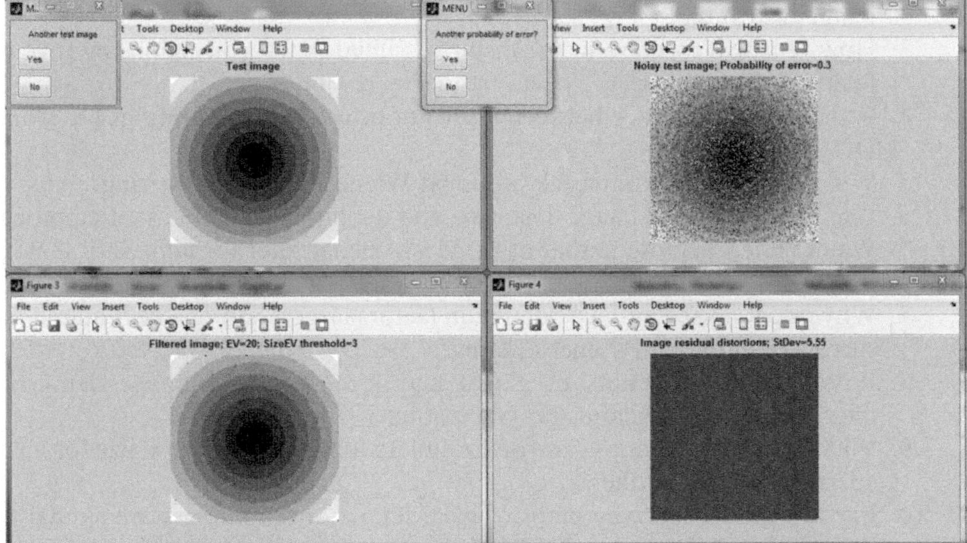

Figure 8.35. Filtering impulsive noise: an example of final display.

8.9.2 Filtering impulsive noise

This exercise demonstrates a rank filter for cleaning impulsive noise. The filter works in the window of 3 × 3 pixels and uses for detecting distorted pixels a parameter *Size-EV*, which, for each pixel, is the number of window pixels that belong to its EV-neighborhood. The borders of the EV-neighborhood are the user-defined parameter. When *Size-EV* is lower than a certain user-defined detection threshold, the pixel is considered as being an isolated outburst and its gray level is replaced by the average of those pixels of 3 × 3 neighborhood, which are not found to be distorted.

The program works in two passes: detection of distorted pixels (first pass) and correction of detected pixels (second pass). As test images, either one of three prepared test images or any other image from the image database can be used. At the start, the user is prompted to select a test image, set the probability of error for simulating noise, borders of EV-neighborhood and the threshold size of EV-neighborhood for detecting distorted pixels (figure 8.34).

An example of a final display is presented in figure 8.35. The experiment can be repeated with modified filter parameters for achieving a better result or with another test image.

Questions for self-testing

1. How would you explain the reduction of the number of non-zero beans in histograms of images after correction of their non-linear gray scale distortions (figures 8.4 and 8.5)?
2. How sensitive to noise in the distorted signal is the correction of gray scale image distortions?
3. How sensitive to noise in the distorted signal is the correction, by inverse filtering, of the imaging system frequency response?
4. Is there any difference between results of moiré noise filtering in DFT and DCT domains?
5. What is the major drawback of global Wiener denoising filtering?
6. Can one assert that image denoising and deblurring capability of empirical Wiener filters is close to that of the ideal Wiener filter for high SNRs? Why this is so?
7. Why might noise variance estimation factors larger than one be required for successful empirical Wiener filtering?
8. If you compare results of global and local adaptive image denoising filtering, what distinctions do you see first?
9. What recommendations can you formulate for setting window size for local adaptive denoising filters?
10. Explain the reason why maps of local filter transparentness are similar to those of image local standard deviations, such as shown in Figure 5.7.
11. Why do local adaptive denoising filters exhibit edge preserving capability?
12. How can one interpret images of difference between noisy input and filtered images for local adaptive denoising filters from the point of view of characterization of filter performance?
13. What filtering artifacts have you noticed in local adaptive denoising filtering?
14. Which modification of local adaptive filters for processing of color images, 2D filtering of separate to R, G, B image component, 2D filtering of separate to Y, U, V image component, filtering in 3D DCT spectrum of image R, G, B components or filtering in 3D DCT spectrum of image Y, U, V components appears more efficient in terms of noise suppressing and edge preserving capability?
15. Do the mean-EV and median-EV image denoising filters exhibit an edge preserving capability?

16. Does the optimal value of the threshold size of EV-neighborhood for detecting distorted pixels in the Size-EV-based impulsive noise filter depend on the probability of pixel distortions (probability of error)?
17. On what property of images do the optimal borders of EV-neighborhood depend in the Size-EV-based impulsive noise filter?

Chapter 9

Methods of image enhancement

9.1 Introduction

Image enhancement is processing aimed at assisting visual image analysis and facilitating image-based decision making. This usually requires certain purposeful distortions of row images, such as emphasizing some details and eliminating others, displaying hidden pixel attributes, making details which are invisible due to low contrast or other factors, visible, visualizing numerical image parameters, outlining borders of objects, etc. Image enhancement is an essentially interactive process carried out under expert user control.

Exercises collected in this chapter, represent most typical methods of enhancement of achromatic and color images (figure 9.1).

9.2 Enhancement of achromatic images

Exercises in enhancement of achromatic images are listed in the start menu shown in figure 9.2. They implement various methods of image contrast enhancement and edge detection.

9.2.1 Contrast enhancement

The following four methods of contrast enhancement are suggested for the training: *unsharp masking*, *Pth law image spectrum enhancement*, *P-histogram equalization* and the *method of local cardinalities*. The first two methods enhance contrasts of image details by means of amplification of image high-frequency spectral components in the transform domain, and specifically, DCT domain. The last two methods display pixel attributes other than gray levels, specifically pixel ranks and cardinalities, which also result in image contrast enhancement. For all exercises, a set of prepared test images is suggested. The use of any other images from the user's image database is possible as well.

doi:10.1088/978-0-7503-1233-2ch9

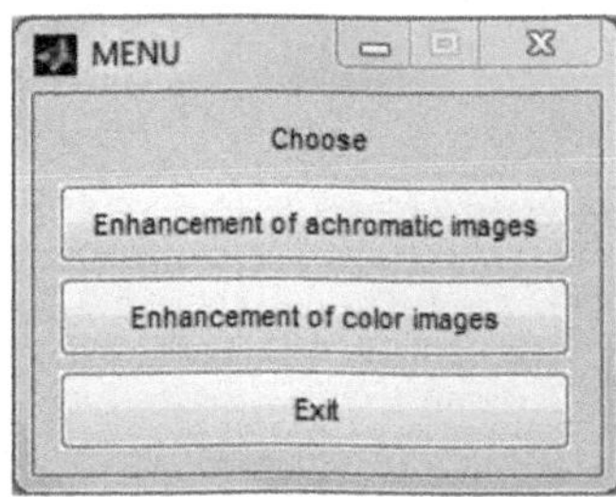

Figure 9.1. Image enhancement: start menu.

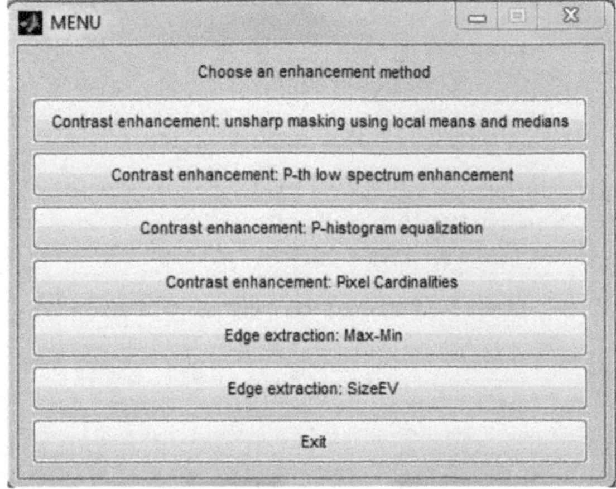

Figure 9.2. Enhancement of achromatic images: start menu.

Contrast enhancement: Unsharp masking using local means and medians

Unsharp masking is one of the earliest methods of image enhancement. It dates back even to pre-computer era photography. Unsharp masking consists in computing and displaying for visual analysis the difference between the image and its unsharp (blurred) copy generated by one or another image smoothing method. Due to this subtraction, low frequency components in the image are weakened, and, therefore, the weight of image low-intensity high-frequency components in the image spectrum is correspondingly amplified.

The two simplest and fastest image smoothing methods, smoothing by local mean and local median (see exercises in chapter 5), are implemented in this exercise. At the program start, a list of test images is displayed and the user is prompted to set vertical and horizontal dimensions of the smoothing window (figure 9.3). One this is done, the program displays the chosen test image, two processed versions of the test image, i.e. its differences with local means and local medians computed in the chosen window, and a difference between local means and local medians themselves. The latter illustrates distinctions between local means and local medians for different images. An example of the final display for this exercise is presented in figure 9.4.

Figure 9.3. Unsharp masking: start menus.

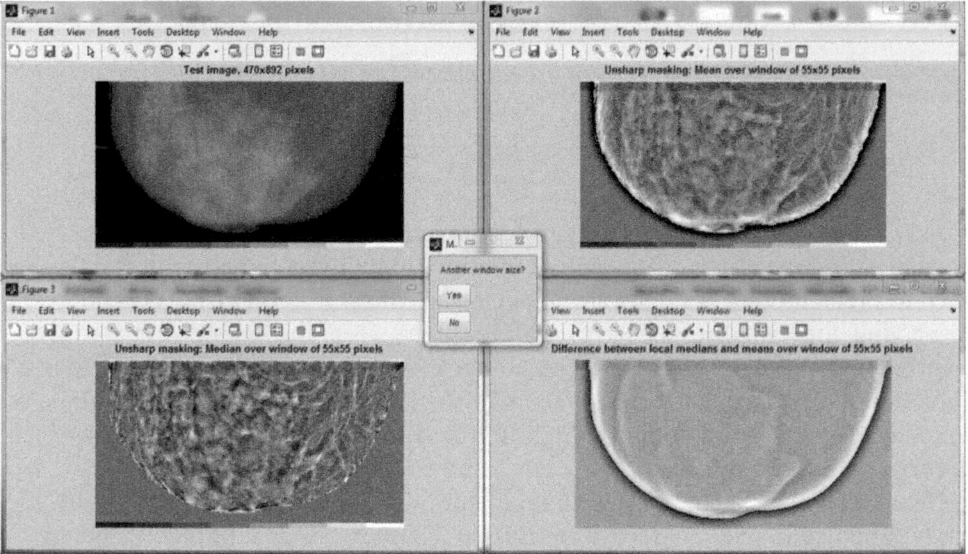

Figure 9.4. Unsharp masking using local image means and medians.

Contrast enhancement: P*th law spectrum enhancement*

*P*th law image spectrum enhancement is also an image enhancement method that redistributes image energy in favor of its high-frequency components. This is achieved by means of rising absolute values of image spectral components to a power $P \leqslant 1$. The exercise allows evaluating efficiency of both versions in

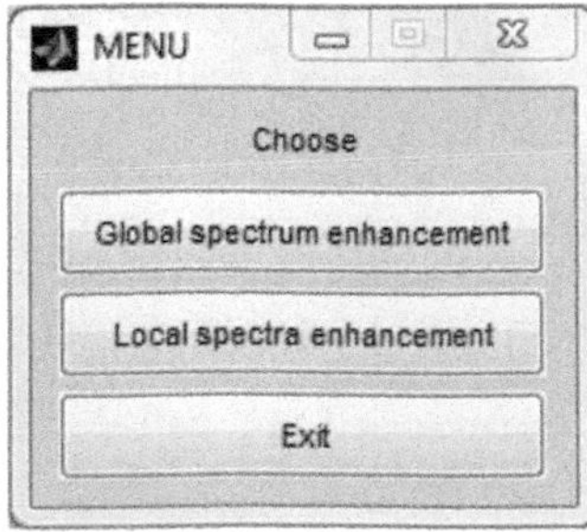

Figure 9.5. *P*th low spectrum enhancement: menu.

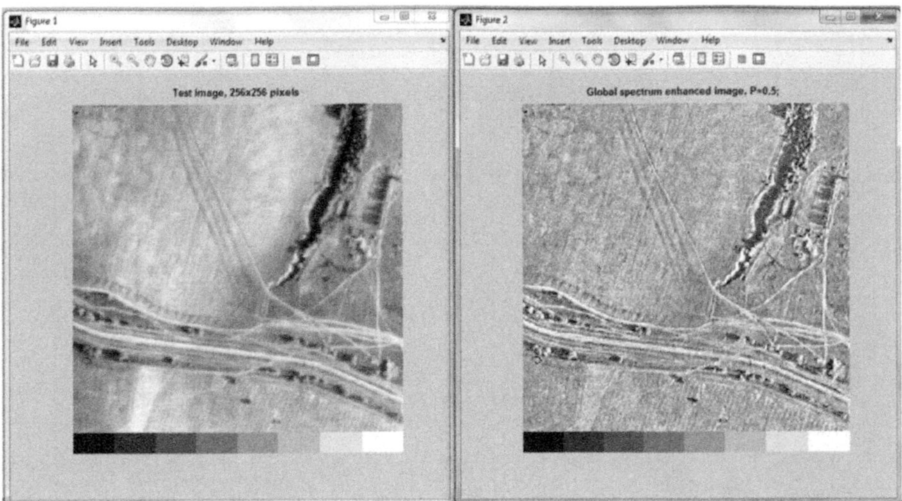

Figure 9.6. *P*th law global spectrum enhancement.

application to various pre-prepared images or to images from the user's image database (see the list in figure 9.3). The method can be applied both globally to the entire image spectrum and locally in a moving window (figure 9.5).

For global spectra enhancement, the user is prompted to specify the spectrum enhancement parameter $P \leqslant 1$, and the program displays the chosen test and processed images (figure 9.6).

Local spectrum enhancement is supplemented in the exercise with an opportunity to simultaneously suppress additive noise in images using a local adaptive filter similar to that studied in chapter 8. Hence, it requires, in addition to the spectrum enhancement parameter $P < 1$, specification of the sliding window vertical and horizontal dimensions, filtering threshold and spectrum amplification factor $G \geqslant 1$. The latter multiplies *P*th law modified local spectral components left after thresholding (figure 9.7). An example of a final display is shown in figure 9.8.

Contrast enhancement: P-*histogram equalization and pixel cardinalities*

P-histogram equalization and *pixel cardinalities* are contrast enhancement methods that deal with pixel ranks and cardinalities as pixel attributes (see exercises in section 5.4.1).

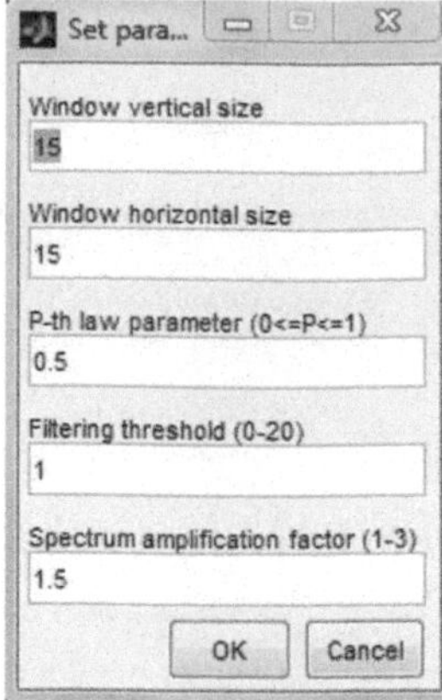

Figure 9.7. Pth law local spectra enhancement: filter parameter menu.

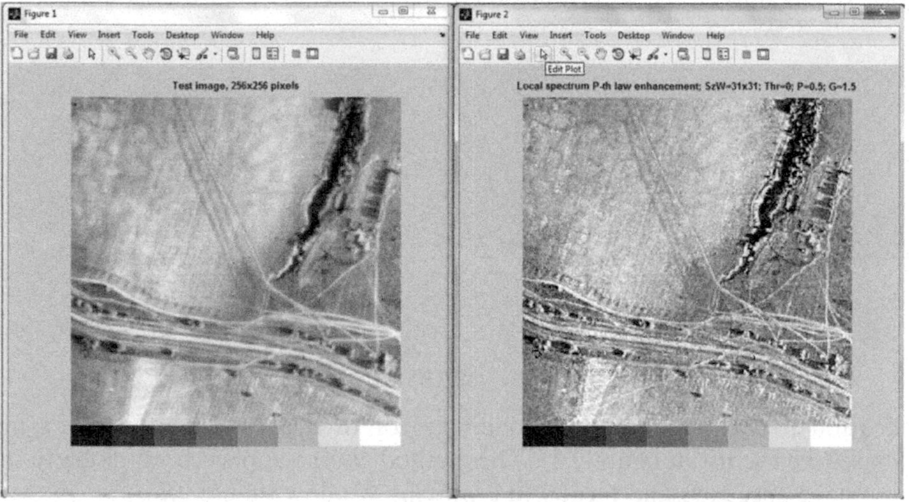

Figure 9.8. *P*th law local spectrum enhancement: initial test and enhanced images.

P-histogram equalization is a generalization of the popular method of image *histogram equalization*. Whereas in histogram equalization pixel gray levels are modified according to a look-up table built by means of the cumulative summation of the image histogram, in the *P*-histogram equalization the look-up table is built by means of the cumulative summation of histogram bins raised to a power P, which can be any real number between zero and one. The case $P = 1$ corresponds to the regular histogram equalization. When $P = 0$, the actual pixel gray level range is linearly stretched to the entire image dynamic range 0–255. Intermediate values of P provide a kind of 'softened' histogram equalization.

At the start, the user is prompted to choose a test image from a list shown in figure 9.3, and the way of applying the method, globally and locally (figure 9.9).

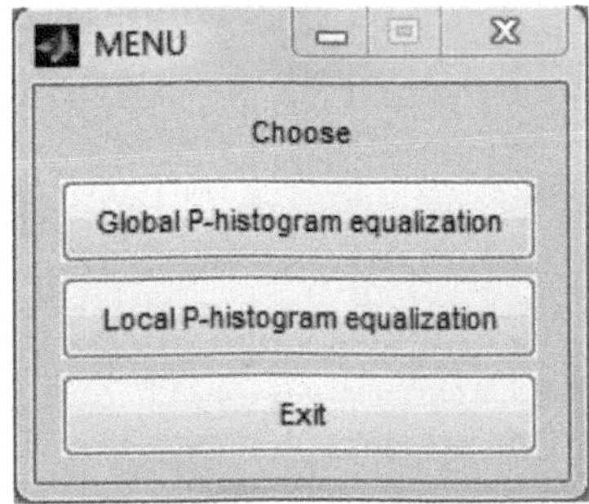

Figure 9.9. *P*-histogram equalization: start menu.

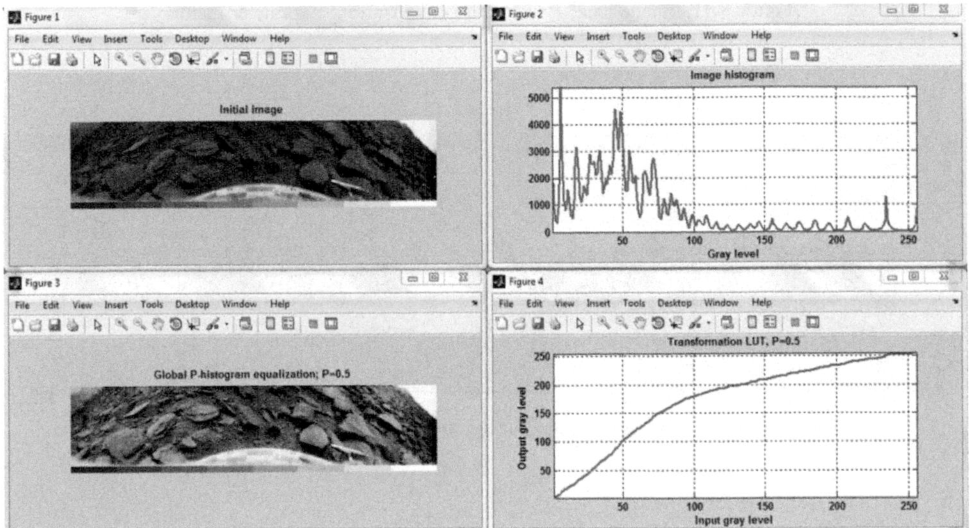

Figure 9.10. Image global *P*-histogram equalization.

For global *P*-histogram equalization, the user is prompted to set the value of the parameter *P* and displayed are the chosen test image, resulting image and plots of initial image histogram and of the transformation look-up table (figure 9.10).

For local *P*-histogram equalization, window horizontal and vertical dimensions are user defined parameters (figure 9.11) and displayed are the initial and resulting images (figure 9.12.).

An alternative image histogram based contrast enhancement method is the method of computing and displaying image cardinalities, i.e. replacement of pixel gray levels by the number of pixels that have the same gray level (with the corresponding normalization). This can be applied either globally to the entire image frame (figure 9.13) or locally in a moving window, as illustrated in figure 9.14.

For some images, the results of displaying image local cardinalities are more suitable for visual analysis if they are displayed in a compressed dynamic range. This option is offered at the end of the exercise. For image dynamic range compression, *P*th law transformation with $P = 0.3$ is applied to image gray levels.

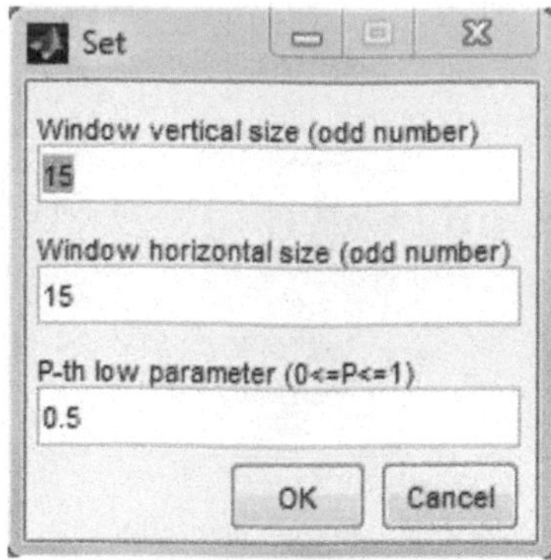

Figure 9.11. Image local *P*-histogram equalization: parameter menu.

Figure 9.12. Image global *P*-histogram equalization: final display.

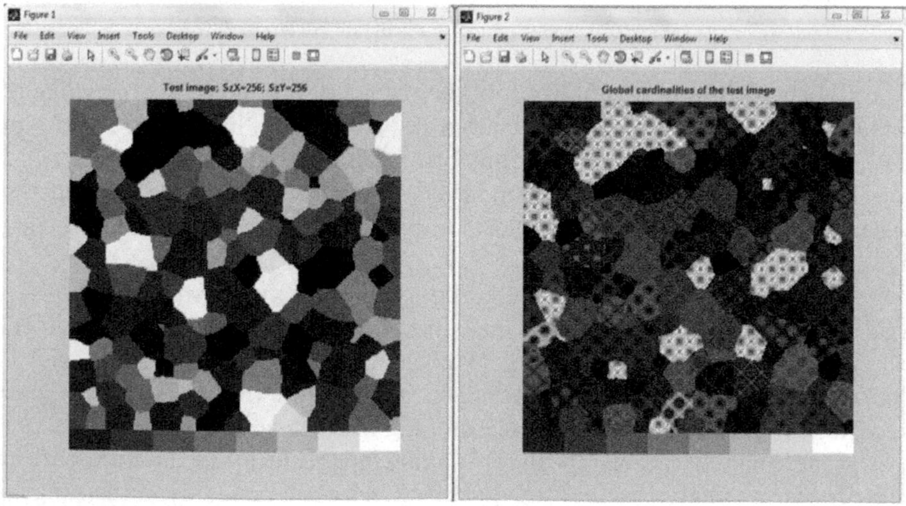

Figure 9.13. Image global cardinalities: initial test and processed images. The pattern seen in the processed image has too low a contrast to be visible in the initial image.

Figure 9.14. Image local cardinalities: initial and processed images. Fine structures invisible in the initial image become visible in the processed image.

9.2.2 Edge extraction: Max–Min and Size-EV methods

As an image enhancement method, edge extraction is processing aimed at extracting and visualizing information on object borders. There are numerous edge extraction methods. Most of them are based on various kinds of differential operators and are sensitive to orientation of borders. In this section two simple, robust and insensitive to edge orientation methods are offered for training, *Max–Min method* and *Size-EV method.*

The Max–Min method consists in computing differences between maximal and minimal gray levels of pixels within a moving window. The Size-EV method consists in computing the number of pixels that form, in a moving window, the EV-neighborhood of the window central pixel. For the Max–Min method the program requires setting vertical and horizontal dimensions of the moving window (figure 9.15). For the Size-EV method, it is necessary to set, in addition to the window dimensions, upper and lower borders of the EV-neighborhood (figure 9.16). In both cases initial test images and edge extraction results are displayed. Because results of edge extraction may have very large dynamic range, which hampers their proper display, an option is offered of displaying the results in a compressed dynamic range, as in the previous exercise for image local cardinalities. Examples of final displays are illustrated in figures 9.17 and 9.18.

9.3 Enhancement of color images

9.3.1 Introduction

Most methods of enhancement of color images are extensions of achromatic image enhancement methods to processing individual RBG or YUV components of color

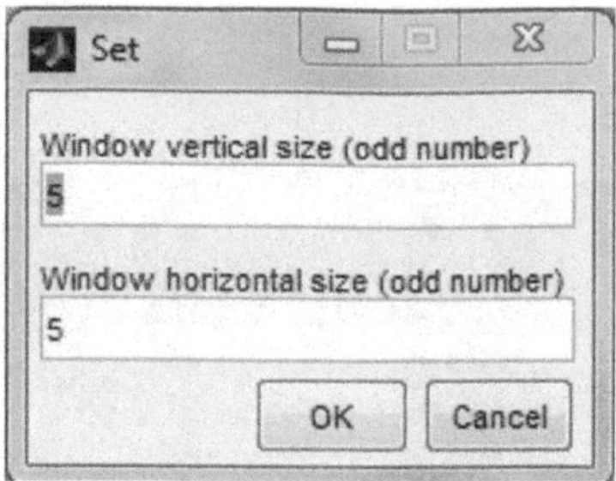

Figure 9.15. Edge extraction, Max–Min method: parameter menu.

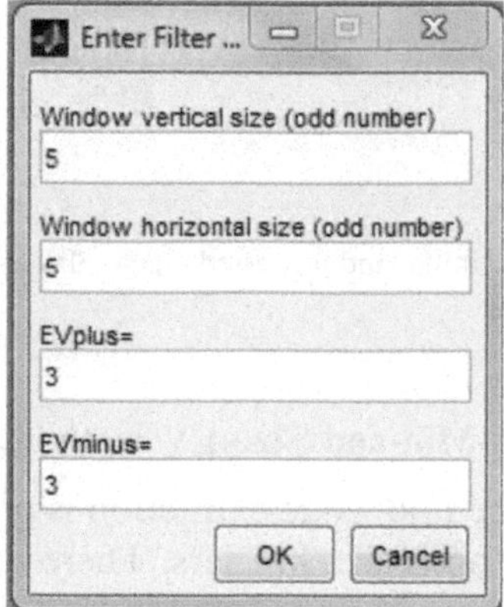

Figure 9.16. Edge extraction, Size-EV method: parameter menu.

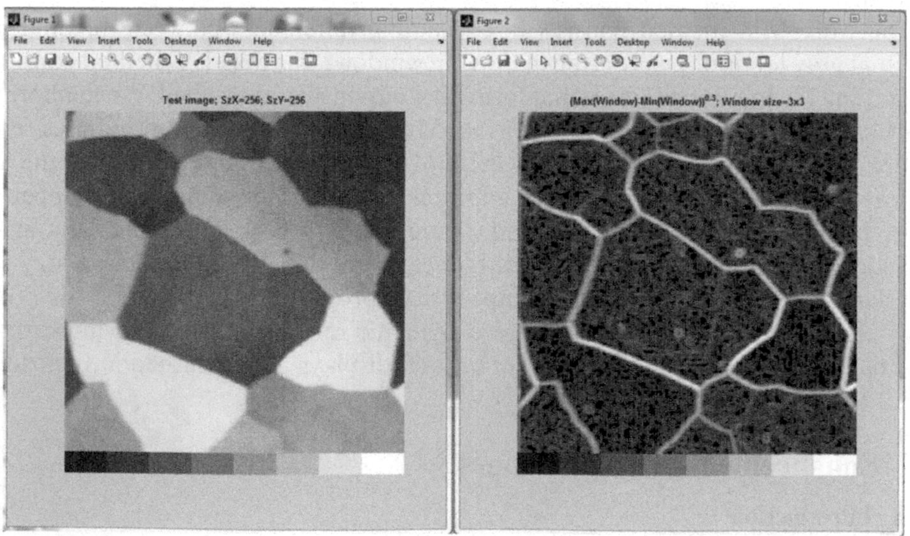

Figure 9.17. Edge extraction, Max–Min method: initial test image and processed image displayed in a compressed dynamic range.

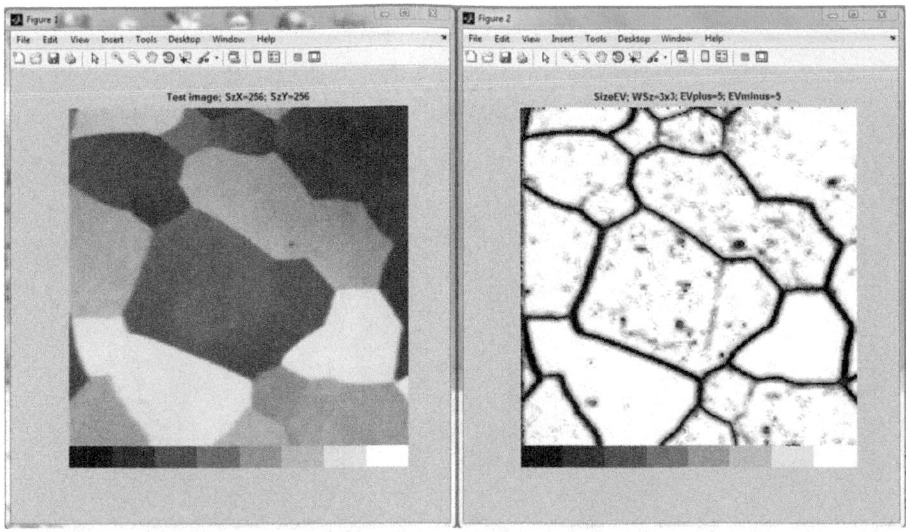

Figure 9.18. Edge extraction, Size-EV method: initial test and processed images.

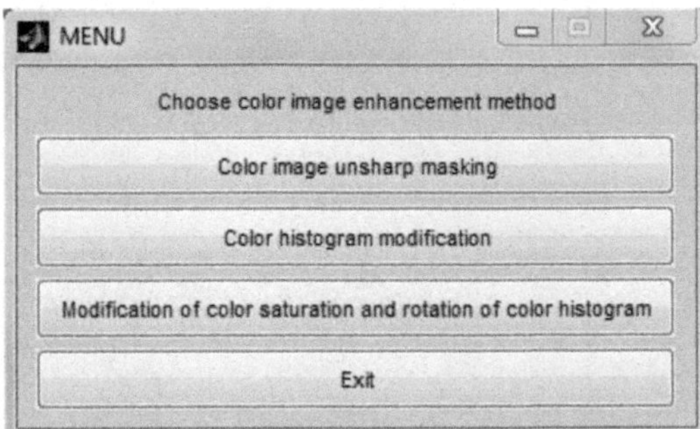

Figure 9.19. Enhancement of color images: start menu.

images. In this section, two such methods are presented for training and comparison: unsharp masking and histogram modification. From methods specific for color images, a method of modification of color saturation and rotation of color histogram is offered. The start menu for these exercises is shown in figure 9.19.

Color image unsharp masking

At the start, the user is prompted to choose for experiments either one of the prepared test images or an image from the image data set, then to choose a method for unsharp masking, unsharp masking of RGB or YUV image components, and then to set parameters for unsharp masking: dimensions of the filter window for computing local means and local medians and amplification factor of the difference between the initial image and its local means or medians to be added to the initial image (figure 9.20).

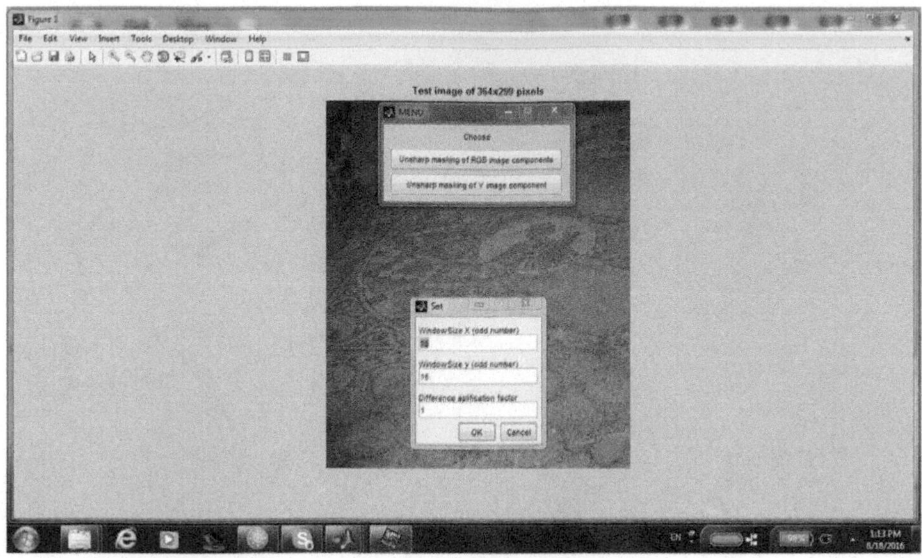

Figure 9.20. Color image unsharp masking: start menu.

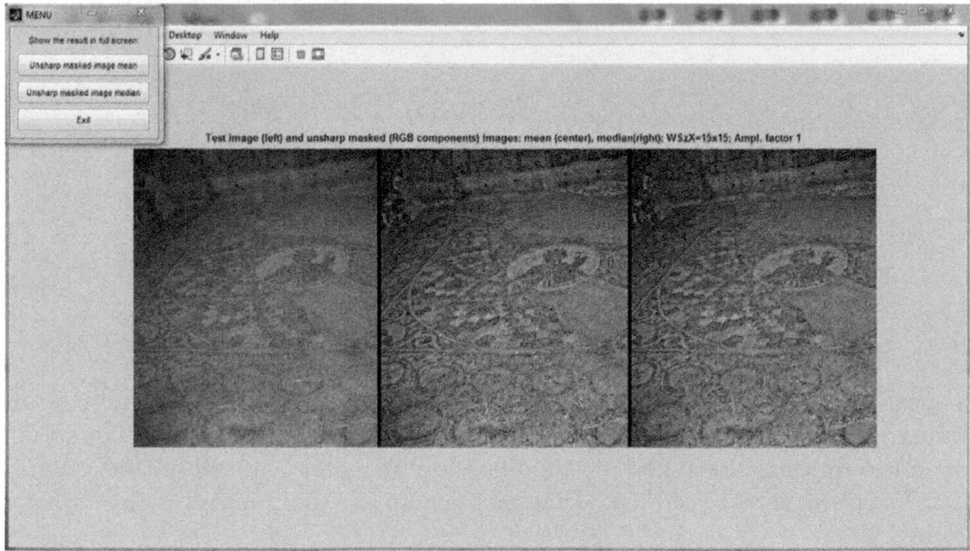

Figure 9.21. Color image unsharp masking: test image and its unsharp masked of its RGB components by local means and local medians versions.

Then the program computes local means and local medians of image RGB component in a sliding window of chosen size and adds to the image components their corresponded differences with local means and medians times the chosen amplification factor. The results are displayed side by side, as shown in figure 9.21, and an option of displaying the unsharp masked images full screen for detailed

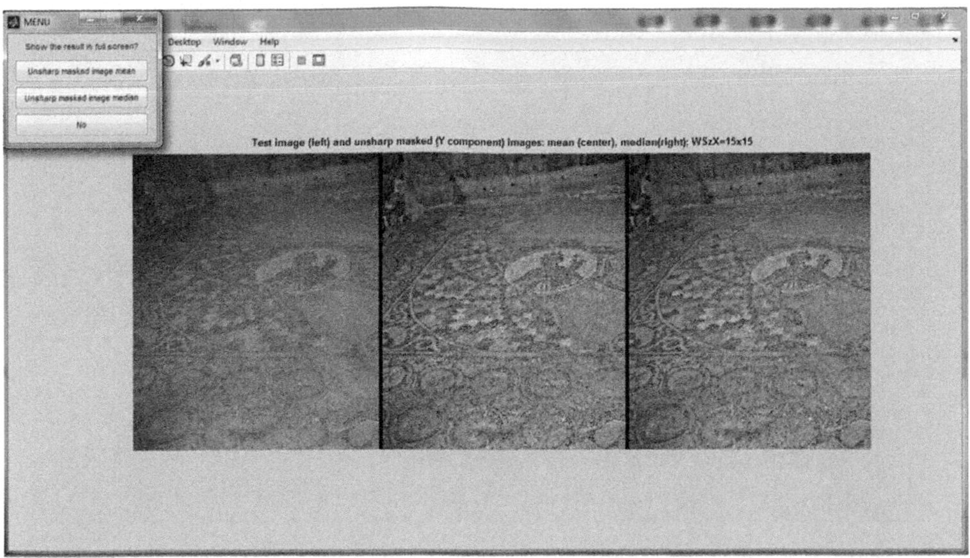

Figure 9.22. Color image unsharp masking: test image and results of unsharp masking of its Y component by local means and local medians.

Figure 9.23. Color histogram modification, global histogram RGB *P*-equalization: start menu.

comparisons is offered. The experiment can be repeated with other parameters or with another image. In a similar way the exercise can be carried out solely with unsharp masking of the image Y component (figure 9.22).

Color histogram modification

The exercises in color histogram modification enable comparison of global and local *P*-histogram equalization applied to the color image individual RGB components

Figure 9.24. Color histogram modification, local histogram RGB *P*-equalization: start menu.

Figure 9.25. Color histogram modification, global histogram RGB *P*-equalization: a final display.

and to the color image Y component. For processing RGB components, the user, after choosing a test image and the type of operation, global or local equalization, has to set the *P*-parameter for global equalization (figure 9.23) or processing window horizontal and vertical dimensions and *P*-parameter for local *P*-equalization (figure 9.24).

Once the necessary settings are completed, the program displays for visual evaluation initial and processed images, side by side or one above another, and, in the other panel, color triangle histograms of both images (figures 9.25 and 9.26).

Figure 9.26. Color histogram modification, local histogram RGB *P*-equalization: final display.

Figure 9.27. Color histogram modification, global histogram Y component *P*-equalization: start menu.

P-histogram equalization of the color image RGB component enhances both spatial and color contrasts. The second exercise in this group, 'Color image Y component *P*-histogram equalization', enables one to separately control spatial contrasts and color contrasts. The former are controlled by means of Y component *P*-histogram equalization, the latter are controlled by amplification of image color differences encoded in color image U and V components. As in the first exercise, processing can be applied globally to the entire color frame or locally, in a moving window. For global processing, *P*-parameter of *P*-histogram equalization and amplification factor for color differences have to be set (figure 9.27). For local

Figure 9.28. Color histogram modification, local histogram Y component *P*-equalization: start menu.

Figure 9.29. Color histogram modification, global histogram Y component *P*-equalization: results of processing.

processing in a moving window, vertical and horizontal dimensions of the processing window are additionally requested (figure 9.28).

Processing results are displayed in the same way as in the previous exercise: initial and processed images side by side or one above another and corresponding color triangle histograms (figure 9.29 for global processing and figure 9.30 for local processing).

Figure 9.30. Color histogram modification, local histogram Y component *P*-equalization: results of processing.

Figure 9.31. Modification of color saturation and rotation of color histogram: start menu.

Modification of color saturation and rotation of color histogram

This exercise is intended to demonstrate how one can manipulate with color saturation and modify image colors by means of changing the distance of pixel color vectors from the center of a color triangle and by rotation of color vectors around this center. At the start, the program prompts one to choose a test image, displays the chosen image, computes and displays its color triangle histogram and prompts one to set color saturation factor and color vector rotation angle (figure 9.31). The result of processing and its color triangle histogram are displayed side by side with the test image and its color triangle histogram (figure 9.32).

Figure 9.32. Modification of color saturation and rotation of color histogram: processing results.

Questions for self-testing

1. In what sense do unsharp masking and *P*th law image spectra enhancement improve image suitability for analysis?
2. What is common and what are the distinctions between unsharp masking and *P*th law image spectra enhancement methods?
3. Does unsharp masking have any association with correcting imaging systems transfer functions?
4. What are the distinctions in appearance of images obtained by unsharp masking using local means and local medians?
5. Why does *P*-histogram equalization result in enhancement of contrasts?
6. Does displaying pixel cardinalities exhibit any edge extraction capability?
7. How does the appearance of edges extracted by Max–Min and Size-EV methods depend on the window size and, for the Size-EV method, on the borders of the EV-neighborhood.
8. Can the local cardinalities method be regarded as a special case of the Size-EV method?
9. In what cases is color image enhancement by means of processing image YUV components rather than RGB components preferable?

CPSIA information can be obtained
at www.ICGtesting.com
Printed in the USA
BVOW07*0945021216
469570BV00001B/8/P